THE NEW MIDDLE AGES

BONNIE WHEELER, *Series Editor*

The New Middle Ages is a series dedicated to transdisciplinary studies of medieval cultures, with particular emphasis on recuperating women's history and on feminist and gender analyses. This peer-reviewed series includes both scholarly monographs and essay collections.

PUBLISHED BY PALGRAVE:

Women in the Medieval Islamic World: Power, Patronage, and Piety
edited by Gavin R. G. Hambly

The Ethics of Nature in the Middle Ages: On Boccaccio's Poetaphysics
by Gregory B. Stone

Presence and Presentation: Women in the Chinese Literati Tradition
edited by Sherry J. Mou

The Lost Love Letters of Heloise and Abelard: Perceptions of Dialogue in Twelfth-Century France
by Constant J. Mews

Understanding Scholastic Thought with Foucault
by Philipp W. Rosemann

For Her Good Estate: The Life of Elizabeth de Burgh
by Frances A. Underhill

Constructions of Widowhood and Virginity in the Middle Ages
edited by Cindy L. Carlson and Angela Jane Weisl

Motherhood and Mothering in Anglo-Saxon England
by Mary Dockray-Miller

Listening to Heloise: The Voice of a Twelfth-Century Woman
edited by Bonnie Wheeler

The Postcolonial Middle Ages
edited by Jeffrey Jerome Cohen

Chaucer's Pardoner and Gender Theory: Bodies of Discourse
by Robert S. Sturges

Crossing the Bridge: Comparative Essays on Medieval European and Heian Japanese Women Writers
edited by Barbara Stevenson and Cynthia Ho

Engaging Words: The Culture of Reading in the Later Middle Ages
by Laurel Amtower

Robes and Honor: The Medieval World of Investiture
edited by Stewart Gordon

Representing Rape in Medieval and Early Modern Literature
edited by Elizabeth Robertson and Christine M. Rose

Same Sex Love and Desire among Women in the Middle Ages
edited by Francesca Canadé Sautman and Pamela Sheingorn

Sight and Embodiment in the Middle Ages: Ocular Desires
by Suzannah Biernoff

Listen, Daughter: The Speculum Virginum *and the Formation of Religious Women in the Middle Ages*
edited by Constant J. Mews

Science, the Singular, and the Question of Theology
by Richard A. Lee, Jr.

Gender in Debate from the Early Middle Ages to the Renaissance
edited by Thelma S. Fenster and Clare A. Lees

Malory's Morte D'Arthur: *Remaking Arthurian Tradition*
by Catherine Batt

The Vernacular Spirit: Essays on Medieval Religious Literature
edited by Renate Blumenfeld-Kosinski, Duncan Robertson, and Nancy Warren

Popular Piety and Art in the Late Middle Ages: Image Worship and Idolatry in England 1350–1500
by Kathleen Kamerick

Absent Narratives, Manuscript Textuality, and Literary Structure in Late Medieval England
by Elizabeth Scala

Creating Community with Food and Drink in Merovingian Gaul
by Bonnie Effros

Representations of Early Byzantine Empresses: Image and Empire
by Anne McClanan

Encountering Medieval Textiles and Dress: Objects, Texts, Images
edited by Désirée G. Koslin and Janet Snyder

Eleanor of Aquitaine: Lord and Lady
edited by Bonnie Wheeler and John Carmi Parsons

Isabel La Católica, Queen of Castile: Critical Essays
edited by David A. Boruchoff

Homoeroticism and Chivalry: Discourses of Male Same-Sex Desire in the Fourteenth Century
by Richard E. Zeikowitz

Portraits of Medieval Women: Family, Marriage, and Politics in England 1225–1350
by Linda E. Mitchell

Eloquent Virgins: From Thecla to Joan of Arc
by Maud Burnett McInerney

The Persistence of Medievalism: Narrative Adventures in Contemporary Culture
by Angela Jane Weisl

Capetian Women
edited by Kathleen D. Nolan

Joan of Arc and Spirituality
edited by Ann W. Astell and Bonnie Wheeler

The Texture of Society: Medieval Women in the Southern Low Countries
edited by Ellen E. Kittell and Mary A. Suydam

Charlemagne's Mustache: And Other Cultural Clusters of a Dark Age
by Paul Edward Dutton

Troubled Vision: Gender, Sexuality, and Sight in Medieval Text and Image
edited by Emma Campbell and Robert Mills

Queering Medieval Genres
by Tison Pugh

Sacred Place in Early Medieval Neoplatonism
by L. Michael Harrington

The Middle Ages at Work
edited by Kellie Robertson and Michael Uebel

Chaucer's Jobs
by David R. Carlson

Medievalism and Orientalism: Three Essays on Literature, Architecture and Cultural Identity
by John M. Ganim

Queer Love in the Middle Ages
by Anna Klosowska

Performing Women in the Middle Ages: Sex, Gender, and the Iberian Lyric
by Denise K. Filios

Necessary Conjunctions: The Social Self in Medieval England
by David Gary Shaw

Visual Culture and the German Middle Ages
edited by Kathryn Starkey and Horst Wenzel

Medieval Paradigms: Essays in Honor of Jeremy duQuesnay Adams, Volumes 1 and 2
edited by Stephanie Hayes-Healy

False Fables and Exemplary Truth in Later Middle English Literature
by Elizabeth Allen

Ecstatic Transformation: On the Uses of Alterity in the Middle Ages
by Michael Uebel

Sacred and Secular in Medieval and Early Modern Cultures: New Essays
edited by Lawrence Besserman

Tolkien's Modern Middle Ages
edited by Jane Chance and Alfred K. Siewers

Representing Righteous Heathens in Late Medieval England
by Frank Grady

Byzantine Dress: Representations of Secular Dress in Eighth-to-Twelfth Century Painting
by Jennifer L. Ball

The Laborer's Two Bodies: Labor and the "Work" of the Text in Medieval Britain, 1350–1500
by Kellie Robertson

The Dogaressa of Venice, 1250–1500: Wife and Icon
by Holly S. Hurlburt

Logic, Theology, and Poetry in Boethius, Abelard, and Alan of Lille: Words in the Absence of Things
by Eileen C. Sweeney

The Theology of Work: Peter Damian and the Medieval Religious Renewal Movement
by Patricia Ranft

On the Purification of Women: Churching in Northern France, 1100–1500
by Paula M. Rieder

Writers of the Reign of Henry II: Twelve Essays
edited by Ruth Kennedy and Simon Meecham-Jones

Lonesome Words: The Vocal Poetics of the Old English Lament and the African-American Blues Song
by M.G. McGeachy

Performing Piety: Musical Culture in Medieval English Nunneries
by Anne Bagnell Yardley

The Flight from Desire: Augustine and Ovid to Chaucer
by Robert R. Edwards

Mindful Spirit in Late Medieval Literature: Essays in Honor of Elizabeth D. Kirk
edited by Bonnie Wheeler

Medieval Fabrications: Dress, Textiles, Clothwork, and Other Cultural Imaginings
edited by E. Jane Burns

Was the Bayeux Tapestry Made in France?: The Case for St. Florent of Saumur
by George Beech

Women, Power, and Religious Patronage in the Middle Ages
by Erin L. Jordan

Hybridity, Identity, and Monstrosity in Medieval Britain: On Difficult Middles
by Jeffrey Jerome Cohen

Medieval Go-betweens and Chaucer's Pandarus
by Gretchen Mieszkowski

The Surgeon in Medieval English Literature
by Jeremy J. Citrome

Temporal Circumstances: Form and History in the Canterbury Tales
by Lee Patterson

Erotic Discourse and Early English Religious Writing
by Lara Farina

Odd Bodies and Visible Ends in Medieval Literature
by Sachi Shimomura

On Farting: Language and Laughter in the Middle Ages
by Valerie Allen

Women and Medieval Epic: Gender, Genre, and the Limits of Epic Masculinity
edited by Sara S. Poor and Jana K. Schulman

Race, Class, and Gender in "Medieval" Cinema
edited by Lynn T. Ramey and Tison Pugh

Allegory and Sexual Ethics in the High Middle Ages
by Noah D. Guynn

England and Iberia in the Middle Ages, 12th–15th Century: Cultural, Literary, and Political Exchanges
edited by María Bullón-Fernández

The Medieval Chastity Belt: A Myth-Making Process
by Albrecht Classen

Claustrophilia: The Erotics of Enclosure in Medieval Literature
by Cary Howie

Cannibalism in High Medieval English Literature
by Heather Blurton

The Drama of Masculinity and Medieval English Guild Culture
by Christina M. Fitzgerald

Chaucer's Visions of Manhood
by Holly A. Crocker

The Literary Subversions of Medieval Women
by Jane Chance

Manmade Marvels in Medieval Culture and Literature
by Scott Lightsey

American Chaucers
by Candace Barrington

Representing Others in Medieval Iberian Literature
by Michelle M. Hamilton

Paradigms and Methods in Early Medieval Studies
edited by Celia Chazelle and Felice Lifshitz

The King and the Whore: King Roderick and La Cava
by Elizabeth Drayson

Langland's Early Modern Identities
by Sarah A. Kelen

Cultural Studies of the Modern Middle Ages
edited by Eileen A. Joy, Myra J. Seaman, Kimberly K. Bell, and Mary K. Ramsey

Hildegard of Bingen's Unknown Language: An Edition, Translation, and Discussion
by Sarah L. Higley

Medieval Romance and the Construction of Heterosexuality
by Louise M. Sylvester

Communal Discord, Child Abduction, and Rape in the Later Middle Ages
by Jeremy Goldberg

Lydgate Matters: Poetry and Material Culture in the Fifteenth Century
edited by Lisa H. Cooper and Andrea Denny-Brown

Sexuality and Its Queer Discontents in Middle English Literature
by Tison Pugh

Sex, Scandal, and Sermon in Fourteenth-Century Spain: Juan Ruiz's Libro de Buen Amor
by Louise M. Haywood

The Erotics of Consolation: Desire and Distance in the Late Middle Ages
edited by Catherine E. Léglu and Stephen J. Milner

Battlefronts Real and Imagined: War, Border, and Identity in the Chinese Middle Period
edited by Don J. Wyatt

Wisdom and Her Lovers in Medieval and Early Modern Hispanic Literature
by Emily C. Francomano

Power, Piety, and Patronage in Late Medieval Queenship: Maria de Luna
by Nuria Silleras-Fernandez

In the Light of Medieval Spain: Islam, the West, and the Relevance of the Past
edited by Simon R. Doubleday and David Coleman, foreword by Giles Tremlett

Chaucerian Aesthetics
by Peggy A. Knapp

CHAUCERIAN AESTHETICS

Peggy A. Knapp

palgrave
macmillan

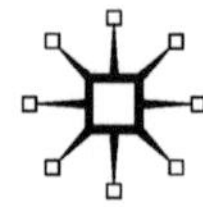

CHAUCERIAN AESTHETICS

First published in 2008 by
PALGRAVE MACMILLAN®
in the US—a division of St. Martin's Press LLC,
175 Fifth Avenue, New York, NY 10010.

Where this book is distributed in the UK, Europe and the rest of the world, this is by Palgrave Macmillan, a division of Macmillan Publishers Limited, registered in England, company number 785998, of Houndmills, Basingstoke, Hampshire RG21 6XS.

Palgrave Macmillan is the global academic imprint of the above companies and has companies and representatives throughout the world.

ISBN-13: 978–0–230–60668–5

Library of Congress Cataloging-in-Publication Data

Knapp, Peggy Ann.
Chaucerian aesthetics / Peggy A. Knapp.
p. cm.—(New Middle Ages)
Includes bibliographical references.
ISBN 0–230–60668–7 (alk. paper)
1. Chaucer, Geoffrey, d. 1400—Criticism and interpretation.
2. Aesthetics, Medieval. 3. Chaucer, Geoffrey, d. 1400. Canterbury tales. 4. Chaucer, Geoffrey, d. 1400. Troilus and Criseyde. 5. Tales, Medieval—History and criticism. I. Title.

PR1924.K56 2008
821′.1—dc22 2007051105

A catalogue record for this book is available from the British Library.

Design by Newgen Imaging Systems (P) Ltd., Chennai, India.

First edition: August 2008

10 9 8 7 6 5 4 3 2 1

Printed in the United States of America.

Tranferred to Digital Printing in 2010

CONTENTS

PREFACE

Like all great works of art, the *Canterbury Tales* and *Troilus and Criseyde* are open to many kinds of analysis, and answer many kinds of questions. Those I have chosen to ask in this book are: why have these poems given so much pleasure over so long a time and why is it right to call that pleasure "aesthetic"? I have always enjoyed reading Chaucer, and the longer I attend to the poetry and the world to which it was originally addressed, the more fun it gets. It's work as well as play, of course, just as working on a backhand tennis stroke is—you have to keep extending your reach in order to enjoy the game.

The founding premise of aesthetic intuition is that beauty mediates between idea and appearance; it brings the sensible and the intelligible simultaneously into play in a felt personal response that can be shared and explicated without being amenable to logical proof. This premise, older than Kant but central to his *Critique of Judgement,* underlies my attempt to display the interanimation of sensible detail with intelligible order in Chaucer's two long poems. There are, of course, many construals of Kant's treatise, and I have used his famous "moments" as incitements to discovery rather than attempting to prove my own construals definitive. I have also tried to adapt the Kantian analysis of beauty to our current concerns; for example, Hans-Georg Gadamer's work has helped to theorize our involvements with the art of the past, Ludwig Wittgenstein's with intellectual play, and Antonio Damasio and Daniel Dennett's with cognitive theory.

I have incurred so many debts to other medievalists over the years that I cannot thank them all here or even in the footnotes. The New Chaucer Society's meetings and publications over the years have involved me in rich, vigorous discussions of the Middle Ages. I have incorporated some paragraphs from essays previously published; the editors of *The Chaucer Review* in the Special Issue on Aesthetics (2005), Mario Di Cesare of the Pegasus Press (*New Perspectives on Criseyde*, 2004), and the University of Minnesota Press (*Imagining a Medieval English Nation*, 2004) have given their permission for their use in this extended argument. I am grateful to

Alastair Minnis for his support of the whole project, to Douglas Brooks and Paul Hopper for their careful readings of certain chapters, and to Andreea Ritivoi, Kellie Robertson, and Michael Witmore for many helpful conversations about aesthetics. My students at Carnegie Mellon, again too many to name here, have greatly enriched my appreciation of the playful, philosophical Chaucer this book celebrates. To study with perceptive young people like these, over many years, makes Gadamer's case that historical horizons are fluid rather than fixed and every generation has to interpret the past and its art anew.

Chaucerian Aesthetics is dedicated to two scholars who have been my constant companions in its evolution: my son James Andrew Knapp knew Kant before I did and saved me from many intellectual wrong turns. My husband James Franklin Knapp read all the drafts and discussed all the details, right down to phrasings. I can never thank them enough for the inspiration and support they have given my *werk* and the *verray felicitee* with which they have filled my life.

CHAPTER 1

INTRODUCTION: WHY AESTHETICS?

What is intelligible is also beautiful

S. Chandrasekhar

A history without imagination is a mutilated, disembodied history

Jacques Le Goff

The headline for the *New York Times* science section on September 24, 2002 was "Here They Are, Science's 10 Most Beautiful Experiments." Why is the word "beautiful" used to value experimental work? There must be an assumption that beauty has something important to do with scientific knowledge. Werner Heisenberg was explicit about this when he claimed that "if nature leads us to mathematical forms of great simplicity and beauty—by forms I am referring to coherent systems of hypotheses, axioms, etc.—to forms no one has previously encountered, we cannot help thinking that they are 'true,' that they reveal a genuine feature of nature."[1] One often sees such an idea assumed casually, as when in the *Science Times's* discussion of the nature of a subatomic particle, Dr. Lee Roberts points to "logical and aesthetic flaws" in the older theory, and Dr. Frank Wilczek sees the new theory as "more unified and more beautiful" than the old one.[2] The beauty referred to in these remarks is not that of the phenomena (natural beauty) but that of ideas. Philip Fisher argues that ever since the Greeks investigated geometry and proportion, the apprehension of beauty has been seen as close to the operations of scientific discovery; Plato, for example, sees it as "mediating between idea and appearance."[3] It is therefore appropriate that those sciences using sense data to deduce underlying (or overarching) principles should employ the same value-laden word the ancients did to mark their achievements. Saint Bonaventure makes a similar case from a different perspective when he writes that "beauty is nothing other than numerical equality or a certain relation of parts" (*pulcritudo nihil alius esy quam aequalitas numerosa*) that causes "delight" since God made both the well-proportioned world and the human mind that perceives it.[4] These comments imply that beauty unites the sensible with the intelligible to produce a particular form of pleasure and satisfaction grasped through imagination. In literary study, this perspective, acknowledged so frequently in modern science and medieval thought, has been neglected and even traduced of late. It ought to be recovered.

In this book I want to acknowledge the riddling, elusive manner of beauty's hold on us and yet attempt to reclaim aesthetic concerns for the study of Chaucer.[5] My purpose is not to provide an authoritative definition of either medieval aesthetic principles or those appropriate for our moment, but to point to a cluster of ideas (family resemblances, as Wittgenstein would call them) proper to the pleasure associated with beauty in each of these social formations. Evidence of the intellectual traditions available to Chaucer's world points to some diversity of outlook, but also to some congruences. Contemporary thinking about beauty is more sharply divided and I will begin by levering the case for an updated aesthetics against the exclusive concern with ideology critique so evident in current academic circles of late. Rather than sign on to any ready-made contemporary theory, I will attempt to fuse some relevant thinking about the imaginative grasp of and regard for textual art into an eclectic mix useful for the study of Chaucer now. Part of my purpose is to rescue delight in beauty from the aestheticism of an "art for art's sake" trend in the visual arts that seemed to have severed traditional connections with ethics, science, and philosophy. More recently all formal study of art has been accused of severing those connections, in effect isolating it from the "real world." Ideology critique in particular has treated aesthetics and beauty as bad words, consigning taste to the illiberal category of elitism, denying intrinsic aesthetic worth entirely on the grounds that all value is socially constructed, and discounting intellectual pleasure. This critique justifiably confronts the pretensions into which art criticism had sometimes fallen and enables important disclosures about the art itself, especially about its situatedness in its original contexts. What it leaves out is attention to the power exerted by beauty.[6] If aesthetic considerations are to be reintegrated into critical discourse, they must acknowledge the complex interactions between art and the social formations attendant on its making and first reception, as well as the equally complex relations, between that art and our time.

Aesthetics as an inquiry is, of course, both larger and smaller than the study of art. The particular kind of pleasure that surpasses simple gratification of the senses and eludes the certainties of conceptual thought can be found as well in contemplating nature and life experiences—Fisher calls that pleasure "wonder," remarks on its "drive toward intelligibility," and concludes that that intelligibility "lies in a profound use of the visible that outwits the conditions of visibility itself."[7] Fisher is particularly interested in natural beauty, especially the rainbow, and Kant is too, his *Critique of Judgement* taking examples of the sublime, for example, entirely from nature rather than art. If aesthetics is not just about art, neither is art approached only through aesthetics. The study of art can, and often does, reveal facts about the past, make speculators rich, or suggest a palette for painting the living room. Sometimes it provides the cultural capital to qualify someone for a special ingroup. Because aesthetic responses are subjective and cannot be established through argument, I will not be able to offer rules by which Chaucerian aesthetic effects may be judged, although it will be clear that I think that aesthetics as a "mode of intelligibility" (Jacques Ranciére's term)[8] for approaching his fictions is rewarded.

Chaucer's work rewards such study because criticism and theory surely have some responsibility for investigating why certain objects remain impressive after the material and cultural conditions that produced them have undergone important changes.[9] The modern reception of the *Canterbury Tales* and *Troilus and Criseyde* make them good test cases for confronting the ideology-only camp because of their continuing readability in spite of such changes. Chaucer himself expressed worry about the "gret diversite" in writing and speaking English during his lifetime; he seems eager to be clear ("that none myswrite") and lyrical ("Ne mysmetre for defaute of tonge").[10] He wanted his poem to invite both understanding and pleasure. Ideology critique has persuaded many academic readers to suppress their own pleasure in reading, to regard their affective and intellectual involvement in texts like Chaucer's as guilty secrets, betrayals of right-minded social principles. The guilt arises in part from the role "major authors" have been accused of playing: inaugurating a tradition in English writing, and enhancing English as a "literary language" only appreciated by elites, but claimed by them to be universal. It also arises from current biases in favor of "the sublime" over the homier "beautiful," for those who account for the aesthetic register at all.[11] If principle demands the museums be burnt, it will hardly do to enjoy a poet who writes with a certain "autonomy from both ideological programs and social appropriations," as Lee Patterson puts it.[12]

My aim in this chapter is to defend pleasure in beauty against its detractors and pleasure in the beauty of Chaucerian texts against a particular kind of historical determinism. My aim in the book as a whole is to consider the imaginative style of *Canterbury Tales* and *Troilus and Criseyde* as rewarding to aesthetic attention in terms of both medieval structures of feeling and our own. To "think with" Chaucerian fictions, we need not posit a universal human nature, for universalism and sealed-off ideological situatedness are not the only alternatives we have in confronting the past. Although no conceptual argument can *prove* anything to be beautiful, when we are impressed by beauty, we want to share our pleasure—we do this all the time in "real-life." Chaucerian texts that produce wonder by "outwitting" their surface visibilities can best be shown through readings of their features, and this is the work of chapters 3–7. I make the claims I do in the mode of witness. Elaine Scarry says we want (and want others) to be "looking in the right direction when a comet makes its sweep through a certain patch of the sky."[13]

Aesthetics and Ideology

Considering Chaucerian texts within the "regime of the aesthetic" is in one sense unnecessary, since many readers are delighted by them now and apparently were in the fourteenth and fifteenth centuries as well.[14] It is recent academic discourse concerning them that has downplayed delight in favor of critique. The "antiaesthetic" of the Frankfurt School has been tirelessly cited as the position of socially responsible academic criticism. Adorno's "no poetry after Auschwitz" and Benjamin's "every document of civilization is a document of barbarism" are quoted with an ex cathedra finality intended to unmask the naiveté of aesthetic analysis with its admission of pleasure.[15] As Oscar Kenshur writes, "Ideological critique, at least as far back as Hobbes, undertakes to show that what purports to be good actually operates in the service of interests."[16] Recently, such critique prides itself on unmasking the ways in which literary art reinforces aspects of hegemony by offering the bribe of beautiful form. Kenshur goes on to argue that the claim to an intuitive grasp of social good that found ideology critique is not unlike the claim of an intuitive grasp of aesthetic effects. Both are vulnerable to historical changes and neither should be cause for embarrassment.[17]

Adorno has said much more about art than his famous pronouncement about Auschwitz. His unfinished *Aesthetic Theory* takes a position closer to the one I wish to advance here: that the direct experience of art and the intellectual understanding of it must be seen as reciprocal and treated dialectically, and that aesthetic attention is immanent to immediate response.[18] Adorno's "where art is experienced purely aesthetically, it fails to be fully experienced even aesthetically"[19] could be turned around as "where art is experienced purely ideologically, it fails to be fully experienced even ideologically." This is because "purely ideological" analysis rarely attends adequately to form. Form "is the coherence of the work of art" and what saves it from eclipse by ideology, as Denis Donoghue puts it in his analysis of Adorno's position.[20] The strong version of ideology critique takes as its goal "seeing through" the text, unmasking its ideological investments and resisting the way it has papered over the contradictions of the regime or institution it supports or the social argument it makes. But even those who set out to resist Chaucer's ideological alignments, I would argue, should examine the particular forms that produce the luminous, memorable details and rhythms that rendered it ideologically powerful in its own time.

Kant's first major assertion in the *Critique of Judgement,* that aesthetic experience is capable of disinterest, is basic to the strong version of aesthetic theory and a lightening rod for ideology critique. Kant writes: "The delight which determines the judgement of taste is independent of all interest."[21] This position rests on the disinterestedness of the appeal of art to other personal and social aims; it moves one, but not toward a practical action in the "real world," not even moral action as long as the response remains an aesthetic judgment. Note that neither Kant's aesthetics nor the position of ideological critique alleges that art *has no interests*; both point to modes of attentiveness. The *Critique of Judgement* acknowledges the possibility of the uses to which art may be put (and chooses most of his examples of the beautiful from the natural realm); the point is that our aim in finding them beautiful makes a different claim on attention (*CJ*, p. 14).

Exclusive acceptance of either aesthetic or ideological attention is dismissed by Raymond Williams in *Marxism and Literature* on somewhat different grounds than Adorno's. The aesthetic realm, Williams notes, has traditionally been a refuge from the relentless descent of everything into instrumentality—a realm in which one forms images and makes judgments of what is not immediately useful—in short, where one imagines freely ("free" here distinctly in the arena of Kant's "disinterest"). On the other hand, says Williams, capitalism has appropriated for instrumental ends, containment of unrest, for example, even this speculative feature of art.[22] Medievalists know that other social formations have done so as well. Williams describes a standoff between "ideology" and "aesthetics" that is still recognizable in current debates:

> If we are asked to believe that all literature is "ideology," in the crude sense that its dominant intention (and then our only response) is the communication or imposition of "social" or "political" meanings and values, we can only, in the end, turn away. If we are asked to believe that all

> literature is "aesthetic" in the crude sense that its dominant intention (and then our only response) is the beauty of language or form, we may stay a little longer but will still in the end turn away. (*ML*, p. 155)

He goes on to conclude that a range of intentions and effects must be acknowledged in dealing with literary objects, and I certainly agree, but my emphasis here is on reconsidering the "regime of the aesthetic" (Ranciére's term) to include the way ideologically inflected horizons of understanding shape the invention and interpretation of any work. In other words, I want to see ideological intuitions as immanent to aesthetic effects in Chaucer's work. My emphasis will, therefore, fall on the gains that accrue to Chaucer criticism from a renewed respect for aesthetic pleasure, aligned, but potentially polyvalent, in its real-world effects.[23]

To regard all art as hopelessly enfeoffed to the current regime is to argue that it never rouses imagination to incite or accept social change, that dominant culture can completely saturate understandings of the world, an idea Williams rejects (*ML*, p. 125). Complete saturation would predict that texts written under a particular set of ideological conditions cannot challenge or transform those conditions—cannot, in the Middle Ages for example, provide imaginative pleasures that do not lead to established pieties. Criticism like that of Paul de Man, would call the undisciplined pleasures of literary texts, those that evade direct decoding, "mere local seductions," distracting readers from systematic truth claims.[24] Even when textual intentions are strongly marked ideologically, the aesthetic play of fictional representation is constitutionally ill-suited to replicate ideology flawlessly, as both D. W. Robertson Jr. and de Man (from very different starting points) argue that it does. Yet to define art as neutral in ideological struggles is to deny its social power and relegate its aesthetic effects to affective responses leaving no mark on thought or action, a thought to be rejected by anyone who knows the history of *Uncle Tom's Cabin*. There is no necessary contradiction in claiming that a given verbal text may be credited with social effects for particular readers without relinquishing its claim to enhancing imaginative freedoms. In other words, any text may be written under the influence of ideological tenets (good ones or bad) and may be read in the light of them, but that neither constitutes nor forecloses its claim to beauty. As Kenshur puts it, "to see that a symbolic structure emerged in a specific historical situation to serve a specific ideological role does not necessarily deprive it of its cogency or intellectual potency."[25] Its cogency may even reassert itself later under different conditions.

There is another sense in which aesthetic judgments are less than disinterested from the point of view of ideology critique, which reads

Kant's notion of taste as merely a screen for indulging arbitrary and self-aggrandizing class authority, merely the preference of elitist persons and groups, taught to those who wish to enter the club. Rather than the result of judgment set free from interest, it is precisely *interested,* a judgment made (or at least expressed) in order to achieve some practical goal (pass the exam, get the degree, impress the boss). Such a public display of taste is called cultural capital and is subject to the same critique as other class interests.[26] Pierre Bourdieu's *Distinction* offers a fascinating account of twentieth-century French people's preferences in art and social practices (like blowing one's nose), treating taste as that which "brings together things and people that go together" in class terms.[27] Although there *are* situations well explained in terms of cultural capital, it is not clear to me, living in the United States, where one would spend the capital accrued by admiring literary art. *Distinction* explains artistic taste, when taste is regarded as "what I like and feel comfortable with"; it depends less on the characteristics of the object than on "who else likes it." In his "Postscript," Bourdieu acknowledges that his book is a wholesale rejection of Kantian "purity," but it seems to me that his account misses Kant's point about disinterestedness, both because the *Critique* nowhere alleges that art can serve only a "pure" aesthetic purpose and because *Distinction* must deny the subjective pleasure that seems to take one by surprise, what Fisher calls "wonder."[28] Thus Bourdieu cannot account for why the older objects of "elite" taste came to belong to that category in the first place, nor can it account for aesthetic experiences in emerging genres like television serials. To insist that taste is *nothing but* affiliating oneself with a social group is to deny the pleasures of the sensible (calling them seductions, as de Man does) in order to render intelligible a text's position in the power game.

Pleasure in beauty, according to Kant, does not arise from its congruence with rational concepts, yet it brings rational faculties fully into play. The good is understood conceptually: "having a concept of the thing represented is not necessary for calling it beautiful, but to call a thing good, there must be a concept of what it is" (*CJ*, p. 46). The escape of aesthetic judgments from concepts, especially those of social or moral logic, is yet another of its tenets objectionable to ideology critique. What pleasure can there be in a Chaucerian text clearly on the wrong side of an important issue? What if the poet lets Alison get away with adultery in the *Miller's Tale* (offensive, perhaps, to certain early audiences and today's "evangelicals") and seems to praise Griselda for an inhuman and inhumane exercise of patience (offensive to feminists of all stripes)? Can any art be seen as beautiful, aesthetically pleasureful, or even as art, when it does not meet one's standards for probity? Since ideology is now regarded (even outside the Marxian circles that first elaborated it) as one's lived relation to the real, it is difficult to claim that ideology is completely absent, that one's entire relation to the world is put aside in favor of aesthetic vision. And since ideology is not just a system of acknowledged beliefs, it may exert its influence when least expected. Kant's posited evasion of conceptual fixity may not be entirely possible in all cases, but for ideology critiquers, it is always a wrongheaded indulgence in an imaged world with incorrect suppositions about power, class, or gender. They grasp the text in terms of concepts and find it wanting, precisely because it is the nature of beauty to overflow any perfect match with concepts. This has been a problem concerning textual art at least since Plato's *Republic.*

But even when ideology is not the center of attention, literary art invites conceptual consideration because the linguistic sign consists of both signifier and signified.[29] The involvement of concepts on this level has given rise to a separation between the language of poetry and that of prose, the former evading conceptual boundaries because of its incantatory power. Both Adorno and Williams dispute this opposition, claiming that literary prose, too, evades direct conceptual claims. Williams insists that the "specific feelings, specific rhythms" presented only in the form of imaginative literature be acknowledged and welcomed, rather than reduced to fixed systems (*ML*, p. 133). In other words, concepts are called into play by text, but are kept *in play.* Gadamer's description of the Kantian relation of text to concept in *Truth and Method* is that "both in creator and recipient" there is "no other way of grasping the content of a work of art than through the unique form of the work and the mystery of its impression, which can never be fully expressed by any language" (p. 53). Reading in this way, the aesthetic force of a fiction is both felt and returned to the social world, but under the aegis of play (*TM*, p. 103). Denial of this principle of play in aesthetic intuition has distorted recent criticism, often marking it as the smug culmination of the world's long search for knowledge: "this poem may have seemed beautiful, but I see how incorrect it actually is." Imaginative experience that appreciates the force of ideology (knowing that both writer and reader are, in some measure, subject to it) can confront it and negotiate with it.[30] Response to the world of a particular moment in the past is a good corrective for the hubris of presentism. A surface respect for the power of ideology blinds us to that of aesthetics, a deeper respect for it informs aesthetic effects. While ideology critique relies solely on the intelligible reduced to concept, the mode of imagination through which we respond to art calls upon the sensible and the intelligible in tandem.

Kant's idea of "subjective universality" has also come under attack from ideology critique. "The *beautiful* is that which, apart from a concept, pleases universally" is his summary of the "second moment" (*CJ*, p. 60, italics original). It follows from disinterestedness in that claiming beauty means claiming it for everyone, whether or not it represents or produces material or even moral benefits. Since it rests on imaginative grasp rather than logical deduction, it must be subjective, yet Kant pointedly argues for its universality. A position like this seems strained to the breaking point, resting as it does on the assumption that imaginative powers, even when free from rule-bound reason, tend to be alike from one person to another: someone who experiences aesthetic delight *is entitled to posit* a like response in others.[31] Furthermore, it assumes that the subjective state involved can be in some measure communicated. Although one cannot argue another person into experiencing aesthetic pleasure (since logical force does not apply), one can call attention to the possibility, and the power of beauty strongly impels one to do so.[32] Claiming something to be beautiful is a good faith demand that others too enjoy it, but that demand could be mistaken either because the object is merely agreeable or because it serves the claimant's unacknowledged interest. Kant's insistence on the universality of taste, then, is not that aesthetic judgments are based on rationally definable characteristics or even that they are *right,* but that they are universal claims not made on behalf of interests. In an eighteenth-century enlightenment and democratizing impulse, Kant sought to free the judgment of taste from the aristocratic and clerical domains that had exercised it earlier by referring it to a wider public sphere, potentially a sphere "for everyone,"—just the implication Bourdieu dismisses. The claim to "subjective universality," even in what I take to be Kant's terms (i.e., stripped of its imputed claim that everyone *will* find pleasure in the same forms), must be modified in a contemporary aesthetic especially with reference to historical change.

Nowadays we are very much aware that mental habits are at the same time intimately personal and socially constructed, subject to the vagaries of history. Raymond Williams calls this oscillation between private and social "structures of feeling," "characteristic elements of impulse, restraint, and tone.... a social experience which is still in process, often indeed not yet recognized as social but taken to be private." Art and literature are "often among the very first indications that such a new structure is forming" (*ML*, pp. 132, 121–27, 133). Structures of feeling are *experienced* as natural and intimate, the way one's own corner of the world works, but they are also *structured* and the patterns into which they fall are conditioned by society and firmly situated historically. Subjectivities cannot be regarded as "universal" across time and space in the light of such a social patterning, but Williams also argues against the tyranny of such structures: "No dominant social order ever in reality includes or exhausts all human practice, human energy, and human intention" (p. 125). Again the powers of imagination, sometimes called up through the formal strategies of literature, are called upon to break the lock of historical situatedness. I will consider this issue further in the next section, by exploring the value of substituting "horizon " for "situation" in carrying out interpretive work.

Aesthetics and Historical Understanding

An updated aesthetic must supplement the attention to historical change neglected by the *Critique of Judgement.* Since Kant's account of the apprehension of beauty, with its implication of unmediated effect, deals inadequately with art distanced by history, an aesthetic theory useful to Chaucerians will have to supply it. I will turn to Gadamer's hermeneutic principles to investigate how historical distance may be acknowledged without abandoning aesthetic reflection. Much of Gadamer's work may be said to consider interpretive issues in close relation to aesthetic ones. In *Truth and Method,* he calls the experience of beauty "an enchantment and an adventure," and he begins the essay "Aesthetics and Hermeneutics," by acknowledging art's accessibility across time:

> For of all the things that confront us in nature and history, it is the work of art that speaks to us most directly. It possesses a mysterious intimacy that grips our entire being, as if there were no distance at all and every encounter with it were an encounter with ourselves.... Only in a limited way does it retain its historical origin in itself.... the aesthetic consciousness can appeal to the fact that the work of art communicates itself."[33]

This looks very much like Kant's subjective universality, but the essay goes on to argue that although the work may be said to "occupy a timeless present," it nonetheless requires hermeneutics—"the art of clarifying and mediating by our effort of interpretation what is said by persons we encounter in tradition"—to make it intelligible to later generations (*PH*, p. 98). Hermeneutic practice generally has the character of translation in that it "bridges the distance between minds and reveals the foreignness of the other mind" (pp. 99–100). Art presents a special case; it speaks not only about a past world, but also about the reader's own world and must be "integrated into the self-understanding of each person" (p. 100). Both textual understanding and aesthetic experience are instances of being, and, as Gadamer has insisted all along, "being that can be understood is language" (p. 103). Hermeneutics, he asserts in *Truth and Method*, came about because of a "rise of historical consciousness"

(*TM,* p. 165). These positions unite historical and aesthetic issues with the strategies of hermeneutics.

The Gadamerian mediation between earlier lifeworlds and those of modern readers mandates historical inquiry into material and intellectual contexts (*TM*, p. 247) and is particularly important for a poet like Chaucer. The scholarly effort to construct responsible images of the past is part of the hermeneutic project, since these are neither objectively given histories that we can simply assent to nor persfonal understandings we can rely on once and for all. Instead they are fluid and open to new knowledge of both Chaucer's world and ours. If the book of history is a fragment (p. 199) to which each generation has its particular access and particular blindness, the hermeneutic project is never complete, the "context" never fixed in place. From Gadamer's standpoint, even if we could know Chaucer's world and intention exactly, "Not just occasionally but always, the meaning of a text goes beyond its author," and understanding is productive rather than simply reproductive (p. 296). This is the principle of *Wirkungsgeschichte,* which holds that any historical vantage point "determines in advance what seems to us worth inquiring about" (p. 300), enabling genuine, but never complete historical analysis.[34] It is linguistic in that language presents an understanding of being. Gadamer does not deny that an era holds specific conditions of possibility—horizons of possibility—but he does not construe that as an impenetrable barrier to later understanding. The response to a work hermeneutically "translated" is a fusion of horizons between past and present readers, and, once accomplished, that fusion allows the direct aesthetic response alluded to above: the "mysterious intimacy that grips our entire being, as if there were no distance at all and every encounter with it were an encounter with ourselves." It is therefore possible for us to both understand Chaucerian texts in our own way and intuit new shapes that lead to our own pleasure in their aesthetic effects.

Regarding past writing under the concept of horizons enables more intimacy with it than the notion of sealed-off "situations of ideological possibility" favored by ideology critique. Horizons are only imaginable as moving with the observer, as connection between past and present—no isolated past horizon and no fixed horizon in the present. Every current understanding "is always a fusion of these horizons supposedly existing by themselves" (*TM*, p. 306). To fuse horizons is to "regain the concepts of a historical past in such a way that they also include our own comprehension of them" (p. 374). Although this may sound like altogether conceptual work, Gadamer represents it as fluid and conversational. Hans Robert Jauss similarly refers to its unavailablility in objective or even objectifiable form, to either its author or later recipients.[35] Ranciére's "aesthetic regimes of art," systems that work by "coexist[ing] and intermingl[ing] in the works themselves," shares some of these elements.[36] The point is that, in dealing with a Chaucerian horizon, we are not observing a fixed or obvious mental universe. Gadamer and Jauss regard the hermeneutic process as basic to aesthetic grasp and offer a way to include historical reflection in it: the logic of the hermeneutic circle.

The hermeneutic circle is usually called on to describe how individual works are interpreted through an "oscillating movement between whole and part" (*TM*, p. 191). Gadamer's description of this process works from hypothesis to its confirmation or modification. Following Heidegger, he identifies a style of reading: "interpretation begins with fore-conceptions that are replaced by more suitable ones. The constant process of new projection constitutes the movement of understanding and interpretation."[37] Gadamer's argument expands the circle to include the historical horizon of the whole work and discusses how broad a context should be included as fore-conception. In the case of Chaucerian texts, the circle can be continually enlarged to include a broader sense of medieval culture (resulting from new findings in social and cultural history) and of verbal suggestiveness (resulting from developments in literary theory and historical linguistics). The process is recursive, but the implied circle is not vicious because at each moment it challenges the very prejudices that allowed the process to be entered into. Although this is not Kant's language for apprehending the purposiveness intuited in the aesthetic object, it is congruent with his description of the aesthetic idea, "the representation of the imagination which induces much thought, yet without the possibility of any definite thought whatever, i.e., *concept,* being adequate to it" and without the possibility that language will render it "completely intelligible" (*CJ*, pp. 175–76). The recursiveness of Gadamer's circle might be taken as a gloss on Kant's denial of art's confinement to a stable concept in accounting for divergent readings of valued texts.

As we build our mental representations of Chaucer's first audiences (and at this point cultural studies, even as ideology critique, has much to teach), we try to imagine structures of feeling without necessarily claiming them as our own. Much criticism fails to accomplish that feat successfully and, in any case, each generation has to do it over again. Byron called Chaucer's fiction "obscene and contemptible"; Gwynn called the fabliaux "gross ribaldry" and Skeat thought them regrettable.[38] Chaucer's work appears to different audiences in different shapes and with different emphases, and therefore tends to command aesthetic attention and provide aesthetic pleasure for different reasons. In addition, the research of the past few decades has uncovered so much about the social formation of Chaucer's time that we see the elements of many of his tales differently now, and we may find them aesthetically effective for different reasons.

But the fact that very specific historical conditions (social, ideological, literary) contributed to the *Canterbury Tales* and *Troilus and Criseyde* by no means dictates that they cannot convey meaning and excite audiences in a different dispensation. History changes "lived relations to the real" (Althusser) and "structures of feeling" (Williams),[39] but it doesn't change everything at an equal rate, and some felt rhythms seem to recur in disguised forms centuries later. The return to history itself involves historical imagination, and Gadamer's style for using modifiable fore-conceptions to frame interpretation provides a powerful way to induce it. Fusing horizons—sometimes speedily, sometimes entailing years of effort—can end up enabling aesthetic pleasures that suppress neither historical origins nor contemporary lifeworlds.

Gadamer's manner in linking hermeneutic activity with historical imagination brings to mind Kant's sense of the beautiful as involving the whole mind in pleasureful activity. The escape from determinate concepts supports his frequent recourse to the "freedom" of imagination. Eluding fixed concepts allows art to bear playful relationship to the "regime of truth" dominant at its making. George Levine asserts that "however absorbed into dominant ideological formations the aesthetic has been, it has always served also as a potentially disruptive force, one that opens up possibilities of value resistant to any dominant political power. (The danger of a relatively free art in totalitarian countries is the most obvious evidence for this.)"[40] I agree with this observation, but not because beauty is always and everywhere aligned with "immutable truth" or because "aesthetic harmony" is "intrinsically subversive," but because dominant ideological and aesthetic systems cannot be counted on to stay in place over time.[41] Once an art object is grasped by imagination, it can escape even its most tractable service to the social regime that nourished it. Another, now discredited, Kantian term "genius" is related to Levine's point. Genius is, for Kant, an "animating principle in the mind," an idea that induces thought while overflowing any concept that might contain it and lying just beyond the confines of ordinary experience, not learned and taught like other mental powers, but rather visited upon an author absent a defined will or method; it is a presiding guardian, a "Genie" (*CJ*, pp. 175–76). The stress here is on the freedom of imagination to escape from the confines that govern ordinary thought. It follows from disinterestedness (freedom from willfulness) and purposiveness without purpose (freedom from conceptual logic). Like the rest of Kant's analysis, genius suggests that imagination can recognize and foreground the products of others uncompelled by rule. It also suggests that historical situatedness does not prevent its pleasure for subsequent generations. Later readers are imaginatively enabled to participate in worlds with institutions and structures of feeling different from their own.[42]

That the aesthetic is somehow reserved for the free play of thought—a kind of mental utopia or "national park" for the mind[43]—is widely, if grudgingly, granted by people who find themselves on very different sides of current questions of ideology and literature. Sartre defended art as the realm of freedom, and Lukacs distinguished it from the practical on the one hand and the magical on the other. In a more internal sense of freedom, Freud calls the aesthetic form of a work of art a bribe that enables us to overcome our compulsions and that frees us from our own anxieties. For the radical ideology critiquer, though, this mental latitude is fostered by modern states precisely to buttress a form of personal individualism that is both illusory and hostile to collective projects. On that point, Northrop Frye, Fredric Jameson, and Raymond Williams, all from different angles, stress the force of literature's "meditation on community." Indeed, if the constraints of social/cultural life are so confining that it is truly impossible to meditate on the community or see empathetically into the lives of others in unfamiliar communities, every libratory project is doomed from the start and "demystification" in the service of social goals is pointless.

Different works induce this freedom in different ways, but readers who deny it altogether must also reject the element of newness or emergence (in Raymond Williams's sense) as a feature of art.[44] They can explain repetition—the "o sentence" Robertson finds in *Troilus and Criseyde* or the "divine recapitulation" Eco's character Jorge defends in *Name of the Rose*—better than change in either life or art. Where change presents itself is in imagination, first in the isolated imaginings of authors and readers and then, perhaps, in new structures of feeling for a generation. The arena of freedom I am positing for art is both personal, in that it is experienced by one onlooker at a time, and social, in that it arises from and flows back into a social imaginary related to (but not saturated by) ideology. Aesthetic force is not of course the sole spur to social change, but neither is it inert in the mix of forces that impel it. And it is not a simple reflecting mirror for the dominant. The simultaneous appeal to understanding and imagination is described by Paul Ricoeur as "the free play of possibilities in a state of noninvolvement with respect to the world of perception or of action."[45] It is in this state of noninvolvement that we try our new ideas, new values, new ways of being in the world."[46] This principle holds for both Chaucer's world and our own.

Medieval doctrine both distrusted the freedom of imagination as fantasy and honored it when controlled by reason as necessary to intellection. It will be a central term in this book because imagination that becomes art implies some blend of the sensible and the intelligible, a starting point for an aesthetic that we can share with Chaucer and his earliest readers. In the next chapter, I want to comment briefly on the intellectual traditions concerning beauty and imagination entertained in Chaucer's era and then see where contemporary horizons can be reconciled with those traditions and where they cannot. What I hope will emerge is an array of working principles for the analysis of the *Canterbury Tales* and *Troilus and Criseyde* in an aesthetic mode.

CHAPTER 2

CHAUCERIAN RESOUN YMAGINATYF

And thus the whole world can enter into
the human soul through the doors of the senses.

Saint Bonaventure

nat by resoun sensible of demyng, but by resoun ymaginatyf.

Chaucer's *Boece*

I need to answer the objection that Chaucer's own era could not have considered aesthetic questions because the category of thought designated *aesthetic* was not introduced until Alexander Baumgarten's *Aesthetica* in 1750, nor made central to European thinking until Hume, Kant, Schiller, and Hegel took it up.[1] People who would not quibble with using the word *ideology* as an analytic category bearing on issues earlier than *its* appearance as a term in the eighteenth century, or *unconscious* before Freud, cannot argue that these matters were not in the intellectual world before the current terms were in use. "Sweetness" (*dulcis, suavitatis*), as Mary Carruthers has pointed out, carries the notion of "sense-based knowledge" and is consistently used "to make a positive judgment about the positive effects of a work of art."[2] But the argument may be that there was no *systematic thinking* about beauty and art in the Middle Ages, and this I intend to dispute. Aesthetics concerns the nature and perception of the beautiful, and medieval thinkers inherited rich, though not undisputed, theories from Plato, Aristotle, and Plotinus, building on that inheritance, primarily to reconcile it with the claims of Christian theology. Authors like Chaucer used it to reflect on their own poetic strategies, which, as Vincent Gillespie concludes, display the "most sustained and subtle responses" to medieval aesthetic theory.[3]

This brings us to a third objection, this one most fully associated with D. W. Robertson, Jr.: the medieval "universe of discourse" was so different from our own that intuitions of meaning and aesthetic responses alike are rendered unreadable without abandoning our expectations for meaning and enjoyment.[4] Judson Boyce Allen, working from similar premises about the unanimity of medieval sensibilities, denies the possibility of aesthetic response that resembles post-Kantian notions of pleasure.[5] Received traditions (including Robertson's Fathers and the incipits used by Allen) figure as important considerations as we construct medieval horizons of understanding (Gadamer), but they do not have the final word on what Chaucer and his various audiences understood, and they should not be used to devalue our own responses. I agree with Robert Edwards that, even for the Middle Ages, they are neither "a proper account of what authorship and literary form mean in the aesthetic understanding of a work," nor a "metalanguage" operating above the poetry. His book concludes with the assertion that poetry "operates within a double truth—a world of sustained imagination intensely conscious of its own complexities and limits."[6] It is not ahistorical to think our own ways into that imaginative realm with all the resources we have.

My object in making this glancing foray into the tradition Chaucer inherited is to fashion a notion of what was thinkable within medieval horizons. The horizon of the thinkable is, of course, historically bounded for any era (although I think Robertson and Allen overstate the case), but I do not present these traditional influences (except for that of Boethius) as conscious constraints on Chaucer while he was working. The subject is vast, but even this brief survey reveals the latitude and subtlety within traditional thought on imagination and art. The emphasis of my account will fall on Augustine's largely Platonic mode, Aquinas's Aristotelian style, and Bonaventure's mysticism.

Chaucer Imagining

Augustine is everywhere aware of beauty.[7] Although ascribing beauty to anything is for him a high form of praise, a link with an attribute of God and his creation, the *Confessions* shows him suspicious of "lower beautiful creations" (*pulchra inferiora*), which tempt us to love them for themselves instead of for God, and to weep for their demise without reference to the divine plan (4.13). Verbal and dramatic arts were seductive for Augustine from an early age, when he loved inane tales [the Trojan horse, for example] and hated truer more useful studies like arithmetic sums (1.13.22). As a student in Carthage, he was moved by the theater, but in the *Confessions*, he condemns his tears for suffering lovers, judging them to be a waste of true pity, since the plays merely mimicked misery (1.13.20–22). His love of the nobility of Cicero's style initially prejudiced him against the surface "lowliness" of Scripture (*sed visa est mihi indigna quam tulliane dignitati compararem*), the truth and nobility of which was only revealed through humble attentiveness (3.5.9). These superficial beauties are castigated by the saved Augustine as he writes, but he reveals his deep respect for their power as he relates the spells they had cast over him. As a mature Christian, he loved the metaphors of the Bible, finding them pleasurably open to renewed contemplation. Yet one might discern a hint of guilt even in this pleasure: "But why it seems sweeter to me than if no such similitude were offered in the divine books, since the thing perceived is the same, is difficult to say and is a problem for another discussion."[8]

Number and suitability are Augustine's keys to both kinds of beauty. In music, "beautiful things please by proportion" just as they do in architectural matters.[9] These are Platonic ideas, of course, which refer to mathematical and musical perfections, but for Augustine, as for most medieval thinkers, they are reinforced by the phrasing "weight, number and measure" of Wisdom (11.23). This leaning acknowledges the sensible delights of well-proportioned objects, but true or higher beauty is the intellectual grasp of "simple and intelligible numbers."[10] Although there are innocent aesthetic pleasures to be taken from both natural and humanly constructed sensible objects, the serious beauties of the world are properly used by reason to contemplate the revealed, but difficult truths of Scripture and the church.

> Quomodo ergo, si essemus peregrini, qui beate uiuere nisi in patria non possemus, eaque peregrinatione utique miseri et miseriam finire cupientes in patriam redire uellemus, opus esset uel terrestribus uel marinis uehiculis, quibus utendum esset, ut ad patriam, qua fruendum erat, peruenire ualeremus; quod si amoenitates itineris et ipsa gestatio uehiculorum nos delectaret, conuersi ad fruendum his, quibus uti debuimus, nollemus cito uiam finire et peruersa suauitate implicati alienaremur a patria, cuius suauitas faceret beatos, sic in huius mortalitatis uita peregrinantes a domino, si redire in patriam uolumus, ubi beati esse possimus, utendum est hoc mundo, non fruendum, ut inuisibilia dei per ea, quae facta sunt, intellecta conspiciantur, hoc est, ut de corporalibus temporalibusque rebus aeterna et spiritalia capiamus.
>
> [Suppose we were wanderers who could not live in blessedness except at home, miserable in our wandering and desiring to end it and to return to our native country. We would need vehicles for land or sea which could be used to help us reach our homeland, which is to be enjoyed. But if the amenities of the journey and the motion of the vehicles itself delighted us, and we were led to enjoy those things we ought to use, we should

> not wish to end our journey quickly, and, entangled in a perverse sweetness, we should be alienated from our country, whose sweetness would make us blessed. Thus in this mortal life, wandering from God, if we wish to return to our native country where we can be blessed we should use this world and not enjoy it, so that the "invisible" things of God "being understood by the things that are made" may be seen, that is, so that by means of corporal and temporal things we may comprehend the eternal and spiritual.][11]

The beauty of the world we journey through is only a vehicle, the right-minded use of which is instrumental to spiritual understanding and moral probity. Throughout *On Christian Doctrine*, even the figures of Scripture are to be enjoyed only for the sake of the spiritual homeland toward which they move us. It should be noted as well that Augustine provided this defense of moral reasoning in a beautiful and memorable metaphor of his own.

The idea that God is traceable through his creation is the sustained focus of Bonaventure's *The Mind's Road to God*, but Bonaventure is generally more lyrical about and less suspicious of sensible beauty than Augustine:

> Relucet autem Creatoris summa potentia et sapienta et benevolentia in rebus creatis secundum quod hoc tripliciter nuntiat sensus carnis sensui interiori. Sensus enim carnis aut deservit intellectui rationabiliter investiganti, aut fideliter credenti, aut intellectualiter contetemplanti. Contemplans considerat rerum existentium actualem, credens rerum decursum habitualem, ratiocinans rerum praecellentiam potentialem.
>
> [There shine forth, however, the Creator's supreme power and wisdom and benevolence in created things, as the carnal sense reports trebly to the inner sense. For the carnal sense serves him who either understands rationally or believes faithfully or contemplates intellectually. Contemplating, it considers the actual existence of things; believing, it considers the habitual course of things; reasoning, it considers the potential excellence of things.][12]

This passage is interesting in that the "things" of the sense world remain under scrutiny throughout the process; they are the "eternal art" of God's creative act (1.3). As he contemplates the natural world, Bonaventure, like the founder of his order Francis, sees both its immediate delight and its power as a sign, although sense is just the first rung of the ladder upwards; (*scala Iacob, primum gradum ascensionis collocemus in imo, ponendo totum istum mundum sensibilem nobis tanquam speculum, per quod transeamus ad Deum* [1.9]). The beauty of things testifies to God's power, wisdom, and goodness because their forms result from divine "seminal reasons" (*rationes seminales*), which can be contemplated not just *through*, but also *in* things (1.14). The delight experienced in the presence of beauty also bespeaks the seminal reasons and the human mind, as an image of God, is designed to respond to it (2.1).[13] Mental powers used in rational inference rather than in direct observation also participate in "eternal art" so that purely logical statements can be true even if the elements to which it refers do not actually exist (3.3). (This idea of a *via rationis* that could operate without reference to observable reality was still being debated at Oxford in Chaucer's time.)[14] Although this tenet usually functions as a justification for rational deduction, it might be used on behalf of fiction as well. Chaucer's "hertes line" (of which more later) may be such a case.

Like Augustine, Bonaventure stresses weight, number, and measure in considering "things in themselves": "All delight, however, is by reason of proportion" (omnis *autem delectatio est ratione proportionalitatis* [2.5]). "And thus the whole world can enter into the human soul through the doors of the senses" by apprehension, delight, and judgment; (*Et sic totus iste mundus introire habet in animam humanam per portas sensuum secundum tres operationes praedictas* [2.6]). The delight that induces admiration for the order of the universe is in this (broad) sense formal. It is not surprising, then, that he attributes beauty in humanly created objects to good construction and faithfulness to the reality they imitated, which allows the representation of a monster, ugly in itself, to be praised for beauty.[15] Bonaventure quotes Augustine's treatise on music to emphasize his conclusion that beauty results from formal properties (2.10). As sense experience, the beauty of the world is immediately delightful on account of its proportion, but it is also a vast forest of signs: "so that through the sensibles which they see they may be carried forward to the intelligibles which they do not see, as if by signs to the signified" (*ut per sensibilia. quae vident, transferantur ad intelligibilia, quae non vident, tamquam per signa ad signata* [2.11]). This passage echoes *On Christian Doctrine* directly in positing a world full of divine footprints, but it differs in maintaining so full a respect for the initiating *things*.

For Thomas Aquinas, as for both Augustine and Bonaventure, the world of sense impressions is the beginning of knowledge and understanding; his detailed analysis of the powers of the mind keep sense impressions—phantasms—in the picture during "higher" levels of intellectual endeavor. "The intellect is constantly looking to see what the senses are doing, and is constantly instructing the internal senses on what to do next, as Robert Pasnau puts it."[16] The "cooperative venture between sense and intellect" begins with perception (aided already by intellect), judges the perceived forms species, packs them away in memory for use by imagination, and continues to use them for conceptual thought. God and the angels do not need these images (phantasms), but human beings do.[17] Moreover, the imagination is itself active, forming for itself "the image of an absent object, or even one never seen" (*imaginative format sibi aliquod idolem rei absentis, vel etiam nunquam visae*).[18] This productive power of imagination would seem to apply to both visual and verbal imaging.[19] This attention to verbal classifying allows Pasnau to discuss (compellingly, I think) Aquinas as attacking the problem Wittgenstein called aspect recognition, "seeing as."[20] Although he sees Aquinas's practice of discriminating between the parts of a "seemingly unified event" like seeing, he "is pursuing the same project that engages contemporary cognitive scientists."[21]

Seeing, along with hearing, is central to Aquinas's description of beauty "whereas a thing is called beautiful when the mere apprehension of it gives us pleasure" (*pulcrum autem dicatur id cuius ipsa apprehensio placet*). Umberto Eco identifies this passage as the key to Aquinas's aesthetics.[22] The formal attributes of beauty are presented within a discussion of the attributes of Christ in part I of the *Summa theologiae*: *integritas, proportio sive consonantia, claritas*. Integrity of form is concrete reality, this particular thing, not just something of this species. Proportionality seems a nearly mathematical concept, but Aquinas broadens it to account for the psyche perceiving it and the "connotative code" through which a particular culture might read it, including a set of literary conventions.[23] Clarity—shining with both uniqueness and participation in universality—seems the most immediate attribute of a beautiful object (that which pleases when it is seen), yet that very radiance also holds the key to the further aesthetic pleasure of interpretation.[24] Man-made art is described in terms of imitation: "an image is called beautiful if it represents a thing, even an ugly thing, faithfully" (*Unde videmus quod aliqua imago dicitur esse pulchra, si perfecte repraesentat rem quamvis turpem*).[25] This old and widely held proposition insists on verisimilitude while denying that art produces merely decorative (or as Kant would say "agreeable") effects. When he is not invoking mimetic art, Aquinas expresses the usual medieval ambivalence about imagination, writing of imaginings inspired by angels, but also of demonic visions, some revealing or seeming to reveal the future. These are especially likely to occur during sleep, when the storehouse of phantasms overcomes the common sense that usually keeps them "quiet."[26]

I present these overlapping, but not identical, comments on beauty and imagination to suggest the esteem in which beauty was held during the Middle Ages as an attribute of the divinely and humanly created world, as a "forest of signs," and as a potentially misleading ensnarer of loyalties. These influences were felt in disseminated ways throughout the late medieval period and doubtless fell within Chaucer's mental horizon. But the *Consolation of Philosophy* was directly known and pondered by Chaucer early in his writing career (late 1370s, early 1380s) as he produced *Boece*, his complete translation of it. This is not to say that everything Chaucer wrote was adjudicated by his scrupulous involvement with the *Consolation*, but that he had thought carefully about it before and while he wrote.

Boethius treats beauty with mixed awe and suspicion, much as Augustine had. Most of his references to it come from Lady Philosophy's unmasking of *false* beauties like those of precious gems, lovely fields, and fine clothing when desired as possessions. Their beauty may be admired as belonging to them—"apayed of [pleased with] hir owne beautes," but owning them does not bless the human owner, whose particular beauty is reason, and who ought not be sorry to lose them (2. prose 5). False social "beauties" like undeserved status are also castigated, and physical ones are transitory. But beauty, false or true, is presented as the object of desire.[27] Boethius seems eager to leave sensible details behind as he guides readers from the beauty of Lady Philosophy's garment and its dirtied and torn condition to the significance of the wear and tear of history on innately appealing truths. Like Augustine, he is in a hurry to see *through* the sensible layer, while Bonaventure seems unashamed to love the sensible world, and Aquinas argues that mind returns to the phantasms even after their intelligibility has been glimpsed.[28] Boethius includes the usual stress on the control of imagination by the "higher" faculties of reason and intellect, but the treatise also keeps imagination in the realm of judgment throughout cognition. Chaucer's translation phrases this point thus:

> Also ymaginacioun, albeit so that it takith of wit [sense impressions] the bygynnynges to seen and formen the figures, algates althoughe that wit ne were nat present, yit it envyrowneth and comprehendith alle thingis sensible, nat by resoun sensible of demyng, but by resoun ymaginatyf. (V, prosa 4, 200–210)[29]

The phrase "resoun ymaginatyf" seems to me a resonant locution for considering Chaucer's practices in relating observed reality and rational activity to authorial creation.[30]

Beauty instructs through imagination; that is its value in much medieval thought. Roger Bacon describes the beauty of literature as its power to "move the soul unexpectedly," making it particularly useful in exploring moral terrains.[31] Properly contemplated, it inspires cosmic appreciation and love of goodness. Abbot Suger even elevated gems to the realm of moral inspiration, speaking of the decorative elements of the church, "the loveliness of the many-colored gems has called me away from external cares, and worthy meditation has induced me to reflect, transferring that which is material to that which is immaterial, on the diversity of the sacred virtues."[32] But imagination might also instruct wrongly. The oscillation between exalting beauty for its inducement to insight and opposing it to reason as fostering illusion is perhaps the most striking feature of Chaucer's inherited tradition.

Chaucer knew both aspects of that tradition through his translation of *Boece*, but he also heeded what must have been a commonplace of medieval thought: before you can do anything, you have to imagine doing it. Chaucer's extended metaphor for imagination (from Geoffrey of Vinsauf's *Poetria Nova*) comes at the end of Book I of *Troilus and Criseyde*:

> For everi wight that hath an hous to founde
> Ne renneth naught the werk for to begynne
> With rakel hond, but he wol bide a stounde,
> And sende his hertes line out fro withinne
> Aldirfirst his purpos to wynne.
> Al this Pandare in his herte thoughte,
> And caste his werk ful wisely or he wrought.
> (I.1065–71)[33]

This fundamental role for imagination—sending out the heart's line to remember things about building houses and to assess plans in terms of purposes—is one we share; when we observe a Pandarus or an Iago planning in this way we say, "what an imagination," and when a project of our own flops, we say, "that was a failure of imagination." The concrete, but highly suggestive, image of mental probing as sending down a plumb line from the heart to measure depth and get the angles straight before acting, building, or writing is itself a contribution to medieval theories of imagination.

In spite of the suspicion and potential censoring of the doctrinal positions of the late fourteenth-century church, fictional art was too useful to be foregone in inducing the laity to piety. Chaucer's Pardoner proves by his success that "lewed peple loven tales olde; / Swiche thynges kan they wel reporte and holde" (VI.437–38), a position in keeping with Aquinas's insistence on keeping images in play throughout cognition. Fictions of all kinds proliferated in the late medieval Church filling devotional manuals and sermons with "fals fablis," as Wyclif called them, many from the pagan past and only lightly dusted with Christian moralizations. The trick is to recycle or invent stories that would lead seamlessly to the intelligible truths of the faith. Outside the church too, this was a flourishing time for verbal art in both poetry and prose not to mention the guidebooks on producing it effectively.

Medieval aesthetic understandings, while not altogether assimilable to a single "theory," consistently depend on attempts to wrest intelligibility from sense experience. Even supposing the mental horizons of the long period we call the Middle Ages have been circumscribed by these major writers' ideas (a by no means obvious move), some latitude for responses in medieval reception must be granted. Both the natural world and the human mind that contemplates it were designed by God, both exhibit traces that lead to Him, and are immediately delightful and (with contemplation) instructive. Platonists are wary of lingering over sensible details once they have been found intelligible; mystics quite hospitable. The beauty of creation and human artifacts results from harmonious proportion, sometimes stated abstractly, as mathematical or musical, but sometimes as the formal (but less rule-bound) presentation of an indwelling idea. Verisimilitude is praised, even in depicting monsters, but nonmimetic invention (as in the case of nonexistent monsters) can also be beautiful, lending a certain legitimacy to imagination, which is regarded as both the formation of observed realities not present and the exercise of fantasy when controlled by the higher faculty of reason.

The medieval record presents a clear picture of the distrust with which imagination was regarded. Both objects in the world and the man-made creations of art and delusion are present to the mind as imagination. In *De Musica*, Augustine distinguishes everyday images retained in memory from "phantasms" or *imaginium imagines* created by the mind. He admits the possibility of "true phantasms," but distrusts them.[34] The virtual image as a concept is as old as Plato and Aristotle, and Sidney made it prominent in poetics with his "nothing affirmeth," but the Middle Ages had its suspicions of images unfettered to scriptural or real-world reference. Peter Haidu summarizes such suspicions: "fiction is man's disruption of language from its divinely ordained intentionality." It has "undergone a subtraction of its divinely determined purpose." Once language is used without its extra-linguistic reference, it becomes, whether mimetic or a simulacrum of the world, "essentially unbound and unpredictable."[35] At worst, it becomes imagined in the sense of imaginary or phantasmagoric, possibly sent by the devil; at best, the monsters imagined by writers and cathedral stone masons deserved to be called beautiful although they were found in neither nature or Scripture. In Chaucer's generation, the issue was polemicized by Lollard's wholesale objections to images, statues, and "fables" alike.[36] These disparate claims gave rise to waves of uncertainty throughout the period.

The *Canterbury Tales* registers such distrust of imagination and its kinship with fantasy. When Mercury appears to Arcite in a dream, his image and message are tinged with threat. His "slepy yerde" is held upright, in power over the prone Arcite, and Arcite recognizes that he looks as he did when he killed Argus. Arcite, though, reads his instruction to end his woe by going to Athens as helpful encouragement. Imagination in this case is seductive and in the event destructive, and so it is in the *Miller's Tale*. John the Carpenter entertains Nicholas's carefully architected fiction of the flood as a truth (thinking that "verraily" he may see the water come "walwynge"), but

> Men may dyen of ymaginacioun,
> So depe may impressioun be take.
> (I.3612–14)

John suffers a broken leg, but if he had died in the fall from the ceiling, it would have been the result of his enthusiastic participation in the fictional *image* of the flood Nicholas presented.

Within medieval horizons of understanding, imagination grasped beauty in terms of verisimilitude, coherence, proportionality, and luminosity, but against a backdrop of distrust of those very properties as available for seduction or error. Practical discourses, like pulpit oratory and devotional guides, could not get along without the use of imaginative narratives, but there was always the chance that they might escape their exemplary functions and produce scandalous thoughts. When we attempt to understand Chaucer's world and the aesthetic effects his fictions might have had for his first audiences, this vocabulary aids us in opening unaccustomed perspectives on art, but in the end we call on our own theories of imagination. As Alastair Minnis writes concerning both visual and verbal forms, "People cannot think without images; people cannot remember what they thought without images; people cannot plan for the future without images."[37] And scholars cannot historicize without imagination: "A history without imagination is a mutilated, disembodied history," as Jacques Le Goff puts it.[38] First we will construct (imagine) a horizon for our late fourteenth-century writer and then be in a better position to assess which effects on his earlier audiences are available within current horizons. I will begin with distrust.

Imagining Chaucer

Currently we seem to hold a high estimate of imaginative reach—Mary Carruthers begins *The Book of Memory* with a striking contrast between descriptions of Aquinas's vast memory and Einstein's creative imagination. "When we think of our highest creative powers, we think invariably of the imagination" is the first sentence of her book, yet, like medieval people, we both love and hate imagination.[39] Public discourse debate on issues like "recovered memory," "eyewitness testimony," the social effects of filmed violence, and the truth-value of anything "fictional" registers our era's vacillations about the tangled webs that bind perception to reality, personal predisposition, and even delusion. In many academic circles, the impression of giving in to the "enchantment" of literary art is widely seen as an embarrassing indulgence in what is personally agreeable. Some recent critics (even when they are not pledged to ideology critique) make resistance to the imaginative element in fiction into a kind of moral probity. De Man, for example, has been praised for writing criticism that made difficult texts still more perplexing by resisting their seductiveness and deliberately staying out of their virtual lifeworlds. Many more practice one of the several styles of "hermeneutic of suspicion," in Paul Ricoeur's celebrated phrase, reading "against the grain" without having read with it. Sometimes this stance is presented as political watchfulness, sometimes simply as the chutzpa of showing that the critic knows what the author was up to and can demystify its ideological interests. The structures of feeling involved in unstinting praise alternating with deep distrust for imagination are reminiscent of those I have traced in the Middle Ages.

If we share with Chaucer's era both fascination with and distrust of imagination, we also share the general notion that aesthetics addresses the interlace between sensible pleasure, artistic beauty, and contemplation of its intelligibility.[40] Why an object should appear delightful in the first place, though, sometimes marks the difference between medieval men and women and ourselves even where natural scenes are involved. We are more acutely aware that much pleasure in nature is historically conditioned—we know that until the eighteenth century, mountains were generally considered unsightly and smooth geographic regularity seemed pleasing.[41] Our own natural environment is constantly subjected to the commodification which hypes even remote natural areas and commercializes them whenever possible, straining the sense of spontaneous delight (yet for all that, nature is never spent). We also regard imaginative creation and reception somewhat differently.

The phrasing resoun ymaginatyf of Chaucer's *Boece* suggests that reason and imagination are more intricately enmeshed than is implied by the medieval commonplace that reason properly dominates over imagination. Carruthers reads the traditional use of *cogitatio* as also thoroughly involved with images and emotional colorings rather than signaling anything as "abstractly rational as the modern word 'thought'" for the medieval commentators who gave it so much priority.[42] If this is right, the control of imagination by reason means something less tilted toward logical systematicity (and perhaps less suspicious of imagination) than is usually assumed. Carruthers' investigation of the deep and intricate involvement of memory and imagination in the Middle Ages yields two propositions bearing on my argument here: that words and visual images are made to stand in for one another in memory, and that these "mental images" are figures for understanding rather than pictures of reality.[43] On the first point, Carruthers produces models of the mnemonic techniques developed by cultures with far less access to books than we have. Often they involve "laying down" visual images in "cells" imprinted in the mind for later access, as when Paul likens the virtues to a Christian's armor.

In our own era, this meshing of consciousness itself with image-making and emotion is coming to prominence in some academic communities. It is the theme of neuroscientist Antonio Damasio's *The Feeling of What Happens* and figures significantly in philosopher Daniel Dennett's *Consciousness Explained*.[44] The medieval account of mental picture-making can be placed beside contemporary theorizations by Damasio and Dennett on imagination, which of course are based on different assumptions. Carruthers' second point stresses that these mental representations are "verbal" rather than realistically pictorial because they signal ideas; the images serve as functional clues or signs that form the basis of cognition. It will be a continuing motif of this book that Chaucer's aesthetic effects are achieved through this more interactive idea of imagination and reason, just as his phrase "resoun ymaginatif" predicts. This mental horizon may be attributed to some in Chaucer's earliest audiences, and is available to us through our quite different conception of mental life.

Imagination and memory can be envisioned as if something is physically imprinted on the brain when we remember, as in medieval thinking (Carruthers) or as if we create a continuous internal movie, in Damasio's description of mental life.[45] Dennett's *Consciousness Explained* goes further toward Artificial Intelligence and away from the notion of a "central processing" unit called "mind," distinguishable from the brain. Considering what we know of brain functions, Dennett argues that we must substitute a myriad of brain subsystems, the "multiple drafts" theory, for the movie in the mind model or what he calls the "Cartesian theater."[46] Can effects of art like those in question here be registered in this discourse? Respect for the human resources necessary for perception and invention certainly can; Dennett writes, "When we understand consciousness [in this way]—when there is no more mystery—consciousness will be different, but there will still be beauty, and more room than ever for awe" (*CE*, p. 25). Here is how it works: much more is coming from the world than we have the capacity to process, so we take in only as much as will satisfy our current "epistemic hungers" and, when we hallucinate or dream, the subsystems that retain and combine these impressions will supply only as full an image as is hungered for at that moment. "Epistemic hunger" leads Dennett to the principle of thrift—the brain takes in what it "needs" and the seer is satisfied that she has been offered the whole visible scene. This version of thrift—restated as "an image is created from words suggesting just as many characteristics as it must to provide satisfaction"—has interesting implications for fiction. Since I think of Chaucer as a preeminently thrifty poet, I will use it throughout to comment on his effects. Such thrift in art seems to me a mark of its aesthetic appeal, although Dennett does not make that assertion.

Thus it does not seem to me the case that suspicion of imagination arises primarily from the natural sciences. Carruthers is right that Einstein is celebrated for his imaginative reach, and so are the others who designed the "10 Most Beautiful Experiments" (above, p. 2). Even literary imaginings are sometimes echoed or corroborated as procedures or sources of knowledge. A familiar ploy in Dennett's work, for example, is "to construct a certain kind of thought experiment" he calls an "intuition pump" which steadily makes use of the faculty of imagination.[47] "My intuition pumps are, for the most part, intended to help you imagine new possibilities, not convince you that certain prospects are impossible" (*CE*, p. 440). Dennett's respect for imagination and its revelatory power, in league with other mental abilities, is everywhere apparent. The form of his intuition pumps—"Let us imagine that a man. . . ." "Suppose a person were imprisoned. . . ." and the like—take the form of brief fictions with extensive powers of illumination. One might say that each storyteller in the *Canterbury Tales* provides an intuition pump allowing the others to enter the lifeworld implicated in his or her tale and conceive of the emotional and social possibilities it involves.

There is a yet firmer commitment to narrative fiction available in Dennett's model of consciousness, and in Damasio's. Dennett's conclusion about human consciousness is that it is the result of the stories we continuously tell ourselves; each human self is a *center of narrative gravity* (*CE*, p. 418, Dennett's italics). Without positing a mind separate from the brain, or even a "central processing unit" as the stage for the Cartesian Theater, Dennett has proposed a firm and unique self for each of us composed of our individual and usually unpremeditated fictions. Here is Damasio's take on the subject: "The entire construction of knowledge, from simple to complex, from nonverbal imagistic to verbal literary, depends on the ability to map what happens over time. . .one thing followed by another thing, causing another thing, endlessly." And, "Telling stories...begins relatively early both in terms of evolution and in terms of the complexity of the neural structures required to create narratives.... [it] precedes language, since it is, in fact, a condition for language." For Damasio, this reference to language is not a metaphor: "Whatever plays in the non-verbal tracks of our minds is rapidly translated into words and sentences" (*FWH*, pp. 189 and 185). As we become selves, we can construct true stories or lies, beautiful stories or confusions, but what we cannot do is stop talking. No pilgrim on the Canterbury road refuses to tell a story.

In medieval thought, those stories that justly claim beauty exhibit verisimilitude, formal coherence (*integritas*), proportionality, luminosity (*claritas*), and usefulness for moral reasoning. These common threads appear woven together in various ways in the medieval accounts of beauty and are only distinguished here for analysis. For example, form is implicated in Aquinas's third desideratum for beauty, *claritas* (resplendence, radiance, luminosity), "through which being manifests itself," although form is more commonly connected with *integritas*.[48] Like the five-pointed star in *Sir Gawain and the Green Knight*, these features blend with and sustain one another. Although the contemplative mode of a mystic like Bonaventure differs from that of a contemporary critic, I think that these ideas can be juxtaposed with modern notions of imagination and beauty (even those like epistemic hunger, intuition pumps, and centers of narrative gravity) to help us grasp how Chaucerian art might have appeared to medieval audiences and might still appear. To start with, our horizons blend in rejecting the school of thought that elevates fully achieved works to an "aesthetic realm" in which the art becomes its own and only explication, unique and graspable only through immediate intuition, effectively denying its "drive toward intelligibility."

Verisimilitude

When Bonaventure and Aquinas assert that verisimilitude is so prominent an aesthetic desideratum that a well-represented monster can justly be called beautiful, they cannot be thinking solely of garden-variety mimesis. The implication is that represented objects can be "true to" entities that are only available to mental faculties, not just to those already seen in ordinary experience. Literary criticism is littered with debates about realism; W. J. T. Mitchell writes that "the long tradition of explaining literature and the other arts in terms of representation is matched by an equally long tradition of discomfort with this notion."[49] More recently, a serious challenge to literary realism comes, on the one side, from a strong version of deconstruction, in which the "real" in "real-world reference" is itself undermined by the arbitrariness of the link between sign and signifier and literature becomes entirely self-reflexive. On the other side is the voice from ideology critique that makes the connection between the representations of the text and the "real-life" thoughts and actions of its readers so close that it binds them, usually to an unsavory status quo. As an observer of the life around him, Chaucer has always been numbered among the realistic writers, right up there with Dickens, impelling scholars to comb the archives for the "real" Harry Bailey and the "real" Roger Ware. Again like Dickens, Chaucer's style of realism is identified with certain ideological positions, not without justification, impelling scholars to note, for example, the similarities in shoe styles and clerical practices between the pilgrim Parson in the *General Prologue* and Lollard "poor priests." Hume's assertion that imagination has the propensity "to turn ideas into living impressions, to arouse actual passions and to experience them,"[50] seems eminently appropriate to Chaucer's fictions. The *Canterbury Tales*, particularly leaves the impression that we are seeing something of what medieval England was actually like, and from the many perspectives of many storytellers.

The Wittgensteinian idea of the language game comes in handy in considering these multiple perspectives. Instead of looking at language as a repository of fixed meanings for discrete signifieds, Wittgenstein thought of words as participating in the various scenarios of practical life, never sealed off from the realm of thought: "To imagine a language is to imagine a life-form."[51] Interpretation begins with the attempt to determine just which game is being evoked in any text or utterance. Wittgenstein's language theory abandons mimesis as reflection in favor of reference to a culturally established common understanding. John Gibson points to the fact that the language in each game attests to shared standards of representation, a "broad backdrop of agreement" ("the wonder of agreement" is his term) against which disagreement can be staged.[52] We can disagree about the length of something, but agree to play the game of measuring and respect the standard metre in Paris (*PI*, p. 21). Games do not all share one particular property, but exhibit a "family resemblance," an array of features some of which are exhibited by each member of the family (*PI*, p. 27). This perspective seems particularly apt for looking at Chaucerian texts, since the closeness to everyday life and the hint of fun in the idea of games suggests Chaucer's fusion of social concern with humor. Yet the teasing way his art eludes *concepts about* "life-forms" keeps us from regarding it as merely didactic.

Resoun ymaginatyf, then, never merely reflects observed scenes and beliefs. We might say that each perspective, however close to a "social reality" contextual evidence might make it seem, is presented only fully enough to satisfy epistemic hunger. Chaucer adopted a strong theory of imagination is his "hertes line" meditation in *Troilus and Criseyde*, discussed above, and his occasional use of "engyn," for the imaginative faculty, points in the same direction.[53] The range of "engyn," from an exact synonym for imagination as a faculty of mind to clever mental planning and then to physical machines, suggest that Chaucer could think of imagination as an active, even an aggressive, intellectual process rather than a passive repository for sensations given by the "real world" or by the angels and devils. In the *Second Nun's Tale*, a traditional reference is made to the three faculties of mind—man's "sapiences three—/ Memorie, engyn, and intellect" (VIII.338–39). Cecile is explaining how God can be single yet in three persons by likening Him to the triune composition of human mind.[54] In *Troilus and Criseyde*, Pandarus has all he can do with "engyn" and "loore" to keep lovesick Troilus from dying (II.565), implying ingenuity. Pandarus's second use of "engyn" gives the term more range as Pandarus swears Troilus to secrecy, partly to protect Criseyde's name and partly because the charge of treachery would be brought against him if it were known that the affair had come about through his "engyn" (III.275). The added implication here is that of a contrivance, like that sought by the lover standing outside the garden in the *Romaunt of the Rose* trying to come up with an art or "engyn" to admit him.[55]

In the *Merchant's Tale*, Chaucer presents what might be considered a commentary on the picture-forming aspect of imagination. The Merchant describes January thinking about womanly beauty as *like* setting a mirror in the market place. "Heigh fantasye and curious bisynesse" (note the activeness implied by "bisynesse") characterized the first phase of his search as he watched "many a figure pace / By his mirour" (IV.1584–85), using imagination "to arouse actual passions and to experience them," in Hume's phrasing. His passion lights on May, and his love ("blynde alday"—"always," but a nice pun on daytime reality) portrayed in his bed at night, her imagined beauties of body and deportment. Boethius presents this aspect of imagination as a first step in cognition, that faculty of mind that "comprehendith oonly the figure withoute the matere" (V. Prosa 4, 150–60). In January's case, little is done to modify by reason or intelligence the "fantasye" (the word itself appears twice in thirty-five lines) in which he revels. The *Merchant's Tale* might be read as an account of willful fantasizing unmasked, a misuse of imagination out of touch with its ordinary references to the world outside the self, although Chaucer does not use the word "imagination" in this account.[56] Whether there can be any such thing as realism in a verbal text, and to what extent Chaucer is a realist will be visited with emphasis on persons in chapters 3, 4, and 5.

Coherence, integritas

Literary verisimilitude is made possible by the power of imagination to form mental pictures and interpret the world actually before us, causing us to *see* what we experience *as* a specific something, something already carrying meaning. Aquinas's *integritas*, the appearance of an object *as a particular shape*, foregrounded, is his first qualification for beauty. This is what Wittgenstein calls "aspect formation" (*PI*, pp. 166–79). In spite of its different explanations of mind, medieval thought also held that mental images serve a functional rather than a strictly mimetic purpose, as Carruthers asserts. The celebrated rabbit/duck picture clarifies the extreme case of the aspect problem. When seen as a rabbit, the image is coherent and adequate to trigger thoughts about real rabbits, but when it is subsequently seen as a duck, it surprises by providing a completely different animal referent just as coherent as that of the rabbit without changing the simple outlines of the image. Wittgenstein refers to the sudden recognition as the "dawning" of an aspect (its *Aufleuchten*). This slightly metaphoric suggestion of light should be taken, I think, to link aspect formation with *claritas* as well as coherence. It is bound to interpreting the world and it links fiction to the concerns of the "real, but it is always an imaginative activity, not a passive mirroring."[57] I find the idea of aspect recognition useful in thinking about whole texts as well as images within texts, providing a ground for asserting textual coherence, which is a condition for aesthetic apprehension in both medieval and contemporary thinking. We may see shapes that differ from those of Chaucer's first audiences, but we still read for *integritas*.

Even ordinary visual or linguistic sign systems do not, therefore, elicit fixed interpretations—imagination has to *see* them *as*. The reflective pleasure of art depends on grasping the work *as something*, that is, on formulating what it is we are looking at, sometimes more than once. For the Middle Ages, this last point may be linked not only with Aquinas's requirement for *integritas*, but also with the kind of generalized neo-Platonic intuition of "the forms" that hovers around Bonaventure's meditation. In its more work-a-day style, *Philosophical Investigations* goes on to play with the idea that someone could be "aspect blind," able to see, but without the normal intervention of imagination that recognizes or assigns forms and classes of things.[58] Before *Philosophical Investigations* appeared, Jorge Luis Borges had played with a similar idea in "Funes the Memorious," the story of a boy whose fall from a horse rendered his memory so acute that each impression was separate, and "he was disturbed by the fact that a dog at three-fourteen (seen from in profile) should have the same name as the dog at three-fifteen (seen from the front)."[59] Later, Annie Dillard also wrote about "aspect blindness" caused in the cases she discusses by the surgical cure of lifelong blindness. On their sudden entrance into the world of the sighted, most people's new vision, "pure sensation unencumbered by meaning," presented itself "as a dazzle of color-patches." They found it "tormentingly difficult" and sometimes defeating. What they had to do much later in life, and more quickly than other people, was to develop that function of imagination that foregrounds images and interprets them.[60] Funes and the newly sighted had lost their resoun ymaginatyf. This active way of seeing seems to be Benedict Anderson's way of using the term "imagination" when he writes of the nation as an amorphous, scattered group *coming to appear to itself as* an "imagined community."[61] Chapter 7 discusses the *Canterbury Tales* as an imagined English community.

Evidence that Chaucer could see perception as in need of imagination's intervention in its Wittgensteinian sense of aspect recognition is found in the Knight's account of Palamon objecting to Arcite's *seeing* his shocked change in color (his *bleynte*) and his "A" *as* distress over his imprisonment. He resents Arcite's lecture on enduring that seems to have no remedy: "Thou hast a veyn ymaginacioun," and discloses the real cause of his suffering as the wound of love.

> This prison caused me nat for to crye
> But I was hurt right now thurghout myn ye
> Into myn herte, that wol my bane be.
> The fairnesse of that lady that I see
> Yond in the gardyn romen to and fro
> Is cause of al my criyng and my wo.
> (I.1095–1100)

Beyond Chaucer's imagining his Knight and the Knight imagining Palamon, we have two acts of imagination here: Arcite imagines Palamon's suffering *as* an effect of his imprisonment, and Palamon imagines the effect of seeing Emelye *as* the construct familiar to courtly culture: an arrow has entered through his eye and pierced his heart, undetected by the outside world. What Arcite sees (quite understandably) as an enactment of the complaint against Fortune, Palamon sees as a spontaneous reaction to Venus's aggressive attack. Which form the perception takes has consequences: Palamon conflates Venus's influence over his seeing Emelye with thinking of Emelye *as* Venus herself ("soothly"), putting himself at a disadvantage rhetorically when Arcite claims he loved her first *as* a woman.[62]

Proportionality

Every medieval commentator on beautiful man-made objects stressed, as we have seen, proportion: weight, number, and measure. Augustine is quite forthright in describing good proportion as the formal arrangement of the parts of a beautiful whole. Taking (admittedly small) hints from Aquinas, we can link these formal elements with literary conventions in the case of verbal art and see idea and expression as fused. He writes, "For this kind of proportion is not form, as people used to think, but rather the disposition of matter to receive form.... It follows that when the disposition of matter to receive form is present, then so is form."[63] Bonaventure's assertion that the forms of beautiful things result from divine "seminal reasons," also makes form part of a living universe (1.14). Current thinking about the aesthetic must also rest on analyses of form, but cannot insist on its dependence on divine order or even natural growth. Elaine Scarry considers the problem that beauty, long linked with the sacred, may appear weakened when we can no longer take the sacred for granted. She concludes, "What happens when there is no immortal realm behind the beautiful person or thing is just what happens when there is...the perceiver is led to a more capacious regard for the world."[64] I will include this sense of "capacious regard" in analyzing how Chaucer's vision of late medieval England, especially in terms of persons, maintains its aesthetic effects.

If the first question about literary form posits that a coherent shape lifts itself from its background, the second concerns the characteristics of that shape. At least from Aristotle onward, narrative forms have been considered in terms of plot and genre. Kenneth Burke's *Counter-Statement* defines formal excellence in terms of the audience: "form is the creation of an appetite in the mind of the auditor, and the adequate satisfying of that appetite"[65] stands early in the tradition of reception aesthetics. It echoes both Augustine's analysis of church sculpture (in which shapes must be elongated or foreshortened to accommodate the eye of the onlooker) and Aquinas's emphasis on the importance of the observer ("Clarity is the fundamental communicability of form, which is made actual in relation to someone's looking at or seeing the object").[66] Considering the *Canterbury Tales* and *Troilus and Criseyde* in terms of genre and reception is especially useful, since both are of acknowledged interest to Chaucer. His narratives often specify genre (the first such specification in English writing)[67] and he attends to the expectations of readers in, for example, warning the "gentils" in his fictional and real-world audiences that the Miller is going to tell a "churles tale." These two principles are of course interdependent; genre sets up a constellation of predictions that may or may not be fulfilled, or may be fulfilled in unexpected ways. Particularly relevant to Chaucer's work are elements of newness and surprise in managing formal configurations. His fictions take meaning from the tradition with which they are implicated without entirely reproducing it—Gadamer bases his hermeneutic principle exactly on "a polarity of familiarity and strangeness" (*TM*, p. 295). Jauss describes genre in terms of the hermeneutic circle: "The new text evokes for the reader (listener) the horizon of expectations and rules familiar from earlier texts, which are then varied, corrected, altered, or even just reproduced."[68] Genres may be seen, then, as Wittgenstein's language games: romances resemble one another, but not in all traits.

The plot of *The Knight's Tale*, for example, invites suspense about how so evenly matched a competition for Emelye's hand will be adjudicated, perhaps related to the *demande d'amore.* But when Arcite, Palamon, and Emeleye all receive exactly the boon the words of their petitions have literally requested, the tale evokes surprise. (It might be argued that Theseus also gets what he asks for but not what he wants from the artists who decorated his celebratory temples—the gods, yes, but the "smyler with the knyfe"?) *The Miller's Tale* is built on a comic inversion—the denial of getting what was asked for: John wanted Alison to himself and aided her seducer, Nicholas lusted for the "lower body stratum" pleasure of uncommitted sex and was injured in his lower body, Absalom sought a romantic kiss. Within each tale the characters' expectations are surprisingly answered, within the *Canterbury Tales* the contrast between them implicates the life-worlds of their tellers, and for readers, the design of whole work evokes the social formation of late medieval England. Chapter 3 explores the question of whether or not aesthetic effects are in general served by a perfect fit between the text and its implied genre.

Luminosity, claritas

Surprise is a component of *claritas* as well. For Bonaventure the sensible arrests delighted attention in its "shining forth" to show God's power, and Abbot Suger found himself distracted from external cares by precious gems. Beauty is still often described as taking one by surprise, which means that we do not see beauty only where we are looking for it. Scarry refers to this surprise as a "greeting." Beauty is experienced as a summons to stop one's purpose-bound pursuits and an incitement to try to replicate it somehow. She connects the sense of greeting with a long line of poets and thinkers from Homer and Plato on, and specifically with Aquinas's *claritas.*[69] I think too of Fisher's comments on Hamlet's openhearted reception of the strangeness of the Ghost, "And therefore as a stranger give it welcome."[70] The fact that beauty surprises should not, however, suggest that it cannot be seen in something previously known as ordinary. Scarry only saw the beauty of palm trees after years of thinking: "Palms are not beautiful; perhaps they are not even trees,"[71] and I had not noticed the resonance of Hamlet's welcoming the stranger-ghost until Fisher pointed it out. Scarry concludes that granting aesthetic admiration is a generous act that tends to produce "lateral regard" for other items in one's lifeworld.[72] One experience of beauty seems to light the way to another. Luminousness ("resonance" is a close synonym, and sounds more up-to-date and perhaps more appropriate to the verbal domain) is thus, perhaps, the most distinctive attribute of a beautiful thing, since other, more quotidian, objects can be verisimilar, coherent, and even well-proportioned without offering the greeting of the specifically aesthetic encounter.

Luminousness has a particular role to play in the interpretation of historically distant works. Although we have lost a great deal of the factual detail that would reveal medieval life to us, we nonetheless have more facts than we can easily mold into a medieval horizon of understanding. In "I Gather the Limbs of Osiris," Ezra Pound writes, "Any fact is, in a sense, 'significant'. Any fact may be 'symptomatic,' but certain facts give one a sudden insight into circumjacent conditions, into their causes, their effects, into sequence, and law."[73] What artists do is to identify and present this sort of "Luminous Detail" from the life around them. Pound proposes a critical practice that concentrates on details in art that provide such "sudden insight" into lifeworlds, but he does not claim to have discovered the method; he does, however, put a distinctive gloss on the idea: some Luminous Details are "symptomatic," registering "a reflection of the tendencies and modes of a time," but some are "donative," going beyond incorporated understandings, creating something new though it may be drawn from "things present but unnoticed, or things perhaps taken for granted but never examined" (*SP*, p. 25). Both kinds help later generations understand the era, but donative artists think beyond the recognized horizon of their time.[74] Donative artists illuminate both their own milieus and possibilities for the future.

Pound then posits the *virtù* of the artist as what makes him unique and inimitable: *virtù* is "not a 'point of view,' nor an 'attitude toward life'; nor is it the mental caliber or a 'way of thinking,' but something more substantial which influences all of these" (*SP*, p. 28). Pound's choice of the word *virtù* signals his longstanding interest, in medieval and Renaissance Italy, where *virtù* became a key term in Machiavelli's *Prince*, as efficacy, power, ingenuity, active masculine (*vir*) intelligence.[75] One cannot help thinking as well of Kant's *genius*, "the innate mental aptitude (*ingenium*) through which nature gives the rule to art" (*CJ*, p. 168). Among the four writers Pound sees as steering the course of Western tradition is Chaucer, whose particular *virtù* is to see "the variety of persons about him, not so much of their acts and the outlines of their acts as of their character, their personalities" (*SP*, p. 30). The other three are Homer, Dante, and Shakespeare. Like all but Homer, Chaucer "swept into his work the virtues of many forerunners and contemporaries" without disrupting the coherence of his distinctive created world (p. 30). In this way, Pound strives to preserve a sense of historical distance and the importance of shared influences while he insists on the uniqueness of authorial powers. The Luminous Detail lights up history, tradition, and other features of the text simultaneously.

Catherine Gallagher and Stephen Greenblatt have given Pound's Luminous Detail new currency by using it in their explanation of the tight focus on specifics that has characterized new historicism from its inception. While older versions of historicism worked to establish fixed boundaries around past horizons, the newer works against "the determinism that attempts to insist that certain things were beyond conception or articulation, new historicism invokes the vastness of the textual archive, and with that vastness an aesthetic appreciation of the individual instance."[76] The argument against historical determinism, especially in matters of the imagination, is what I am getting at in stressing Gadamer's notion of fluid horizons of understanding. But when they "invoke" both archival vastness and the individual instance, Gallagher and Greenblatt disperse the luminousness of the detail across so wide a field that Pound's sense of *virtù* cannot come into focus. Potentially of course anything can illuminate a period or tradition, not just a work of genius or art (they concede that the value of their chosen details will depend on how convincing they can be in writing and teaching). This mode is now well-represented in academic circles and needs little shoring up, and I want to turn back to something closer to Pound's explanation of his term that imputes special powers to donative writers. My focus is on the vitality of certain details in Chaucer's texts to illuminate those fictions and the resonance of his tales to display medieval lifeworlds and connect with ours.

Odysseus's astonishment on seeing Nausicaa is used by Scarry to organize Book IV of the *Odyssey*, demonstrate Homer's depth in rendering the movements of Odysseus's mind, extol the beauty of trees (because Odysseus thinks at this point of a palm tree), and probe the effects of beauty. I have always been impressed by Chaucer's cacophonous account of Chauntecleer as he was carried into the woods. The widow and her daughters cryed "Out! Harrow and weylaway," and other people joined the chase, as did "Colle oure dogge, and Talbot and Gerland / And

Malkyn with a dystaf in hir hand" (VII.3379–83). Then came the cattle, hogs, other dogs, ducks, geese, and, finally, bees. The passage is loud, bright, and extremely specific. Its immediate appeal is that of closely observed realistic detail, the capstone of which is the image of the bees...uproar. Then it likens the noise to that of a larger revolt, lighting up an incident in contemporary history by comparing the hollering and banging on pans in the barnyard to the attack on the Flemings during the Peasant's Rising. (Is the Rising, too, a mock-epic battle?) In terms of plot, it proves the cock's fearful dream to have been prophetic and throws light backward on both the dream theory and the antifeminism of his argument with Pertelote earlier. Ultimately, the disordered noise mirrors the contest staged in the form of the tale between homiletics and rhetorical tropes for control of our interpretive attention. The passage seems to emit light from inside itself, like Philip Fisher's rainbows and Abbot Suger's gems, and illuminate concerns around it like the biblical similes that delightedly puzzled Augustine.

Usefulness

Scarry finds beauty directly useful toward the ethical imperative of justice, and this feature of her argument converges neatly with medieval thinking on uses of aesthetic experience. Beauty that the Middle Ages approved of was thought of as the gift of a benevolent God and, for the right-minded observer, the first step on the ladder of abstraction toward the Beautiful itself, the Good, and ultimately the Divine. Beautiful narratives are those that point to moral truths. This medieval trust in the convergence of the beautiful and the good cannot be reconciled with most contemporary thinking about aesthetics, and I think that Scarry's case is weaker for her link between beauty and justice than for her claim that recognition of beauty impels an "acuity of regard" that helps us love the world and generously extend regard laterally. One reason that post-Kantian aesthetic reasoning does not elide beauty and goodness is that where the good relies on concepts, beauty does not. Kant's is an essentially secular sense of the independence of aesthetic response.[77] We improve ourselves by attending to beauty because it quickens our love for the world, engages both imagination and understanding, and thereby enlarges sympathies (*CJ*, p. 60), but this resembles Scarry's "acuity of regard" claim, not the claim to justice. A second reason aesthetic effects are no longer seen as directly productive of rectitude is that today we assume less unanimity about what constitutes the good (or even the just) than by medieval culture did, for all its disputes.

"For whatever was written in former days was written for our instruction" (Romans 15.4) or, as the *Nun's Priest's Tale* has it, "al that written is, / To oure doctrine it is ywrite, ywis" (VII.3441–42). Biblical narrative held for Augustine the key to moral rectitude, and in *On Christian Doctrine*, he describes the interpretive strategies that would reveal it. His principle that any scriptural passage leading directly to *caritas* is to be read literally and any that does not must be read figuratively can be seen as prefiguring the circle of nineteenth- and twentieth-century hermeneutics, as Kathy Eden points out.[78] There is, however, an important difference: the "fore-conception" of Augustine's system—the injunction to *caritas*—is never modified. It is always already the overarching guide to a right reading of the parts. It does not arise from the continuing revision of whole in response to parts, but rather on the prior commitment that Augustine himself and the early Church had made to *caritas* as the central doctrine of Christianity. *On Christian Doctrine* interprets Scripture by appealing to many kinds of cultural understandings in late antiquity and, therefore, may be thought of as widening the hermeneutic circle, but nowhere does it question or modify the rule of *caritas*.

The emphasis placed on the moral usefulness of nonbiblical fictions in the Middle Ages required Augustine's method of distinguishing the literal from the figurative for the obvious reason that the literal surface of many pre-Christian stories and folk tales assumed different moral imperatives than *caritas*. Augustine's influence was felt, not only in his method, but in his scriptural justification for using such stories: they are like the treasure the Israelites took with them from Egypt "to put to better use."[79] But of course those treasures had to be managed in order to serve the right ends, so some of the "old tales" in the preaching manuals provided the allegorizations along with the plots. The story of Griselda was told throughout Europe, and its least subtle usefulness—its example of heroic womanhood—was acknowledged by even so ardent a feminist as Christine de Pisan. Boccaccio's telling of it struck Petrarch with extraordinary force, and in retelling it, he consciously sought to place its spiritual import above its "counsel for wives"[80] (and even in the *Decameron*, Dineo's reaction is one of recoil from a human Griselda's patience). The usefulness of Griselda's tale is asserted from within the text of the *Canterbury Tales* itself. The Clerk knew that his story would evoke strong feelings of pathos and admiration for Griselda, and was wary in deriving a specific rule for either men or women. It would be "inportable" for a woman to follow Griselda in humility, he says (IV.1143–44), but intolerable to whom? Is it women who could not bear to submit to the apparent murder of their children or moral philosophers who could not bear to ask them to? His shift to allegory—the ungendered soul's submission to God—renders the clarification moot, but the subtle Clerk understands the interpretive problem he has presented to the pilgrims, including the awkwardness of the analogy between Walter's testing and God's. Yet Harry Bailey goes right on to regard Griselda's meek suffering as a moral model suitable for Goodelief's hearing (IV.1212 a–g). The moral usefulness of the tale is thus not transparently available as *content*, addressed as it is to a divided readership, but it is always useful in some way.

The wide circulation of such tales was allowed, in Peter Haidu's view, because the details that worked against social or doctrinal consensus could be counted as mere "free variation," leaving the core morality of the text untouched.[81] A contemporary aesthetics, though, would emphasize precisely the unsettling element of free play, the refusal of the Griselda story, especially as the Clerk tells it, to fully corroborate any of the concepts it calls to mind. The point is that Augustine knew the Good already and could name and explicate the concept that captures it. The strong version of ideology critique, with its insistence on demystifying the social powers at work behind every telling, easily becomes as circular as Augustine's method in that it relies on a grounding in the value of demystification that is taken as self evident.[82] In some hands, demystification is the *caritas* of postmodernity.[83]

The chapters that follow make use of these ideas with varying emphasis, providing commentary that follows from attention to the aesthetic mode of intelligibility. They examine how Chaucer deploys the various resources of narrative poetry to produce a playful engagement of imagination and understanding, evasive of final conceptualization or reduction to the merely agreeable or interested. Chapter 3 reflects on the dialectic between formal generic "purity" (the satisfaction of an epistemic hunger for form aroused by a particular text) and generic play, mixing, and blurring. Both the texts themselves and the Chaucerian world we construct around and through them are *seen as*, apprehended by imagination, in terms of Wittgenstein's "language games" and the medieval privilege given to proportion. Chapters 4 and 5 posit the same kind of dialectic, in this case between characterizations implying complex persons and those implying iconic types, chapter 4 focusing on personhood in general, and chapter 5 specifically on women. Historical considerations suggest (but do not absolutely mandate) that the very idea of complex interior lives may be less readily available to Chaucer's first audiences than to us, but, again, the play within the aesthetic regime allows for divided reception in both eras. Kant's notion of the aesthetic as "free delight"—free from readers' interests (although each of the pilgrims may be motivated by interest) and free from confinement by concepts—is particularly apt in considering Chaucer's distinctive brand of humor (chapter 6). Kant's distinction between the merely gratifying and aesthetically pleasurable is also relevant. Finally, chapter 7 presents the *Canterbury Tales* as the image of a community discernable as an intricate interlace of social frictions and alliances rendered intelligible and delightful through a formal scheme that, while not reducible to a single concept of the good, provides a socially generous regard for persons, imagined and real.

The commentary in these chapters is by no means the *inevitable* result of aesthetic attention to Chaucer's two long narrative poems. A fixed method with predictable results cannot be inferred from neo-Kantian aesthetics, Gadamerian hermeneutics, Wittgensteinian language theory, or the mixed mode described in chapter 1. Although many of the details that provide insight into medieval English lifeworlds rely on critical work with ideological and historical underpinnings, my readings testify to my reflections on Chaucerian fictions in an aesthetic mode of intelligibility. They are attempts to point to a patch of sky toward which others may be looking when a comet makes its sweep.

CHAPTER 3

PLAYING WITH LANGUAGE GAMES

the best actors in the world, either for tragedy, history, pastoral, pastoral-comical, historical-pastoral, tragical-historical, tragical-comical-historical-pastoral, scene individable, or poem unlimited; Seneca cannot be too heavy, nor Plautus too light, for the law of writ and the liberty: these are the only men.

Polonius *in Hamlet*

It seems to me that form involves the conversion of matter, so far as possible, to spirit. At the moment of conversion, form and beauty seem to be one and the same.

Denis Donoghue, *Speaking of Beauty*

What gives the work of art its relative autonomy from ideology, even though in any given case it may remain intricately involved with it, is just what Sidney argued: it neither affirms nor denies but addresses imagination. Yet the imaginative freedom offered by narrative art arises, paradoxically, from its formal boundedness (Aquinas's *integritas*). It is the bounded *form* of a story, its illusion of creating a self-contained virtual world designed for contemplation, that allows socially disruptive structures of feeling to be encoded as art, disseminated, read, and reread, even though they may threaten, sooner or later, to sneak back into the practical world. The imaginative freedom offered by the hypothetical is both experienced as affective and suffused with active thought, not merely agreeable, but offering an intellectual tussle, sometimes hard won.[1] I will connect that active thinking with Wittgenstein's language games and the Gadamerian hermeneutic tradition.

A good way to think about textual boundedness is to consider genre, as Polonius does when he introduces the players. The world created in the *Canterbury Tales* is immense. It looks like a "poem unlimited" in Polonius's anatomy of kinds—"God's plenty" in Dryden's phrase. Its boundaries keep being breached, finally spilling out into what looks, from one point of view, like the direct moral address of the *Parson's Tale* and the sincere authorial confession of the *Retraction*. Moreover, its protean genre is unique in the English vernacular. Its tradition can be construed as that of the short story collection, like the *Decameron*, an extended estates satire, a national epic, a discourse on sin and salvation, or an expansion of its overarching trope—the pilgrimage of life.[2] All of these generic patterns yield important insights into the frame and the tales, and all have been ably discussed by others: Helen Cooper on the story collection, Jill Mann on estates satire, and Frederick Tupper on the pilgrimage; Glending Olson sees the pilgrimage as the poem's outer and the storytelling contest as its inner generic shape.[3]

Whatever the overarching genre of the *Canterbury Tales* is taken to be, it enables the seemingly contradictory effects of coherence (*integritas*, boundedness) and inclusiveness. Wittgenstein's dictum, "To imagine a language is to imagine a form of life," together with his description of language games, allows us to consider the generic shape of the *Canterbury Tales* as purposive without finally determining its specific, final purpose.[4] In describing this heterogeneity, David Wallace remarks: "No other framed collection contrives to enable so many genres to follow their own laws of operation and hence achieve such a plurality of imaginative worlds."[5] Each pilgrim will have his or her say with the consent of everyone gathered ("by oon assent / We ben acorded" [I.817–18]) and that can be construed as a vision of the ideal speech community, like Jurgen Habermas's, or like William Blake's "mental war" without annihilation. Whether there is a "last word" or not, the proposed "end" is that someone will win the free meal, but everyone will have a seat at the table. The fact that the prize is not awarded (in the manuscripts that survive) preserves the openness of the criteria for the "best sentence and moost solaas" and allows later generations to both imagine how the pilgrims would have judged and they themselves might do so.[6] The pilgrims are presented as a voluntary, self-organized group with some likeness to a guild (as Wallace suggests)[7] and some likeness to an open-air congregation with many guest preachers, clerical and secular. Because its contained virtual world is responsible for aesthetic effects of many kinds, the *Canterbury Tales* may also contribute to changes in structures of feeling in "real-life" by presenting new "forms of life" to lots of people's imaginations.

Each tale within the collection also has distinctive generic marks. As Helen Cooper has pointed out: "One of the oddities of the *Tales* is the overt generic label attached to almost all of the stories in the links, a process that first introduces into English the idea of genre as the key to both writing and to hermeneutics."[8] I agree that Chaucer's texts foreground the idea of generic shapes, and not only in the *Canterbury Tales* but also in *Troilus and Criseyde* and many of the shorter poems, although I will concentrate on the *Tales* in this chapter. I also agree that genre provides a clue for hermeneutics, and in this chapter I want to follow that clue, but not by using a formula for each generic form as the standard by which to make an aesthetic judgment. Kant's dictum about aesthetic shapeliness, "purposiveness without purpose," denies that the beauty of an object results from its perfect adherence to a concept, including, I would think, the concept of a generic form.[9] The coherence of a tale is not dependent on its complete identification with a formal genre (any more than with its complete demonstration of an ideological position). My point, therefore, will not be that Chaucer designs each tale to be read in order to enact its exemplary status as a tragedy or a lai, but that, even as he introduces the importance of genre for interpreting stories, many of these fictions mix and blur those generic distinctions. Some admirably fulfill generic expectations (satisfy epistemic hunger for a certain shape, as Dennett would say), some gesture toward more than one genre, and some take an ironic or parodic stance toward the genre they ostensibly enact. Some of the tales seem generically stable until the context of the pilgrimage in the text or of late medieval life outside the text invite attention. Chaucer does not so much *play language games* in the *Canterbury Tales* as he *plays with them*.

Genre is one of the most useful of the fore-conceptions in the Gadamerian/Jaussian hermeneutic; it serves as an initial guide to organizing the parts and is continually questioned and modified. Raymond Williams reads literary genres as rooted in social relations and, therefore, bound to history, although able to survive social change.[10] I need both these notions. Both of them contrast with certain blanket generalizations of ideology critique like "the novel is a bourgeois form." But they are also distinct from neo-Aristotleian descriptions of fixed genres on the one hand and on the other dismissals like those of Benedetto Croce: there are no "kinds," only direct intuitions that become unique expressions.[11] Today the terms "genre novel" and "genre film" are sometimes used to suggest second-class rank, and it is the unexpected frustration of generic expectations that produces aesthetic *frisson*. I find this apparent disdain for things "well made" is often overstated: we are aesthetically "greeted" (Scarry) by the surprising fulfillment of generic expectations and medieval people are, I think, even more likely to have been so greeted. (And of course, medieval English audiences were probably just beginning to recognize the genres Chaucer mentions in any case.) Wittgenstein's "To imagine a language is to imagine a form of life" was never better exemplified than in these tales—each tale-teller asks the *compaignye* to imagine that particular form of life in which his or her tale can occur. Of course, the pilgrims' "forms of life" are also Chaucerian fictions, presented in various relationships to the "real" lifeworlds of his audiences.

To read genre as a hermeneutic clue, I will begin with some positions associated with Gadamer and Jauss in chapter 1. Understanding the art of the past is a question of fusing old with new horizons, since for Gadamer works of art both bring their worlds with them and refer to the world outside themselves, including the genre expectations of the era in and for which they were written.[12] Moreover, neither the horizon of the text nor that of the modern reader, as Gadamer describes it, is closed; no one "is absolutely bound to one standpoint.... The horizon is something into which we move and that moves with us."[13] The hermeneutic project—the discovery of as much as possible about the implied lifeworld of a distant text—succeeds not by suppressing but by bringing into play the lifeworlds of readers who recursively predict and amend their predictions.

Gadamer's description of the hermeneutic circle involves both interpretation theory and aesthetics. By tentatively attributing a prejudice or fore-conception to the whole as one reads the parts, and then confirming or discarding it, one responds to both its meaning and its beauty, which are inextricable in an achieved work. Gadamer acknowledges the fact that much of the art of antiquity and the Middle Ages served ritual or civic ends, which would seem to exclude it from the disinterested notion of art developed by Kant.[14] But the fact that art may be intended for use does not compromise the disinterestedness of its aesthetic impact when it is grasped as a shape. Since the *Canterbury Tales* is a composite work, the issue of the relations between parts and wholes is thrust upon us from the beginning, and the practice of naming a genre in the headlink strongly encourages certain fore-conceptions, including those involving moral, social, or religious usefulness.

Such literary conventions, especially generic conventions, serve, in Peter Haidu's words, "the appropriate formal embodiment of the shared consciousness between writers and audience."[15] Ideological conditions of understanding, for both author and interpreter, will enter into generic fore-conceptions. Part of the reflective pleasure of art, especially if it is historically distant, involves attempting to fuse mental horizons with those of a past writer and grasp the work *as something*, as a bounded form. "Chaucer is the watcher at every window; and what he sees there is not 'life' alone, for 'life' comes to him ready defined by the perspectives of different literary genres, which for him constitute the multifarious windows of the house," as Cooper puts it.[16] I will begin by discussing two discursive modes (not in themselves literary genres) that form the poles between which Chaucerian fictions may be said to operate: "realism" and "allegory."

Realistic Perspectives

The first thing most people associate with Chaucer is literary realism.[17] There is considerable warrant for this view; the *General Prologue* to the *Canterbury Tales* and the links between the tales are probably the richest sustained evocations of material and social reference in medieval writing. This was acknowledged as early as Francis Beaumont's seventeenth-century praise: "One gifte hee hath aboue other Authours, and that is, by the excellencie of his descriptions to possesse his Readers with a stronger imagination of seeing that done before their eyes, which they reade, than any other that euer writ in any tongue."[18] Morton Bloomfield makes a similar assessment of a Chaucerian realism that presents the world "as it appears to our mind," but he includes "an unbiased presentation of the inner reality of the characters."[19] The language games Chaucer's English is playing and playing with seem congruent with the strong realist tradition of the popular sermon style described by G. R. Owst: "verbal illustration which describes everyday things as seen by a shrewd observer" and "direct and continuous contact with Life" that sets common things "high amid the wider concern of the human mind."[20] But Chaucer's realism also reflects the Oxford intellectual current flowing from the work of William of Ockham which emphasizes "the close examination of life as it is lived and the stress on the dignity of man."[21]

Verbal art that impels people to see something in imagination as if it were appearing before their eyes was and is an aesthetic achievement. Such art falls more readily into Kant's discussion of beauty than of sublimity. He describes beauty as life-enhancing "compatible with charms and a playful imagination," while the heavy-duty alternation of attraction and repulsion of the sublime is "dead earnest in the affairs of the imagination" (*CJ*, p. 91). For the ancients, beauty was counted among the absolute goods, and in Kant's analysis it was of coequal worth with the sublime, which he locates only in natural phenomena. Among post-Kantians, though, artistic beauty became the second, lesser, member of a binary that associated beauty with the feminine and quotidian, and sublimity with the masculine and astonishing. Many current critics have seemed embarrassed by beauty's "good-heartedness."[22] Fredric Jameson posits Hegel's "end of art" as the end of beauty and the takeover of art by the sublime. The Beautiful, then, began to seem mere decoration, unconnected to the realm of the Absolute.[23] And Alan Singer sees the sublime as alienating artistic languages from the "discourse of life."[24] Such trends have privileged the "transgressive" extremes of textual practice. The very qualities for which Chaucer's fictions have been valued all along—their specificity of reference, their incisive descriptions/unmaskings of the social formation, their earthy sanity—have all but barred them from the realm of an aesthetic that concentrates on the extraordinary. Without denying Chaucer some sublime (and transgressive) moments, I want to stress the alliance between beauty and recognizable social experience in his work.

On the other hand, textual forms summon the everyday world only obliquely; their magic is all done with mirrors, which is to say, with signs. Literary reference is to an imagined world that only resembles what is outside the window, but that does not necessarily corroborate a strong version of the deconstructive position that fiction offers merely an "infinite play of signs."[25] The hold on imagination exercised by literary texts must arise from the shared cultural understandings that mandate our largely calling the "same things by the same names," as John Gibson says in explicating Wittgenstein's language theory.[26] The play between textual givens and their referential implications provides gaps for interpretation to fill in by playing the language games of a particular lifeworld, in other words returning us to the fore-conceptions of the hermeneutic circle. Chaucer's contemporaries would have begun reading with fore-conceptions that we must uncover by patient inquiry into material, social, and intellectual conditions. His generation must have seen many of his horizons of understanding as close to their own—"that is just what it looks like," "that is just how such a one would say it"—whether or not they had actually experienced similar events. The tales often seem acutely attentive to points of view; consider the position of the shot window in the *Miller's Tale* or the description of the amphitheater risers in the *Knight's Tale* (Augustine writes of the sculptor who attends to the vantage points his viewers will take (above p. 35). Pleasure is involved in recognizing images as familiar objects reframed. Susan Stewart notes the interest aroused by dollhouses and other miniatures in just this way.[27] But the tales demand an acuity of regard that complicates and extends that pleasure by requiring it to be seen as purposive.

For latter-day readers like us, the pleasure in realistic detail is more complicated. We try to imagine the hermeneutic progress of medieval audiences through a tale (without positing an undivided readership), and are rewarded with the satisfaction of seeing a particular tale take on greater coherence when it is connected with its original contexts. In such cases, the immediate aesthetic effects of the tale are augmented in view of new historical commentary. For example, when the Friar's casual assumption of hatred for summoners is linked to the practices of contemporary archdeacon's courts, we can imagine the effect of his tale on the pilgrims more vividly.[28] We enjoy Chaucer as a realistic poet who modified inherited sources and literary conventions in order to attend to the everyday as he watched his world from many windows.

This appearance of allusiveness to real-life may enhance its pleasure for us latecomers in a quite different way. We are especially attuned to playfulness, deferral, and denial of closure, and connect these indeterminacies with certain values we admire in "postmodern" art. Bonaventure's two justifications for beauty in a created object—good construction (proportion) and verisimilitude—may have appeared in differently imagined shapes then than now.[29] The portrait of the Miller in the *General Prologue* could have passed these two tests easily, its good construction shown in the apparent completeness of the portrait and its truth to life apparent because millers seemed accurately represented by it. We also appreciate the vividness of the picture, but because we are aware of mills as corporations rather than local millers, we puzzle over whether to take the pilgrim Miller as a crude bully or a larger-than-life, third-estate leader of the people ("he broghte us out of towne"). Perhaps we can even credit this sort of play as speaking to at least some medieval audiences some of the time. Such playfulness teaches new ways of reading narrative and, by inference, experience, modifying people's structures of feeling. Judgments of beauty are subject to the logic of structures of feeling in that the beautiful object strikes us as relevant to an intimate world, yet may be capable of modifying the perceived contours of that world.

Allegorical Perspectives

At the other end of a continuum from "realist" lie the various typological genres: allegory, *exemplum*, and fable among them. This cast of mind is often treated as specifically medieval, but Angus Fletcher's *Allegory: The Theory of a Symbolic Mode* stresses the ancientness and omnipresence of the allegorical mode as "a fundamental process of encoding our speech."[30] Hayden White points up the similarity of Freud's account of the dream-work to literary allegory.[31] Wittgenstein's principle that to "imagine a language is to imagine a form of life" is just as relevant to the language of allegory as to that of realism. The self-contained world of the bounded text suggests (either directly or obliquely, as in allegory) a version of the world in which it was created; its formal integrity allows it to become a displaced image of other lifeworlds as well. Although this can happen to any coherent text, it is likelier to happen to allegories, which more strongly address mental life. The Middle Ages did privilege it, of course, elaborating Augustine's practice of interpreting events and figures in the Old Testament as prefiguring the New in *On Christian Doctrine*, adopting allegorical glossing as a way of reading, and eventually producing the fourfold system. Literal, allegorical, moral, and eschatological senses were widely understood by Chaucer's time, and even Wyclif, known for his opposition to the elaborate "glossing" of Scripture, mentions the four levels without disapproval.[32] Dante invoked all four senses in reading Psalms 114 in his letter to Can Grande, but it was much more common to simply distinguish literal from allegorical.[33] For both medieval and contemporary sensibilities, the interpretation of allegory promises the pleasure of untangling an enigma, but *which* features of any given fiction require untangling might differ a good deal, since intricate codes for reading Scripture and nature, now arcane, were then widely available through sermons and devotional texts. Some critics think that the fact that Criseyde's eyebrows met in the middle would have been an *immediate* tip-off to medieval people that she was intended as a malign presence; for modern readers it may simply seem that the text is asking us to imagine a particular face.

Northrop Frye argues that every attachment of moral or philosophical meaning to a text is "allegorical," since the details of the text will always be taken to indicate something about the larger world outside it.[34] Maureen Quilligan, acknowledging Frye's point, makes a stronger distinction between the genre that contains polysemous allegorical texts and allegoresis, the critical process of sorting out the polysemy of various textual kinds: allegory is "indicated by the text" and does not require allegoresis by the reader.[35] Rosemond Tuve, using the term "imposed allegories" rather than allegoresis, agrees that allegory must be there in the text, but she allows that those which are "imposed" can sometimes be so persuasive that they ought not be discarded, as in the case of the *Song of Solomon*.[36] Even if they are later considered to have been imposed, such readings played a substantial role in medieval reading practices, especially from the pulpit, rendering difficult the distinction between a textually compelled allegory and the critical practice of attaching meaning. Suzanne Reynolds describes the trajectory of allegoresis as moving from a rhetorical trope in classical thought to a "programme for reading" in the Middle Ages.[37] In general, allegorization belongs to the intelligibility side of the sensible/intelligible pair we inherit from the Greeks, but it is fruitless to delineate a sharp break between modes rather than a continuous variety of literal and figurative suggestiveness.

A medieval reader's structure of feeling must have been structured by Christian traditions that addressed both timeless cosmic principles and the more uncertain venue of day-to-day partial knowledge. Complex texts like Chaucer's call up images that are both referential and luminous, producing, as Tuve argues, "a major enjoyment felt in the mode of allegory in these periods.... Pleasure in ingenuity surely enters, and pleasure in recognition (both of imagery and concept) was a stronger element still."[38] V. A. Kolve has demonstrated that much of Chaucer's imagery can be read as both realistic and iconographic, "the iconographic image is instead [of merely background] characteristically assimilated to the verisimilar and mimetic texture of the whole."[39] Indeed, the "acuity of regard" (Scarry's term) demanded by beauty invites attaching further meanings to even quite quotidian details.[40] This is the kind of aesthetic pleasure Augustine refers to when he finds himself strangely moved by biblical typology and does not seek to ascribe its power to logical deduction alone.[41] But even the allegorical supertext does not yield deducible concepts automatically.

Varieties of Chaucerian Allegorization

Since the tendency of the allegorical modes is to privilege the intelligible over the sensible, what characters and images "mean" is more important than the details of their appearance or the complications of their actions. They are to be taken, not as things only, but also as signs of other things (*ut aliarum etiam signa sint rerum*), as Augustine put it in *On Christian Doctrine*.[42] Fletcher calls the extreme of this tendency "ritualized" and "compulsive," fueled by the desire to escape the painful ambivalences of experience and appealing to an "excess of reason."[43] At this far end of the allegorical spectrum, intelligibility is all there is—Mr. Vitamin A in our third-grade pageants must exhibit all and only the features of that vitamin, and some school texts in Chaucer's day made similarly one-dimensional proverbs out of complex classical material.[44] Northrop Frye calls this kind of text "a disguised form of discursive writing."[45] But many allegories cannot be read this way—certainly not Chaucer's—and must be addressed by attending seriously to their sensible dimensions.[46] At the "ritualized" pole of allegory, each local item described and each move plotted has a counterpart in the cosmic arena for which it is a sign, and moving between "levels" is frictionless. *Exemplum* assumes a greater dose of historical reality.[47] The saint's life emphasizes historical reality still more strongly, since the legend has a place in the authorized narrative of ecclesiastical history. The "cosmic" level of the beast fable tends toward the everyday, but the animals are still merely signs pointing toward human truths. Often even romances, especially brief, nonepisodic ones, invite reading on levels above the literal in the fourfold hierarchy. We may think of an array of tales ranging from self-conscious allegory, like the Clerk's "This storie is seyd nat for.... But for that" (IV.1142–45) to a seeming romance that tempts us toward allegoresis, like the Wife of Bath's. The sensible in any of these genres may appear in either its "everyday" aspect (seeing something *as* something extant) or its more exotic forms (positing a literal but absent or transcendent something). The fact that allegory presumes alert cognitive attention does not preclude its having a strong emotional effect: "For a Tear is an Intellectual thing, / And a Sigh is the Sword of an Angel King," as William Blake wrote in *Jerusalem*. An underlying theme of this discussion of genre is the simultaneous evocation of sustained thought and strong feeling. Mary Carruthers concludes that the medieval thinking included emotional colorings in *cogitatio*,[48] and Isobel Armstrong advocates including the power of affect "within a [modern] definition of thought and knowledge rather than theorized outside them, excluded from the rational."[49] At the same time, aesthetic attention acknowledges the rational element in textual power without reducing it to a purposive (compulsory or dogmatic) concept.[50]

The Clerk's Explicit Allegory

The Clerk's Tale is often and rightly considered in terms of its scenes designed to evoke pathos—suckling children ripped from their mother's arms, the "sergeant" forced to seem a child murderer, the wife's perfect dutifulness rewarded with banishment and humiliation, her father's long-standing suspicion that his daughter would be repudiated, her final swoon of joy. The "taste for pathos" displayed in much medieval writing might have guaranteed the effectiveness of the Griselda story,[51] but pathos has been recognized since at least Aristotle as a basic ingredient of tragedy, and from a certain angle this tale invokes tragic fore-conceptions only contradicted at the last minute. Yet after subjecting his listeners to wide emotional swings, the Clerk explains the meaning of his tale in the most forthright announcement of an allegorical genre in the *Canterbury Tales*:

> This storie is seyd nat for that wyves sholde
> Folwen Grisilde as in humylitee
> For it were inportable, though they wolde,
> But for that every wight, in his degree,
> Sholde be constant in adversitee
> As was Grisilde; therfore Petrak writeth
> This storie, which with heigh stile he enditeth
> For sith a womman was so patient
> Unto a mortal man, wel moore us oghte
> Receyven al in gree that God us sent.
> (IV.1142–51)

The Clerk here indicates that his tale *was* readable, in fact was addressed, as an exemplary story in which the patience Griselda displays because of her marital status as a wife and social status as a peasant is offered only provisionally, to be translated into every Christian's spiritual duties. At the end, he counters the literal reading: the story is "nat seyd" to establish social relations—it *wouldn't be a good thing even if a woman could do it.*[52] The Clerk's is a deeply coded language game. It depends on invoking expectations for a relatively simple tale of virtue's suffering and ultimate reward (but clouds that expectation with asides questioning Walter's motives), appears to complete Griselda's story as an *exemplum* on wifely obedience, and then shifts to a full allegorical mode in which the peasant girl is a figure for the soul. The form of mental life played out in this game is clerical, of course, but in the course of his tale-telling, the Clerk produces a striking glimpse of peasant life, culminating in the "Luminous Detail" (in Ezra Pound's sense) of the "olde cote" that no longer fits Griselda when she returns to her father. Much biblical exegesis follows this pattern—text first, then its allegorical glosses—and some of it runs the risks the *Clerk's Tale* does in attracting attention to distracting details on the literal level.[53]

For some modern readers, there may be considerable aesthetic pleasure in the switch to another level of abstraction. Suddenly we are relieved of the strain of experiencing the powerful presentation of a repulsive series of events seemingly provided for our edification—we no longer have to try to like a seemingly sadistic male Clerk or an author who holds him up for admiration. We no longer have to try to fuse horizons with a medieval public addressed in this way by a popular tale. We are further gratified by the subtlety shown by the Clerk, first in the clever way he requites the Wife by praising a woman—and not a nun either but a mother—and then by denying that she is presented as a model of *wifely* obedience. But we are, nonetheless, left with the bewildering analogy between a benevolent God and an abusive husband, and between a patient Christian and a collaborating sacrificer of children to an ideal of obedience. This is a story shape that refuses to be confined in a concept. It nicely exemplifies Wittgenstein's sense of *seeing as*, alternatively, a rabbit or a duck.[54]

The case has been made, though, that, except for the pathos, these are not the pleasures Chaucer intended or his early audiences would have experienced. Consider a strong reading of *both* the unfolding *exemplum* and the allegory. D. W. Robertson, Jr. argues that the late medieval lifeworlds were saturated with patristic authority, that medieval fore-conceptions of edification would not have been seriously challenged as readers made their way through the six parts of the tale. He reads "historically" the allegory of Christian patience—"the Christian soul as it is tested by its Spouse"—as based on an undisputed bedrock of values that is not in conflict with the duty of wifely obedience. Instead of noticing Walter's cruelty (in spite of the Clerk's explicitness about it), Robertson praises his husbandly behavior, for example, his unsentimental "love" for

Griselda, his perception of her inner beauty, and the propriety of his role as a testing agent.[55] For such readers there is no sudden turn in significance (no shift from rabbit to duck), but a gentle widening of emphasis—she was an exemplary wife, and later she is an exemplary soul.

I do not deny that there were, and perhaps are, readers who could react this way—there are people who only see the rabbit. They would have to ignore or suppress the Clerk's own embarrassed asides condemning Walter (IV.451–62, 622, 704, 785–87), but an additional reason to reject Robertson's interpretation is based on a still larger and more insistent feature of the Clerk's presentation of Walter. Walter's motive is consistently identified as curiosity and obdurate will. Willful curiosity was recognized throughout the Middle Ages as among the deepest roots of sin.[56] From his subject's point of view, Walter might have seemed like Almachius in the *Second Nun's Tale*, although Almachius believes he is acting on behalf of Roman rule, while Walter's actions are presented as personal and domestic. The serious types, who thought concernedly about the Fathers, do not strike me as being able to turn willful Walter into God without some of the very reservations we might register now, or to regard him as an exemplary "tester" during the *exemplum.* I am, therefore, unconvinced that there is an uncontested "medieval" reading of the tale, that a responsible historicism ought to regard the aesthetic pleasure medieval people would have derived from it to have been as an exemplum of wifely duty. The sensible details presenting the pathos of Griselda's trials are too powerful and numerous to be pressed into the exemplary mold; an epistemic hunger for order and point would have been better satisfied with less detail (as it might have been by Petrarch's telling). Walter's willful curiosity, then, might be considered as a Luminous Detail that confronts a reading of history as deterministic.

The allegory, on the other hand, may have been appealing to Chaucer's first audiences for just that release of tension the Clerk provides in explaining that God sends unexplained suffering which must be borne patiently. Given medieval death rates for children during the first years of life, this snatching of children must have constituted a more readable horizon then, a closer fit with everyday lifeworlds. *We* may be tempted to sue medical people when children die; *they* must have been tempted to blame God. For medieval people, the flash of understanding offered by the Clerk's allegorization may have been its defining aesthetic effect. Recent criticism has seen in it an immanent critique of both allegory and (more powerfully) *exemplum.*[57] Furthermore, there is, for everyone, the pleasure of pondering the ways of the wily Clerk, whichever genre he is seen as constructing. The tale requires concerted intellectual attention, while simultaneously evoking wonder.

The Pardoner's Exemplum

The brief sermon *exemplum* is far more common than the extended allegory. Peter Haidu calls it "a predominant fictional mode, even in vernacular literature, throughout the Middle Ages" in spite of the contradiction between its mode as fiction and its role in ideology.[58] This stamina in exemplary writing suggests that it was a deeply rooted feature of imagination in the Middle Ages. I will begin by exploring a proposed "Chaucerian aesthetic" for reading the *exemplum* in the *Pardoner's Tale*, invoking imagination as both producing images of things not present and interpreting observations of the world in a particular aspect. In the *exemplum*, the images of the three tavern boys, the bright new florins, the box of poison, and many other "things" are brought before the reader's mental eye in a largely referential mode,[59] but I suppose few readers have actually been confronted on a road by an old man completely "forwrapped." These partly familiar, partly bizarre images comprise the sensible aspect of the story.

What are these people and things intelligible *as*? This part is easy at first and then gets harder. The rioters are not unlike people we have seen—pleasure-loving, careless, and inept at reading signs. The servant boy uses a common idiom to explain the "clynke" of the deathknell—"Deeth" has taken their "old felawe"; his mother had told him to beware that one. As the boys go out to kill "Deeth," the cognitive dimension of our response kicks in more vigorously. These images are beginning to look like figures in a grand design. The revelers think they are looking for someone like themselves, someone specific; many readers know they are confusing abstract with concrete realities and enacting a parody of Christ's mission to conquer eternal death. The *exemplum* does not merely invite reading on a nonliteral level, it features characters ruined because they are unable to imagine the nonliteral. The exemplum, in other words, contains a key to its interpretation. Moreover, the Old Man is not easy to see *as*, and critics have not arrived at consensus about his identity. This uncertainty, to my mind, simply raises the level of tension, as the boys treat their elder rudely and further disqualify themselves as victorious over Deeth, deepening what Derek Pearsall calls the "surreal effect" produced by "the mixture of planes of reality, the way in which real people behave as if they were characters in an allegory."[60]

The aesthetic pleasure of the tale is that they *are* characters in an allegory, but we only discovered it after we had thought they were fraternity boys who drank and diced and swore too much and didn't do the work for our courses in reading strategies. When all three are dead at the end of the tale, no garish details about the poisoning victims or the stab wounds are given—we have no visceral repugnance or even pathos to account for. The appeal of specific visual detail has yielded almost completely to cognitive intelligibility. Carolyn Dinshaw argues that "The exemplum is unnecessary to the logical argument of the sermon; it doesn't develop or complicate a point but merely demonstrates it"[61] *Radix malorum est cupiditas.* The Pardoner has already said in so many words that cupidity is death. The fate of the boys merely demonstrates it, perfectly demonstrates it. But it does two other things as well: it demonstrates the dangers of reading "the letter" alone, and poses the puzzle of the meaning of the Old Man. As a result, the *exemplum* enhances orthodox moral teaching with sophisticated aesthetic pleasure. For later generations, even those who do not recognize its force as a moral truth, there is pleasure in the exquisite craftsmanship of the tale, which completely satisfies generic expectations without allowing itself to be swallowed by a concept.

Aesthetic pleasures can be multiplied as we move out from the *exemplum* to the Pardoner's sermon, the Pardoner himself, and finally to the *Canterbury Tales.* The sermon is only offered in play; it is an illustrative enactment, perhaps even a parody, of how the Pardoner addresses people less clever than his current listeners. The sermon type is open to the common understanding, yet the pleasure it produces for the pilgrims, Chaucer's first readers, and for us latecomers is cognitively intricate. The pilgrims are being interpellated (though in the end unsuccessfully, since they reject the relics) as superior intellects whose pleasure is in part that of condescension toward the Pardoner's less worldly victims. But only partly. I think that the breathtaking efficiency of the *exemplum* in presenting a moral truth produces a commensurate awe among the pilgrims, perhaps even in the Pardoner himself.[62] The resulting moment is so intense that it takes the acerbic negotiations of the epilogue to return the group to normal communal relations.[63]

Chaucer's readers, then and now, have further aesthetic involvement with the Pardoner's performance. The *exemplum* thriftily satisfies epistemic hunger, and seems to me deeply moving—it might win the contest. Set in the parodic sermon, it takes on a more sinister quality in which the cleverness of the performance can be enjoyed while the vicious misuse of everyone's moral sensibilities must be deplored. This will create a problem for those medieval readers (and those pilgrims) who have pondered Lollard rebukes to the clergy that echo the Donatist controversies of the early church.[64] The Pardoner has delivered a serious moral lesson in a powerful way, but the context in which he set it has ironized it. The insight that *radix malorum est cupiditas* is clear, but the relation between it and its presentation could be stated as a theological problem: can a reprobate preacher effect a true moral awakening? Add to that the suggestion that the church itself, supposed guardian of the truths of faith and morals, is in diverse ways implicated in the bilking of simple people; even if this Pardoner is himself an impostor, there is such a thing as a licensed pardoner.[65]

For us the aesthetic pleasures of this text are even richer and more intricate. We may not care deeply about the Donatist issue now (although the controversy over Paul de Man's early life in Europe suggests that we might still prefer purity in our gurus), but we are certainly intrigued by the friction between the perfectly realized form of the *exemplum* and the puzzling whirl of sensible details around its telling. Deconstruction produces a distinctive pleasure, and for our generation, the Pardoner's role invites us to deconstruct, demystify, and marvel at the layers we have unearthed. The very elusiveness of the Old Man as a trope reminds us of the Pardoner himself, an undecidable in so many ways,[66] who includes an undecidable in his tale.

The Nun's Life of Saint Cecilia

In a somewhat different style of reframing, we might consider the formal perfection of the Second's Nun's telling of the tale of St. Cecilia as a saint's life. From its first instance, the *Life of St. Antony* (mid–fourth century CE), the saint's life genre has taken "the distinctive history of an individual as a timeless paradigm."[67] Since it posits "historical" personages with considerable seriousness, it combines the sensible and intelligible in a somewhat different balance than the *exemplum*, but resembles it in inspirational power. The *Second Nun's Tale* replicates these traditional elements in the voice of an otherwise uncharacterized "Second Nun" so that there is little to disturb the exemplary quality of Cecilia's actions.[68] "Upon first reading, the *Second Nun's Tale* seems as uncomplicated as anything Chaucer ever wrote," is Lynn Staley Johnson's comment on the tale. What might shift one's angle of vision for this tale is a focus on historical context, a little like thinking of the Pardoner in terms of Donatism. Among female saints, Cecilia is surely one of those most defiant toward institutional authority. Her challenge to Almachius is noteworthy, yet perhaps akin to other saint's lives set in pre-Christian Rome, but she defies parents, husband, officers, and national policy. Johnson's argument is that Chaucer:

> doesn't advocate women preachers. But neither does he criticize Cecilia's ecclesiastical voice. He does not urge that the Church divest itself of its temporalities. And yet the legend contains the outlines of a Christianity as radically simple as any image created by John Wyclif in this period.[69]

It might therefore be said that the Second Nun tells a tale that perfectly satisfies the generic form in which she places it by mentioning the *Golden Legend* in her Prologue, but the local controversy over the positions of John Wyclif shade the tale in a way that turns its exemplary pieties toward reservations about the very institution that sponsors them. Such are the ways, as David Wallace puts it, "in which contemporary history may break into and embed itself in a literary construct."[70] This language game is not being managed by the Nun, but by Chaucer, or perhaps by the pressure of historical events. Seeing *The Second Nun's Tale* in the context of contemporary controversies disturbs the serenity of its emotional effects and raises some of the same questions about the church that *The Pardoner's Tale* does. (There are other hints that such tactics are possible for Chaucer, for example, the Host's objection to the Parson's objection to swearing.) The tale remains exemplary, but its inspiration might be taken to point more than one direction. This is a case in which the timeless *exemplum* is grasped immediately and the "secondary meaning" is the one vulnerable to history. This secondary meaning is presumably not readable at all by a gatekeeping constituency within the late fourteenth-century Church, but an enigma to be recognized (or perhaps felt as an effect) by those touched in some way by the Wycliffite controversies.[71] When the tale was first composed, a stress on apostolic simplicity was considered orthodox and widely shared, but by the time of its inclusion in the *Canterbury Tales* a reading like Johnson's would have embarrassed some and been embraced as an insiders' secret by others. This is a case of risk in fiction, like those Haidu refers to as "free variations" in seemingly pious texts, offering dangerous encouragement to some audiences.[72]

The Nun's Priest's Fabled Beasts

The Nun's Priest's Tale presents still another way of disturbing a generic pattern. The beast fable is the skeleton of the story (announced in lines 2889–81, "For thilke tyme...Beestes and briddes koude speke and synge"), but nearly every available genre is somehow signaled before it is over. Traditionally, the beast fable is a highly readable form; it has a strong plot and a straightforward conclusion that presents its fable wisdom. This instance is a beast fable and also a parody of beast fables. It includes a parody of most of the other genres in the *Canterbury Tales* as well. Pared of its *amplificatio* this tale fulfills its mission admirably: the foolish cock is seized once through the fox's flattery, but uses flattery to outwit his captor in the end. The admonition to both barnyard and other princes is to suspect flattery and learn from previous mistakes. But of course, decisive as that fable is, the Chaucerian tale loads it with so much ornament that it seems to be *playing with* its imputed language game in a kind of immanent critique. The complication of the Nun's Priest's genre does not arise primarily from involving it in a larger historical context (although evidence for that can be adduced), nor from a relationship with its teller, since, like the Second Nun, the Nun's Priest is almost completely uncharacterized in the frame tale, except that he is the *Nun's* Priest, which enlivens the sly and partial misogyny of the tale.

The parodic slant of this tale is owed to its massive echoes of the advice of Geoffrey of Vinsauf's *Poetria Nova.* There is scarcely a figure or ornament described by Geoffrey that does not turn up in the *Nun's Priest's Tale.* The single exception is that Chaucer ignores Geoffrey's dictates on comedy: "Yet there are times when adornment consists in avoiding ornaments, except such as ordinary speech employs and colloquial use allows. The comic subject rejects diction that has been artfully laboured over; it demands plain words only."[73] The sleek, unpretentious example Geoffrey of Vinsauf provides for this point contrasts in every way with Geoffrey Chaucer's. That fact alone plants suspicion that a central issue in the tale concerns effective representation itself. Chaucer is writing about writing, and his unobtrusive Priest demonstrates his thorough knowledge of the tropes and ploys of rhetoric by using them where they will attract attention for their incongruity: the barnyard. He might win the storytelling contest through pure virtuosity. So we might call the *Nun's Priest's Tale* a beast fable larded with immanent critique of the rhetorical tradition that all the other pilgrims had called upon in more measured ways. To put it slightly differently, we might call it a beast fable with an interpolated encyclopedia of the genres used by the other pilgrims. It most particularly satirizes the moralizing tendencies of all the allegorical genres, beginning and ending like a sermon, as it does. But the Host is right this time in his assessment: this is a "murie tale" and the Priest is to be commended for it. It is murie because it binds together the concerns and representational strategies of the other tales, and of much lore in medieval society generally, without polemics, in service to the cause of community within the company. Wittgenstein says that "we are most fully human when we laugh," and it is in this tale that the implications of his term *language games* seem most fully enacted. The distance allowed by the humane cheerfulness of the beast fable might be taken to signal the Priest's undogmatic goodwill toward the other pilgrims.

The Wife's Arthurian Romance

The historical setting of *Wife of Bath's Tale*—the "olde dayes of the Kyng Arthour"—calls up generic expectations for romance. If its tone seems a little too homemade for the genre, Northrop Frye's description of it as nostalgic wish fulfillment adds an interesting twist: although it initially turns up as chivalric, romance wishing, it is historically inflected, sometimes even revolutionary or proletarian.[74] Surely that noncourtly inflection is marked in this tale by the way Alisoun the weaver's wishes are reflected in her Arthurian tale. Inside the text of the *Wife's Tale*, the element of wish is enacted on behalf of the nameless knight/rapist who escapes his punishment through the aid of women, first Guinevere, whose intervention in his trial sends him on his quest, and then the hag, whose answer allows him to complete it. When his unwillingly espoused wife turns into a lovely woman, he is granted a larger wish than he could have formulated earlier. He learns (just barely, and some critics think through mere exhaustion) that he must respect women, so his new wife is not merely beautiful and faithful, but a person in her own right, unlike the victimized virgin who appeared to him only as prey. He gets his "freedom" (as both nonconstraint and nobility) in more ways than he himself could have asked for. The literal level of this tale is completely readable, indeed impressive, without further exegesis.

However, experiencing it seems to tempt us to ascribe broader meanings to it, that is, to indulge in allegoresis.[75] Many of my students object to the tale because the knight got so much more than he deserved, but I think a medieval audience might have *liked* this feature particularly, experiencing it as wonder and seeing in it an analogy to grace as opposed to law. "All the souls that were were forfeit once, / and He that might the vantage best have took [in this case the women, Guinevere, speaking on behalf of the virgin, and the hag] / found out the remedy," says Isabella in *Measure for Measure* (II.ii.73–75). Except perhaps for her digression on Midas (III.952–82), Alisoun tells her tale with a remarkable pointedness that suggests the exemplum even while simultaneously fulfilling and reversing romance expectations (since it is the woman who rescues the imperiled knight). This is a somewhat mixed generic shape in which the contributing forms are fused and mutually supportive, while remaining elusive of final conceptualization.

The compression and control the Wife exhibits in her tale are in obvious contrast to everything else we know about her, especially her rambling disclosures in her Prologue and her more general "wandrynge by the weye" remarked in the *General Prologue* (I.467). Seen in terms of our knowledge of the Wife, her generically near-perfect romance-cum-exemplum seems the fulfillment of her wish rather than the knight's. Read through the hag's interests, the tale is about the power to dispense grace rather than to be granted it. When the seemingly old, lowborn, and "loothly" hag is transformed by the knight's willingness to let her decide the "case" she has set him, the Wife's wish to teach and control men is granted without the physical struggle she and her fifth husband waged in her prologue.[76] That transformation may even be attributed to the psychology of the knight—"educated" he now sees the hag *as* beautiful—he has mastered a new aspect recognition. In telling her tale, the Wife adopts courtly and clerical voices, the courtliness of the nostalgia and wonder of the "olde dayes" of "Kyng Arthour," and the clerical earnestness of her lecture on ethical gentilesse. Yet her "own" earlier voice emerges as well, for example in her account of friars, which is both an observation about history and an insult to fraternal behavior (865–81), and her digression on Midas, which echoes her general prolixity and her tendency in her Prologue include stories damaging to women (952–82). Genre plays an important role in this case. The *Wife's Tale* appears as a definite shape: by itself it seems a duck but in the context of the frames she and Chaucer supply for it a rabbit.

Varieties of Chaucerian Realism

I want to now return to the earlier discussion of verisimilitude, which is, of course, one criterion for aesthetic excellence throughout the Middle Ages. In spite of our suspicion of any fictional image that seems to offer itself as a direct reflection of observed reality (or, for that matter, of the claim that unmotivated observation can be achieved in ordinary life), we cannot "jettison representational theories" in favor of an "infinite play of signs" without losing much of the power Chaucer's fictions exert over imagination.[77] A distinct and apparently extant lifeworld seems to lurk behind almost all the tales, and in those I will address next, sensible detail is particularly close to the ground of everyday life.

The Franklin's Lai

The genre of the *Franklin's Tale* closely resembles that of the *Wife of Bath's Tale;* it also shares themes in that both explore the terms on which an early version of companionate marriage might be established. Although both tales reach their conclusions in part by magic, I see the Franklin's contribution as closer to realism because its primary level seems clearer about the world of time and space (it is located in Armorik, and the characters, unlike those in the *Wife's Tale*, are called by their names) and about the line between supernatural causes and the transformations of human desire. By the end of this tale, it is not clear that any "real" magic has been effected (but then one might say that about the *Wife's Tale* as well if the hag's transformations occurred within the knight's mind). Both tales are comedic in that the characters overcome obstacles to their happiness, but the Franklin more fully invokes the order of nature and the rules of society in producing that conclusion.

The sensible details of the *Franklin's Tale* weigh more heavily than in *exempla*, and the Franklin's generous and experienced, but secular, voice is consistently heard throughout his telling. The initial situation in which "greet emprise" wins the hand of a woman of high birth is hardly unknown in medieval society.[78] Although the private marriage compact (V.741) violates aristocratic/courtly legalisms on the one hand and patriarchal/Christian legalisms on the other, it is justified at length (761–802) by reference to the everyday experiences of married people the Franklin thinks will support his everyday interpretation of patience ("For every word men may nat chide or pleyne" [776]). This is so far from the extravagant definition of patience in the *Clerk's Tale* (and later *Melibee*) as to place this fiction in a realistic conjugal setting—not that there will not be extravagance later in the tale.

This middle register (I think of Frye's low-mimetic) matches the realistic characterization of Dorigen and Arveragus. While one might call Aurelius a man with no more complexity than his role as a lovesick courtier requires, the husband and wife are presented as experiencing their situations in more nuanced ways. Why that seemingly half-serious attempt at softening her blow to the squire's ego is taken so seriously in the tale has been the source of much critical dispute.[79] It seems to me, and to many others, that a literal reading of the crisis will not do; the seriousness of the promise is the *given* of the tale (as is Gawain's return of the ax blow in *Sir Gawain and the Green Knight*), emphasizing the ways the characters will handle the aftermath and making the *Franklin's Tale* a "psychologizing romance" (the term is Charles Muscatine's).[80] The account of their courtship stresses responsiveness and negotiation, not just typecasting. In the design of the tale, her ethical earnestness is nicely contrasted with the classical, pagan phrasing of Aurelius's prayer. Dorigen's mental habit is to consider general precepts and prior cases feelingly, which is why she marshals her long array of female suicides. Her recital of those cases indulges the medieval taste for pathos at too great a length for a shapely story in terms of modern narrative thrift, but one could regard this suffering and hesitation as a feature of her characterization.[81]

Arveragus, too, is treated as someone with an inner life. His dilemma, when Dorigen describes her plight, is solved at great emotional cost, but in keeping with the heavy emphasis on promises he and the tale have maintained. As Carruthers has argued, he will not treat her rash promise less seriously than the other promises in the tale, but he reminds her not to disgrace him, in keeping with the marriage compact.[82] Susan Crane thinks both Arveragus and the Franklin take the compact too seriously, misreading the demands of romance to indicate the suitor's worth by having him say such things in courtship. She concludes that the "Franklin is not entirely in consonance with romance convention."[83] Her view is that the Franklin is placed as an uncertain outsider to the genuine aristocratic code that romance has become. If this is true, those romance conventions tend to make women merely the erotic prey of men, who are free to treat promises to women as "game." The Franklin's unwillingness to do so is one reason I do not see this tale clearly in the generic mode of romance.

In making private oaths the crux of the story does, I think, democratize the romance form (as Frye allows for in his anatomy of genres): the married pair are granted mental lives less controlled by chivalric "honor" (a public virtue) than by personal integrity.[84] Perhaps the Franklin is presenting a deliberate modification of the code he has adopted by telling a tale in which personal integrity becomes the decisive moral force, and perhaps Chaucer is characterizing *him* as a man in just the right relation to society to do so. In spite of its attention to the sensible level, then, this tale turns that very attention to a powerful secular moral: generous respect for the integrity of other people is the real mark of civilized behavior. As in the Clerk's and Wife's stories, the element of wonder, of sudden revelation, is strong, but here the magic that produced it is unequivocally wielded by human beings. The realism of this tale lies in the social/domestic realm and can be read as the contribution of a realistically conceived narrator displaying an emerging structure of feeling.

Fabliau and Lab Report: The Canon's Yeoman's Tale

The Miller, the Reeve, and the Summoner, in particular, acquit themselves so well in deploying the fabliau that they elevate the form.[85] I will discuss these tales in chapter 6, but the *Canon's Yeoman's Tale* presents some interesting problems to consider in terms of fabliau conventions. Convinced by Lee Patterson's argument, I consider the *Canon's Yeoman's Tale* to fall into three parts—*Introduction, Prologue*, and *Tale*—rather than a prologue and a two-part tale, as printed in the *Riverside* edition.[86] Helen Cooper finds its genre unclassifiable, but only because she regards the tale as both parts 1 and 2, while I am treating the tale proper as part 2, and part 1 as the Prologue, in analogy to the organization of the Pardoner's performance. The *Tale* thus considered is a fabliau of the trickster type. The Yeoman satisfies the expectations connected with this genre, which combines very specific "everyday" detail with an overarching lesson about fraud. Intensifying the "realism" of the tale is the fact that we are, like Chaucer's first audiences, curious about what happens in alchemical labs. Not only are the events of the tale described so as to allow the exact nature of the trick to be grasped, but the authority for knowing what an alchemist would use and do is established in the Yeoman's *Prologue*. In introducing the teller, the *Prologue* and *Tale* mesh as neatly as the Pardoner's and the Wife's, and the tale seems more continuous generically with its prologue than in the other cases.

What changes a fabliau introduced with an account of the teller's life (told with "journalistic" attention to everyday reality)[87] to a more remarkable and less bounded genre is its *Introduction*. There the Canon's Yeoman *enacts* a story as it unfolds for him. His decision to address the pilgrims provides its crisis point, since it is the Canon who is the first focus of the Host's attention and the one from whom he expects a tale. The Host is curious about the ragged garments of a man so gifted as the Yeoman alleges his canon to be, and after finding that the two of them live in a "pryvee fereful residence" (VIII.660), Harry Bailey shifts his attention to the Yeoman, inquiring about his marred countenance. The more the Yeoman talks about his life, the less he seems to be "opening" for the Canon, bursting instead with a story of his own. Since he cannot both keep his "lord and soverayn's" counsel and tell his own story, he breaks with his master and joins the pilgrims' *compaignye*. The story of his apprenticeship with the Canon becomes his *Prologue* and the fabliau his *Tale*. Where at first it seemed he intended to sustain the high reputation of his master—the Canon could turn the path they have been following to Canterbury "up-so-down, / And pave it al of silver and of gold" (VIII.625–26)—by the end of the *Introduction* he has disobeyed him and begun to reveal his secrets. The story told in the *Introduction*—in real time—is that the Yeoman decides to go to Canterbury by the communal road of these and other pilgrims rather than to cling to the hope of repaving the way with the Canon's gold and silver. As a result, he becomes a masterless man in the social order of the medieval estates.

The ringing line "Swich thyng as that I know, I wol declare" (VIII.719), situates the genre of the *Prologue* as confession, not only personal but artisanal as well. This Prologue touches imagination as the performance closest to handheld camera realism. Although the Yeoman calls it a tale—"By that I of my tale have maad an ende" (VIII.971)—it has no plotted shape, is delimited by the seven years of the Yeoman's service, and follows no known original. It is, nonetheless, full of ordered knowledge of the craft of alchemy, and some readers have found it so detailed that they suspect Chaucer to have been either a practitioner of alchemy or the victim of one who was; certainly, he had done his research. I find Cooper's term "journalism" particularly apt, not to claim Chaucer foresaw newsprint or documentary, but because for us it seems so close an analogue to the now-popular "biographical profile" or "day in the life" forms. It forces audiences early and late to regard the Yeoman as an able craftsperson and a shrewd observer of the harsh contexts for medieval lives, just as the prologues of the Pardoner and the Wife had done. Unlike the *Wife's Prologue* or the *Pardoner's*, though, it does not disturb the impeccability with which the *Tale* fills out the trickster-fabliau genre.

Historical Tragedy: The **Physician's Tale** *and the* **Monk's Tale**

Inviting mixed generic readings or failing to fulfill generic expectations does not, by itself, of course, produce aesthetic pleasure. The *Physician's Tale* can be read as historical narrative—since history is bound to what happened and Livy was read as history, this seems its strongest claim to authority and coherence (as Strohm has pointed out, this is a *storie* rather than a *tale*).[88] But, in that case, the frequent appearance of moral guidance attached to persons and events (governesses "teche hem vertu" [VI.82], parents set an example [97], sin has its reward [276–82], and forsake sin [286]) invites a reading of its address as an *exemplum*. Moralizing an historical incident is not in itself genre-confusing, but none of these morals really accounts for the outcome of the tale or underwrites its emotional investment in pathos as Virginia begs for her life. The reference to Jeptha's daughter is an inadequate scriptural anchor; the relevant biblical parallel is Abraham's averted sacrifice of Isaac.[89] The moralizations are specifically Christian, but the Roman venue and the stress the tale places on Virginius's high social and legal standing and support from the people disturb the sense of urgency for his sacrifice. If a moralization appears in the tale as an argument, that argument must be logically sustained (coherent), as a necessary, though not sufficient, claim to beauty.

As the Physician presents the tale, it is easier to read the beheading as a display of Virginius's ownership of his daughter's fate than as either Roman stoicism or Christian purity. The bifurcated term *sentence* could function in either a tragic historical account, as legal judgment, or in a moral *exemplum*, as wisdom (the Clerk's reverent words were "ful of hy sentence"). *Sentence*, then, might be read as a textual detail that illuminates generic fracture rather than unity. Apius uses the word three times in delivering his unjust verdict, and it must there mean "legal finding." When Virginius uses it to justify killing his daughter—"Take thou thy deeth, for this is my sentence. / For love and not for hate thou must be deed" (VI.224–25), the Christian meaning should kick in, but for reasons already discussed it cannot. It looks as if generic shapeliness has been deliberately denied this tale, and very likely in order to serve the interests of the *General Prologue* in which the Physician's grasp of life and the world is found wanting. Any aesthetic pleasure the tale provides results, not from its coherence, but from the light its incoherence sheds on the frame tale.

The Monk also fails to make generic expectations work for him. He announces a generic shape very explicitly and then pays too little attention to the limits and opportunities it might have offered. His reference to "olde bookes" and hexameters signals his desire to be thought learned, and his definition of descents from prosperity to misery (VII.1973–82) betrayed by Fortune (1995) may be taken as a common medieval construal. Like the Physician, he attempts to Christianize this essentially Roman description of tragic action, and like the Physician, fails to produce the wonder that accompanies sudden understanding. Either the shockingly unmerited fall of Cenobia or the moral symmetry of Nebuchadnezzar's God-challenging pride brought low would have displayed the Monk's learning and rhetorical power. But he fails to distinguish between them, and further, supplies such trivial morals for some of his examples—his praise of Julius Caesar's modesty-unto-death, for example—that his telling slips into comedy.

The Monk does not fail because he mixes moralizing modes with tragic realism—in tragedies the harsh demands of the world of nature (and sometimes of a malevolent metaphysical principle) cannot be put aside in favor of the wish—but because he misses the point of tragic irony. Some critics deny that such a concept, so important to Aristotle's analysis of tragic form and those of the renaissance and later, was available to Chaucer, but if such a conception was beyond his mental horizon, he could not have written *Troilus and Criseyde*.[90] Because it would seem that Chaucer was aware of the shapes tragedy might take, his failure to provide effective tales for the Monk is likely to have been deliberate. As with the Pardoner's case, stepping back from the tales to the frame enables us to see the Monk as losing his early-established contest with the Knight whom he seeks to challenge (since his birth and learning may allow it) more directly, though less cleverly, than the Miller had. The Knight's interruption may sound slightly naïve, but his is the truer moral compass.

The **Knight's Tale** *and the Triumph of the Mixed Mode*

Several generic shapes can be made out in the *Knight's Tale*, and they are present in an intricately mixed pattern. The consolidation of the power of Athens over the known world and the participation of the gods suggest epic, and the fact that this material was thought of as chronicled event suggests fictionalized history: *storie.* Nearly coextensive with these is the love *debat* which structures many romances and was said to have been inspired by the "courts of love" sponsored by Marie of Champagne. The prominent Boethian passage that triggers and purports to explain the outcome suggests (but this more faintly) a philosophical or providential meditation, like Augustine's *City of God.* The remarkable manner in which the prayers of Arcite, Palamon, and Emelye are answered add an embedded object lesson—be careful what you ask for— to the mix. Here is a tale to be seized on in many ways, and probably was seen variously by different segments of medieval society. Although each of these perspectives modifies the others, none renders any of the others impossible. One could say, for example, that the tale of Theseus's rule is solidified through his handling of the competition between Arcite and Palamon, or that the "Age of Theseus" is an influential context for either the love story or the meditation on Fortune. The point is that Chaucer could combine generic kinds to impressive aesthetic effect—the sudden flash of insight that each supplicant's prayer has been granted completes the Athenian epic and the meditation on Fortune as well as the love story. Like several of the other tales discussed in this chapter, the *Knight's Tale* provides evidence that beauty may be produced either by fulfilling fore-conceptions unpredictably or by invoking several familiar patterns all of which are brought to conclusion by a single gesture, thus predicting the generic complexity of the pilgrims' performances and the *Canterbury Tales* itself. The pleasure involved in such a conclusion seems immediate and sensible, but it also activates a drive toward intelligibility.

The Knight has "umbokeled the male" with a tale worthy of memory in view of both young and old.The formal complexity and proportionality of his story, reaching as it does into antiquity and philosophical abstraction, yet immediate to its teller and listeners, display the Knight's *largesse* of mind despite his sometimes colloquial manner. His tale and later his response to the Monk's "tragedies" call attention to his concern with genre and with the modes of life it signals, inflecting the frame with a broad inclusiveness. The Canterbury story keeps establishing the community the pilgrims have formed and deepening it as more of them reveal their visions of the world. Everybody is entitled to speak, but nobody gets to go on forever—when *would* the Monk have run out of "ensamples"? This communal effort has boundaries, and so does the extensive fiction that presents it. The virtual community has vacillated between deference toward the "authorities"—the Host as "juge and reportour" (I.814) and the Knight as the pilgrim in the highest secular estate—and disruptions like the Miller's successful bid to tell his tale second and the Pardoner's interruption of the Wife. But, by the end, it has held together and even gained a convert in the Canon's Yeoman. The array of genres and the games Chaucer plays with them in this "poem unlimited" are almost as varied and inclusive as the pilgrims he has invented to relate them. In spite of its *integritas* and apparent purposiveness, the *Canterbury Tales* outwits reduction to a final purpose. The next chapter will consider the extent to which we may refer to these pilgrims as individuals, and chapter 7 will take up the nature of their community.

CHAPTER 4

BEAUTIFUL PERSONS

The business of a poet, said Imlac, is to examine, not the individual, but the species; to remark general properties and large appearances: he does not number the streaks of the tulip, or describe the different shades in the verdure of the forest.

Samuel Johnson, *Rasselas*

In every wood in every spring
There is a different green.

J. R. R. Tolkien, *The Fellowship of the Ring*

I was regarding the boat and then the false President-Pasha himself, when I thought to myself that he seemed to be real and that he was beautiful—if these two words can exist together: beautiful and real.

Orhan Pamuk, *The Black Book*

The idea that attention to individual personhood arose during the European Renaissance is part of what Lee Patterson has called the "pervasive and apparently ineradicable *grand recit* that organizes Western cultural history."[1] In Jacob Burckhardt's famous nineteenth-century formulation, medieval man "was conscious of himself only as a member of a race, people, party, or corporation—only through some general category."[2] Chaucerians are likely to find themselves wary of virtually every feature of Burckhardt's assertion, from its notion of a generic "medieval man" and an accessible knowledge of his self-consciousness to the force of its posited general categories. Yet, at the same time, Nancy Partner's twentieth-century working belief that the "deep structure of human experience has remained essentially the same over centuries of changing culture,"[3] implying that such structures persist untouched by child-raising practices or social mobilities, may seem ahistorical from another direction. I have argued earlier that structures of feeling do change over time, sometimes within a generation, but these are not the "deep structures" Partner seems to refer to. This chapter addresses the interpretive and aesthetic effects of allowing the characters of Chaucer's fictions to appear before us as genuine subjects with rich, complex interior lives on the one hand, or enjoying them for the striking alterity of their presentation as types on the other. To write about history and historically distant art is to try to understand both changes from and continuities with current habits of mind. This is genuinely possible, as Gadamer sees it, because our own experience has been formed by "effective history" (an "at work" history: *Wirkungsgeschichte*, see p. 11 above) even when we are trying to isolate some aspect of the past as alien to us.[4]

Chaucer's pilgrim narrators and the characters within their tales often turn to the concept of "privitee." Surely this fact alone signals individual mental life and some measure of emotional complexity. At the same time, we are aware of Chaucer's mode of representing people through the conventions and tropes of his age, which do often stress a particular social location with its attendant obligations and understandings. The *Canterbury Tales* and *Troilus and Criseyde* introduce persons in terms of their roles in the culture and economy of a virtual England or Troy. Furthermore, both fictions regularly display the inner lives of their characters by invoking authorities from the past (as in the Wife's recourse to Jerome's *Adversus Jovinianum*), either their personal past learning or the conventional shared past, or both. The issues in the long and ongoing debate over personhood require a recasting of their terms for my purposes here.

We can assert without contradiction that people have always had nuanced, individual, inner lives, but that their feelings were structured differently from our own in some important ways. The greater respect in which cultural memory was held, in contradistinction to "idiosyncratic" imagination and the consequent turn to quotation from "authority" even in intensely felt, novel, personal circumstances, is one pivot on which this difference may be investigated.[5] Notwithstanding their full subjectivity, medieval people may have represented themselves to others and even to themselves in formulations now difficult to read. Susan Crane reads material manifestations (clothing, coats of arms) as well as poetic signs to tease out the ways medieval people regarded their selfhood. She concludes that, rather than "neatly bounded, free floating coherence, or 'subjectivity,' with its quite different implication of a constrained psychology largely hidden from view.... Performance is a reliable measure of who one actually is."[6] Certainly, much can be reliably read from that point of view, especially in the way Crane allows for nuance, but my tack will be based on language, as, again in Gadamer's phrase, "being that can be understood."[7] A closer look at the mutually implicated terms "consciousness" and "representation" is therefore required.[8]

Cultural practices do, of course, change, and as they change, they provide new modes for experiencing and representing inner life. Differing modes of literacy, for example, provide consciousness with differing materials and differing ways of weaving them together. Consider, for example, the moving story in which Abelard describes Heloise's reluctant entry into the convent of Argenteuil. Through her tears, Heloise quotes Cornelia's offer to commit suicide on behalf of her husband's honor in Lucan's *Pharsalia*.[9] Lucan's words, long since memorized, Mary Carruthers argues, "helped to make up her experience...even, perhaps with irony, in such an extreme personal situation."[10] Carruthers calls Heloise a "subject-who-remembers," positing that access to cultural texts allow her a way to explore and express her situation and feelings.[11] Nancy Partner makes a similar case for the complications of Heloise's situation, although she posits a more commanding interior consciousness for Heloise, seeing her as manipulating the discursive templates around her in order to understand and convey her particular relation to them.[12] This story seems to me an especially poignant instance of "effective history," incorporating tradition into one's felt experience. Not everyone, not even every writer, of course, would be able to produce the impression of a mind so fully in control of her culture's tropes, but if Carruthers and Partner are right about Heloise, they have established that mental life *could* take this form in the Middle Ages. Both scholars seem to be working toward a fusion of medieval and contemporary horizons and accounting for "effective history" from different standpoints, Carruthers by clarifying the conditions under which medieval people could construct identities, Partner by showing how much is to be gained by positing a "post-Freudian" vantage point.

Whatever features we impute to the self-consciousness of "medieval people," we must admit that for us the only access to it is through representation, the modes of which *are* historically constituted. This admission is not, however, the counsel of despair. We commonly read certain representational strategies as signaling states of inner life that are not directly expressed in dialogue or action in postmedieval, and especially contemporary, representations. We also read signals of this kind in "real-life" and yet, in the strictest sense, we have only a tenuous grasp of the inward states, even of the people we know best. There are, of course, several positions from which a denial of the idea of selfhood, in fiction or in life, may be launched. D. W. Robertson, Jr. writes about one of Chaucer's most interesting characters thus: "Alisoun of Bath is not a 'character' in the modern sense at all, but an elaborate iconographic figure designed to show the manifold implications of an attitude.... That she still seems feminine to us is a tribute to the justness of the ideas which produced her."[13] I will pass over the contradiction between the first and second of these quoted sentences—the first claims nothing but iconographic rhetoric, the second enduring truth to nature—in order to focus on Robertson's denial of personal eccentricity amounting to the pure intelligibility of Chaucer's portraits. His definition of "the modern" is 1962's version of "romantic realism," a realism overinvested in the various shades of green in the forest.

Ironically, Jonathan Dollimore's influential *Radical Tragedy* (1986) denies the illusion of centered selfhood just as vigorously. Where Robertson found his position on the Fathers of the Church, Dollimore justifies his "decentered subject"—a human without a core identity or structure of meaning—on the positions of Foucault, Barthes, and Derrida as a "vision of liberation" from the oppressive social codes that have served to define self-consciousness.[14] In his eagerness to throw off the shackles of capitalist individualism and the denial of collective identifications it has carried with it, Dollimore has written as if early modern playwrights did not acknowledge the existence of individual, self-conscious persons or represent them on stage. Although the tropes he recognizes are different from those cited by Robertson, Dollimore sees the protagonist of Jacobean drama as "the focus of political, social, and ideological contradictions" in society, rather than an instance of personal moral complication. We might say that Robertson posits a premodern representation of the subject, and Dollimore a postmodern. Both seem to me to have confused the ideological privilege humanism gives selfhood with the fact of its persistence.[15]

But today one can go further still in denying the importance of self-consciousness. From the point of view of Artificial Intelligence (AI), Hans Moravec in *Robot* questions the whole idea of consciousness as "the continuous story we tell ourselves...a thin, often inaccurate veneer rationalizing a mountain of unconscious processing." It is an "evolutionary fluke...a far-fetched interpretation of a pattern of tiny, salty squirts" soon to be superseded (in his view we will be turning the world over to our "mind children," aka robots, pretty soon). This is an extreme vision of our "posthuman" condition, but (wacky as it seems to me) its practical consequences are not much more corrosive of values like personal freedom and responsibility than some postmodernist announcements of our being nonagents, written or constructed entirely by social codes. Yet, neither the AI people nor the history-writes-us types actually argue that there is no such thing as self-consciousness, only that it is a dated and retrogressive way of thinking about ourselves; Moravec admits that these stories made of salty squirts are all our generation has to connect us to the universe and to link one of our moments to the next.[16]

Robot appeared in 1999, the same year as Antonio Damasio's *The Feeling of What Happens*. Rejecting the mind/body split, Damasio argues for the "dignity and stature" of our minds, which not only take in sense impressions, but produce images from them and through "the feeling that marks those images as ours" produces consciousness as knowledge. We know that we have seen, heard, and otherwise experienced in the world, and we refer that knowledge to ourselves in an ongoing account Damasio calls a "movie-in-the-brain."[17] This continual consciousness of both self and world is mediated by a feedback loop through the body, the locus of the feeling that accompanies image making; "the brain is truly the body's captive audience."[18] (Compare this with Robert Pasnau's description of Aquinas's *Summa* on mind: "The intellect is constantly looking to see what the senses are doing.")[19] People mature by slowly building a perspective from which to see the world, one that remains relatively consistent and implies some sort of agency.[20] These constructions lie closer to our usual intuition that each of us has a continuous mental and emotional history, and explains why current law regards people who cannot recall and claim their actions as unfit for trial. Damasio's arguments for the essential privacy of mental experience, even in the light of today's greatly improved technology for measuring brain activity's conclusions about selves, are especially congruent with Chaucer's narrative ploys, like the examination of the pilgrims' idiosyncratic linguistic habits, and the insistence on a "privitee" the *General Prologue's* narrator cannot see into.

Burckhardt's description does not absolutely deny medieval people self-consciousness either, but merely denies that they saw themselves as unique and self-defined—their inner lives "lay dreaming or half awake"—under a veil of faith in the groups they belonged to. But if we shift attention to the level of representation, we *can* observe in the Middle Ages a marked adherence to those discursive modes that stylize behavior in the stories people told and listened to. The resilience of the allegorical modes has been discussed, as has Helen Cooper's characterization of Chaucer's life experience as coming to him defined by the available genres: he as "the watcher at every window." The strongest case for Burckhardt's view is that most medieval people looked through fewer windows than Chaucer did and saw in very stylized stories consciousnesses like their own.

But I do not think so. The genres (even without considering Chaucer's) are too various, too malleable, and too open to innovation to allow the conclusion that a fourteenth-century woman, for example, could slip without internal debate into one or the other of the scenarios prepared for her either by estates satire or moral allegory; more than the generic patterns are at stake. The remarkable variety of Chaucer's modes of representation allows us to inquire into how that "watcher at every window" regarded the human person. I want to return now to the term "regard" in terms of Michael Witmore's discussion of it in connection with Reformation-era thought: " 'regard' confers value on the thing regarded, signals interest, awareness, deference and even obligation."[21] Elaine Scarry's defense of beauty, as we have seen, includes the useful phrase "acuity of regard" which both defines an important reaction to a beautiful thing and leads to the habit of "more capacious regard for the world" beyond it.[22] For both Witmore and Scarry, *regard* involves the close scrutiny of an object or event coupled with attention to its implications "beyond itself," which fusion of local (sensible) detail with philosophical (intelligible) import I find particularly evident in Chaucerian texts.

Chaucer lavishes regard on the persons in his fictions. This chapter examines the various ways his narrators—the pilgrim "Chaucer" in the *Canterbury Tales*, the pilgrims who tell tales, and the narrator in *Troilus and Criseyde*—signaled regard toward persons. Characterization in some tales is directed toward typological patterns and in others toward inner lives and emotional idiosyncrasy, as V. A. Kolve has argued about medieval imagery in general.[23] Which mode of characterization turns up in a particular tale has to do with genre, and might be, though, thought of in terms of Dennett's principle of "epistemic hunger": just enough detail about a character is given to assuage the desire evoked by a particular generic shape. Chaucer's pilgrims, in Helen Cooper's view are "not characters of post-Freudian depth, but individualized types controlled by convention—whether they fulfill expectations or contradict them—and by the poetic manipulation of language and imagery."[24] This is both true and inevitable, not only for medieval storytelling, but for all storytelling; linguistic conventions are all we ever have. Yet it is also misleading because the pilgrims are not alike in this matter, nor are the characters in their stories. Cooper herself will speculate throughout her book on the play of motives, conflicts, and predilections involved in the tales. This sounds like the centerpiece of post-Freudian ego theme psychology to me, although my own case for private consciousness does not rest primarily on Freud's propositions, as my recourse to Damasio and Dennett demonstrates.[25]

An emphasis on language and discourse recalls Wittgenstein's style of thinking, in which every utterance is the performance of a language game that evokes the speaker's lifeworld. Chaucer has imagined lifeworlds for the pilgrims in the *General Prologue* and head-links and then presented them as imagining lifeworlds for the characters in their tales; the way they do so then recomplicates our sense of the teller. Some of the pilgrims and *their* characters are presented as types and/or externally, in terms of their adventures, answering the demands of their genres. But for others—and the examples that follow concern these—he imagines and signals rich inner lives. It is this depth and complexity of characterization that Ezra Pound found so impressive that it placed Chaucer among the four "donative" authors of the Western tradition who "draw down" into art something new to the tradition (though based on it) and something previously unrecognized in the "air about him."[26] Pound's description of Chaucer's particular *virtù* is his creation of persons, "not so much of their acts and the outlines of their acts as of their character, their personalities."[27] In this chapter, I want to examine the specifics of Chaucer's regard for his imagined persons by looking into their "confessions," their dreams, and some "luminous details" (Pound's term, which he capitalizes) of their stories, like interior monologues and telling gestures. Such narrative techniques surprise us by providing rich and "sudden insight into circumjacent conditions,"[28] organizing the texts they belong to, and connecting us with Chaucer's imagined and real worlds through their *claritas.*

Forthright Confessions

Michel Foucault's influence has often been registered as emphasizing historical change in the deeper structures of culture and experience. His analysis of the divide between one episteme and another, especially in *The Order of Things*, suggests that "the human" is a significantly different matter at one time than at another.[29] On the other hand, the first volume of the *History of Sexuality* insists on historical continuity, at least in the matter of the medieval discourse of confession and its long aftermath. The institution of confession, he writes, "was inscribed at the heart of the process of individualization by power."[30] As Karma Lochrie puts it, Foucault argues that "confession created an elaborate discourse of secrecy that extended beyond the confidentiality of the confessional to construct our very understanding of the human subject and subjectivity."[31] The "our" here is certainly right and suggests a continuing influence not yet spent. The Fourth Lateran Council's issue of *Omnis utrisque sexus* in 1215 turned attention—established *regard* in this strong sense—for more than a parishioner's actions; it interrogated his or her mental and emotional life in ways that the presuppositions of Roman law had not. Lochrie writes, "Confession did not begin in 1215 with the passing of Canon 21...but its regulations, codification, and formulation as a discourse did."[32] Over time, confessional discourses enhanced the conditions of possibility for experiencing inner life, but the council's edict was merely the necessary and not the sufficient cause. In order to seep into the structures of feeling of ordinary people, of course, it had to be dispersed into the several layers of more localized practice and reach congregation through the parish pulpit. Masha Raskolnikov refers to this dispersal of understandings of selfhood in terms of confession "vernacular psychology."[33] At each stage, of course, there were those who turned religious discernment inward in this way and those who failed to understand it or used it cynically. It is no wonder the process of internalizing religious duty was so uneven and lengthy. In claiming this interiorizing function for confession, Lee Patterson writes of ritualized confession that it "promises a mode of self-representation that can minister to the privation caused by sin by restoring to the penitent an original wholeness."[34] Note that in his account, a person is not merely posited as having an internal consciousness, but as being able to alter it through a sacrament. Confessional discourse was in "the air" of Chaucer's late medieval London, and it served him as a way to imagine and present the inner workings of personality.

The Parson's Tale

Extant penitential guides serve as sources for the *Parson's Tale* and Chaucer translated them with apparent respect. Many in his first reading audiences would have recognized in the tale the sober cast of mind parish priests were expected to follow in eliciting and hearing confessions. (The friar in the *Summoner's Tale* presents a less detailed and conscientious style of "groping" the consciences of his confessants.) The tale is not about caring for people who sin (it is in the *General Prologue* that the Parson's pastoral methods are described); it is an anatomy of the *kyndes* of sin there are. The Parson is the only pilgrim who does not present a fiction—even *Melibee* asks us to consider named persons following out a narrative line, however burdened with "wisdom" it may be. The Parson does not, one might say, participate in the tale-telling contest, but rather reflects upon the forms of life it has represented. His words attend only to the intelligible, addressing himself to concepts (as Bonaventure and Kant both say, the good may be discovered by reason), and not providing, except in passing, pleasurable aesthetic experiences as the others do.

In attempting to link the Parson's confessional manual to the man described in the *General Prologue* and headlinks, many critics find the tale rigid and harsh, even by medieval standards. The Parson is certainly thorough and orthodox in naming the sins and their branches, but it should also figure in characterizing him that he does not mystify the sacrament or try to trick anyone; he tells the pilgrims straightforwardly what he believes about moral life. This sets him apart from what Lochrie describes as the deviousness that was advised to confessors to assure that no secrets would go unconfessed, their tactics sometimes extending to what now would be called entrapment.[35] The pilgrim Parson's very full disclosure of the branches of sin marks him as a teacher, and to some extent mitigates the power relation inscribed in the institution of auricular confession. This fact brings the patient shepherd, who *snybbed* both high and low for obstinate sins, closer to the tale-teller with his elaborate categories. Because his performance is last, he has been taken as a commentator on all the other pilgrims from the vantage point of orthodox teaching—a position that must be balanced by the fact that he too is a pilgrim among the company. In any case, the clerical tenets of prevailing ideological conditions are presented in the *Parson's Tale* in a detailed and orderly way.[36] The Parson's account of the sins and their remedies stresses inner life at every point. Some of the seven are largely matters of mental orientation (pride, envy, and sloth), some result in overt action, but are sinful without being enacted (wrath, avarice, gluttony, lust). In all cases, emphasis falls on the habits of mind that result in sin and the remedy for it is constant vigilance: "penitence of goode and humble folk is the penitence of every day" (X.100). The *Parson's Tale* reveals its teller—provides a confession—as all the tales do, but it is also a confession of faith. In the moral arena, that faith rests on the importance of internal probity and confession that drives sin "from its hiding place in the soul."[37]

The **Wife's Prologue** *and* **Tale**

Several of the pilgrims are always spoken of as providing confessions, the fullest of which are found in the Wife of Bath's and the Pardoner's prologues. The Canon's Yeoman should also be included in this group. These prologues not only clearly locate each of the pilgrims in their "estates," but also reveal personal idiosyncrasies. The conventional roots of each prologue are deeply implicated in the representation of nuanced individual complexity. The Yeoman's disclosures feature his "mystery," alchemy, as Alisoun's do wifehood and the Pardoner's pardoning; they do not present either estates satire or moral censure alone, but the effect of these on particular persons. These three are also linked by the fact that they provide both self-disclosures and critiques of the institutions they have served. Chaucer's text regards them in the language of their types, but constructs as well the "deep structural" effects of their "membership" in associations. This is why the Wife, for example, has sometimes been taken as "an elaborate iconographic figure" and sometimes as a layered, conflicted subject of "post-Freudian" interest.

Most readers of the *Canterbury Tales* feel that the Wife of Bath discloses herself more fully than the other pilgrims and that there is more of her to disclose. Foucault asserts that the regime of confession makes people want to talk about themselves, say more about themselves than their outward behavior would reveal, and Alisoun certainly does do that. In his searching analysis of personal voice in the *Canterbury Tales*, Marshall Leicester describes Alisoun as simultaneously announcing and discovering her selfhood in her *Prologue*.[38] Lee Patterson treats her as the poster girl for it: "What the Wife champions. . .is less the rights of her sex, much less those of her class, than the rights of selfhood."[39] Carolyn Dinshaw writes that the Wife's revelation of her own self-interest mimics that of Jerome and his fellows, in that "the act of appropriating their methods for openly carnal purposes indicts their motivations as similarly carnal."[40] What interests me about these three converging commentaries is that the Wife is figured as the doer: she "classifies and explains herself" (Leicester), she champions the rights of selfhood (Patterson), she reveals the failings of the glossators against whom her argument is levered (Dinshaw). These phrasings testify to the sensible appeal of Alisoun's textual image as an active person (an adventurer in both of its early meanings: someone to whom things happen and someone who seeks out action and incurs risks) and a subject (as both subjected to a patriarchal cultural regime and actor rather than merely object). None of these critics, of course, deny that her figure can also be read as intelligible in some larger scheme afoot in the *Canterbury Tales*.[41] Regard often looks to a cosmic scheme.

On the other hand, as is well-known, substantial portions of the Wife's "confessional" prologue allude to well-known "authorities" on women. Alisoun herself provides attribution to some of them (III.671–80), showing off her capacious memory.[42] At one level, the intelligibility of the Wife's quotations and their attendant ironies are immediately apparent: she is confessing by quoting patriarchal rebukes from both Christian and non-Christian sources (including astrology) and then reports acting out these patterns in her own experiences.[43] Confessional practice would customarily begin with a recital of what one might stand accused of. The *Wife's Prologue*, however, invites readers to look beyond Alisoun's indictment of her own behavior for a fuller intelligibility of the play of motive and regret she reports. Her confession mimes the rhetorical tradition, but her image cannot be confined to the role of that tradition's inert spokesperson. One might take her "confession," like the Parson's, as a profession of a certain species of faith.

Why the Wife voices these damaging affronts to her "sect" in public is a little like why the historical Heloise voices Cornelia's lament from Horace; these women speak of themselves through the words of others.

In explaining what Alisoun reveals of herself, Chaucer's readers have restated the stages of feminist thinking: she repeats Jerome's words because they permeate her society, because they hurt her, because they have taught her how to deal with men, because she is deliberately demystifying them, because in mimicking them she can oppose them. But there is yet another way of seeing her use of Jerome et al. The authorities *meant something* to her about herself; the antifeminism of the past is "effective history" (Gadamer) at work *in* her. She challenges their estimate of female influence, but she cannot escape their having been formative in her own attempts to understand herself and her place in the world.[44] In spite of the irony with which she insults females in the supposed tirades of her first husbands, these commonplaces have surrounded her as she became self-conscious. One does not have to be a scholar to embody effective history.

The *Wife's Tale* is based on the wish that an old and seemingly ugly woman might possess the wisdom that saves the condemned knight and that her gift results in sexual gratification for both of them. This reading in no way pulls the allegorical strand of the tale apart from the individualized wish. The means by which the hag delivers this grace (as I called it in chapter 3) makes an even tighter (more intelligible) link between the personal and the religious allegory that is its cultural content. The hag rescues the knight twice, the first time through the worldly experience Alisoun spoke of at length in her prologue. She knows (or she tells the story to show) that the secular court Guinevere presides over will see the issue of feminine *maistrie* as the right answer. The knight still needs to be saved, however, because he does not understand existentially what he has announced in court to prolong his life. He still believes he must control the marriage he has unwillingly contracted, and he still finds it natural to injure a woman, this time by withholding rather than forcibly enacting sex. The pillow-lecture consists of time-honored truth eloquently stated. It too can be seen as a feature of the Wife's wishes: she wants to be *right*—not just technically (as in the trial), but cosmically. Her confession is ratified by her disclosure in the story that she wants to inhabit a state of grace and confer grace on someone else. She does not make a life of arguing with clerics only because they are wrong and she is hurt, but because she wants to work out a way to be both "wife" and "blessed." Her desire, in all its irreducible complexity, is the mainspring of both her prologue and her tale.

Without compromising the moral allegory her tale has presented, she tells us what she wants, but also why she has not, until the final hard-fought battle with her fifth husband, been able to achieve it in her life. Looking at the relationship between well-known tropes and inner lives, Hayden White reads Freud to suggest that even allegory may be related to unconscious processes. He writes that Freud's "conception of the relation between dream-thoughts and the dream-contents is precisely analogous to that form of poetic discourse...[called] allegorization" (see above p. 49). White's general conclusion is that the tropes of metaphoric language are analogous to the dreamwork and therefore presumably a feature of a kind of transhistorical (or at least very long-enduring) human mental life. Because the links between dream-thoughts (libidinal impulses) and the dream's manifest content (its images) are both personal and cultural (because they make use of cultural symbols), any particular dream sequence and the allegory it resembles will characterize a more or less specific person in a particular culture. Hence, we may see the *Wife's Tale* as an effective general allegory, a performance that bespeaks her place in the estates, and *also* a manifestation of her inmost wishes. At the end of her tale, the hag/Wife is beautiful, both physically and morally, and so is her whole performance. The sensible is addressed so fully and so intricately that generations of readers have pondered her contradictions and recognized her progeny at the supermarket, but she is richly intelligible as well.[45] This commingling of a sensible with an intelligible image is what I am calling Chaucer's aesthetic practice for characterization, and Alisoun is perhaps its fullest manifestation.

The Pardoner's Introduction, Prologue, *and* Tale

Cultural memory troubles the Pardoner in a quite different way. Just as Patristic antifeminism might be said to constitute the Wife's (disputed) definition of femininity, the Pardoner experiences himself as the outlier in a masculine discourse. Lee Patterson stresses that the Pardoner's story is about the constitution of the male psyche: a tale of transgression, castration, and uncompleted penance. In the Pardoner's case the abyss in his inner life, between the peasant-bilking features of his profession and his frustrated wishes, is even wider than Alisoun's. Marshall Leicester argues that in finding the Pardoner such a perfect icon of transgression, we tend to forget that he is also one who understands and "has attitudes toward" the abuses of the church he "serves."[46] Like the Wife, who confesses to the very abominations her culture uses to indict women, the Pardoner enacts the most serious charges leveled by Lollard and orthodox reformers alike against certain aspects of popular religious practice. And like the Wife's contribution, the Pardoner's registers a powerful critique of the institution that provides his authority. But any treatment of his characterization as merely an "iconographic figure designed to show the manifold implications of an attitude" falls short (as in the case of the Wife) of the impression of depth most readers cannot shake off in confronting him.

The Pardoner performs with remarkable self-possession until he gets confused about timing, first seeming to close his mock sermon by announcing that Christ's pardon is best and then offering his admittedly worthless relics. Whether or not he is experiencing a "paroxysm of agonized sincerity"[47] (a phrase I still like for the Pardoner), he certainly has lost his firmness of purpose, inadvertently confessing to deeper regions than can be assigned to an iconographic figure. Chaucer is regarding his created pilgrim with acuity. The Pardoner, in turn, is regarding his own moving exemplum with acuity. His gesture associates him with Christian belief and then immediately with its repudiation—his own lack of faith mirrors the institution's lack of good faith practice. He goes so far that he threatens the fellowship of the pilgrimage by angering one of its "authorities" (the Host) and requiring the mediation of the other (the Knight).

The first part of the sermon inveighs against the sins the rioters in his tale will practice and, therefore, against his own profligate behavior on the pilgrimage. It also introduces the setting in which the action of the *exemplum* will originate, which directs attention to those sins, giving the impression that this will be a sermon against loose living, in which the major irony will be that this preacher also lives loosely. The exemplum serves that scheme, but far exceeds it. It is not about practices but about the orientation of the soul, the relation of the literal to the spiritual. The boys cannot properly regard their enemy Deeth, and the Pardoner deliberately communicates their literal-minded rashness. But what lies behind it is an institutional sin—the Pardoner asks his dupes to attend to the literal bulls, seals, and patents for their salvation, but so does the church he indicts when he confesses his cynicism. The Pardoner himself may be a fake, but the institutional church does in fact offer such pardons. He seems, in his prologue, to be out to impress the pilgrims as powerful and intimidating—rapacious but able to assoil by the authority of his bulls (VI.388)—but, in the larger scheme of things, he is just an operative of a more general cynicism. He is not able to claim the callous scam he works as his own invention. But he does understand it. The tirade against the tavern vices is just the stock-in-trade scary stuff ordinary preachers might use. What turns this uncomfortable blend of confession-cum-boast and institutional critique (again like the Wife's) into a disclosure of striking inward conflict is the *exemplum*.

In telling the story of the rioters, the Pardoner's allegory of destructive greed is perfectly transparent. The Pardoner has made his best claim for his personal force in presenting what he knows to be a bad-faith appeal by him and by his institution. But the very perfection of the story, while he tells it, awakens a partial self-understanding that he represents in the figure of the Old Man. The Old Man candidly states the issues of contrition, repentance, and confession (in fact he confesses to the rioters), but he is unable to "put off the old man" (Ephesians 4.22), just as the Pardoner has confessed to the pilgrims, told them the truth about spiritual grace, and denied his own ability to lay hold of it. To know one's unsaved condition but find oneself unable to grasp grace describes both Pardoner and the Old Man in his tale; it also resembles many of those moments in early modern drama that have served as evidence of its interest in personhood: Faust's anguished "one drop would save my soul, half a drop," Edmund's "some good I mean to do before I die." It may be its resemblance to such moments that earned Pound's admiration for the "donative" aspect of art that anticipates the future.[48]

The physically and morally ugly Pardoner and his self-aggrandizing, yet confessional, tale are not gratifying ("agreeable" is Kant's term). Their claims on aesthetic attention fall within the scope of assertions by Bonaventure and Aquinas that a well-presented monster (even though nonexistent, i.e., fictional) can be beautiful. Modern thought too might recognize the coherence and intensity of his characterization, and a post-Kantian perspective would grant the way it eludes conceptual categories. The Pardoner looks like the moral antitype of the good shepherd, a conscious and confident perverter of the faith, and a social parasite, a powerful man in this world—and so he is. But he *experiences himself* as caught up in the theology he perverts, as merely an operative whose authority comes from that despised theology, as maimed and impotent to either yield to it or oppose it. The figure of the Old Man in the *exemplum* takes the imagination strangely as the partial revelation and partial masking found in current thinking about complex persons, yet does not disrupt the clarity of the allegory. His teasing figure resembles the Pardoner himself, since he knows where death lurks but cannot die, just as the Pardoner knows Christ's pardon is best but cannot accept that pardon. Imagination and understanding are brought into active play in confronting him.

The Canon's Yeoman's Prologue *and* Tale

The Canon and his Yeoman are introduced, sweating, on sweating horses, as they overtake the pilgrims; the Canon's Yeoman is therefore the only teller not occupying a place in the estates scheme laid out in the *General Prologue.* He and his master have lived and worked in hidden lanes (VIII.658), and he has labored directly for wages, "apparently the only wage laborer anywhere in Chaucer—the only person hired to make a commodity," as Britton Harwood has observed.[49] Soon the Canon leaves the group, becoming increasingly restive, "for verray sorwe and shame" because he fears the Yeoman "wolde telle his pryvetee" (701–2). The

Canon's Yeoman at this point seems an individual because he is *alone* and *free* (freed from his master's control—a masterless man). It has been repeatedly claimed that social relations like his underwrite subjectivity itself—and in this case they certainly suggest it—but the further claim that the ideology of individualism was produced by and for capitalist economics and bourgeois politics[50] misleads in two ways. It suggests that there is a relatively clear break (rather than an uneven development) with traditional (feudal) economic relations in the early modern period, and it fails to distinguish between an ideological valuation of individualism and the existence of individuals who can then be represented in art. The Yeoman is a particularly good example of Chaucer's thinking his way into the future of selfhood, but not his only one.

The Yeoman's brilliant description of the major terms and procedures of alchemy (the canon's "privitee"), including a climactic explosion in the lab, shows him to have been alone (but not free) as a worker. It also presents an immanent critique of his craft in terms of its human costs and uncertain results. Everything is lost in the violence of the explosion in the lab; the devil himself seems to be there. The men begin to blame each other for the failure of the experiment: "Somme seyde it was long on the fir makyng; / Somme seyde nay, it was on the blowyng—/ Thanne was I fered, for that was myn office" (VIII.922–24). Each worker has a specific task and bears particular blame for the failure. This scene seems now a forecast of factory workers' relations, but it is presented as *experienced* by the Yeoman and presumably understood by the pilgrims in its presentation of competition, blaming, and private angst.

No wonder that *privetee* occurs in this tale more often than in any other, except the Parson's much longer examination of private conscience. Most instances mark the secrecy that characterizes alchemical work, and it is because he cannot stop the Yeoman from divulging "his pryvetee" that the Canon rides away from the pilgrims' community at the end of the *Introduction* (VIII.701). When he begins to tell his tale, the Yeoman stands in a new relationship to the economy: he is free *from* feudal ties (to the Canon, formerly his "lord" and "soverayne" 590) and free *of* everything he needs in order to pursue his craft.[51] His situation would be tenuous enough in fully capitalist modernity, since the worker *must always sell* and the owner *need not always buy* his labor-power, but in a feudal economy, or one that thinks it is feudal, it is thrillingly dangerous. He may want to link up with the pilgrimage (he rode hard to join the pilgrims and he ended his tale with a religious piety), but at the moment of his telling, he is alone in the manner of a modern subject. It is hard to make him into either the representative of a place in the estates or a moral icon. His personhood is represented as a conscious conflict that forces him to relinquish a "mystery" in which he is proficient[52] and a livelihood that, although it left him in debt, gave him a place in the world. The critique he produces is one he cannot live with ethically, so he joins the pilgrimage, becoming—potentially—spiritually anchored, but socially adrift. Although the Pardoner and Wife confess their own and their institutions' failings, they do not sever themselves from their careers, as the Yeoman does. Subjectivity appears in this case as overt action from which inner conflict may be justifiably construed, but Chaucer also provides some testimony to internal states through what his characters dream.

Dreams

Dreams imply a dreamer, and a dreamer is a likely candidate for an individualized subject. But only a candidate. As A. C. Spearing writes, all medieval dreams presuppose an "interiorated subject," but a "dream's content is not necessarily individualized, for it may claim to offer a vision of absolute truth rather than a glimpse of what is particular to one dreamer's mind and body or...a turning point in his understanding of his waking situation."[53] Chaucer created dreams in the *Canterbury Tales* with a wide range of suggestiveness about individuality and a variety of narrative uses. Spearing claims in an earlier analysis that "Chaucer, more than any other dream-poet known to me, was interested in dreams as they really are...not only in superficial details, but in matters of method and structure."[54] Strongly as I find myself agreeing that Chaucer represents dreams "as they really are," I worry about what this can mean. One can remember (hazily) one's own dreams, hear about the dreams of a few confidants, and take in some dream lore (ancient, Freudian, and post-Freudian). But it would be rash to claim to know the reality of dreams, any more than to know other people's "salty squirts" (the physical basis of consciousness, according to Hans Moravec—see pp. 72–73). But one *can* respond to them as representations and so could Chaucer's earliest readers.[55]

Arcite's dream answers to a form common in epic: the irony of prophesy misread—his return to Athens meant his immediate woe was to be *ended*, as Mercury had told him it would be (I.1391–93), but not turned to joy as he had expected. This handling tends to associate Arcite with other misled protagonists of antiquity rather than distinguish him from them. Here Chaucer is surely playing with the familiar medieval convention of the dream vision,[56] playing because the dream initially suggests the authority of a message from the gods, but ultimately undermines it.

Similarly, though in a more straightforwardly moralizing vein, Croesus in the *Monk's Tale* read his prophetic dream by pridefully thinking that it signified the special care of the gods, while in fact its revealed truth referred to Jupiter as storms and Phoebus as sun while the king's body hung on the gallows (VII.2727–65). The vividness of the manifest content of Chantecleer's dream offered to Pertelote for interpretation initiates Chantecleer's extended "proof" of the prophetic nature of dreams in that tale. The *Summoner's Tale* friar, though, is being characterized in his pretended dream of the ascension to heaven of Thomas's child, told to soften the couple in order to bilk them for money (III.1854–75). This friar demonstrates how far he will go, asserting that two others had had the same dream (it must therefore be prophetic), and building a defense of fraternal holiness on his lie. This performance demonstrates his opportunism and stamina in manipulating the truth and provides emphasis rather than complication for his greed.

Alisoun's Tactical Dream

With Alisoun of Bath, things are far more intricate. One might say that the Wife tells two stories about her wishes: her tale and the dream about Jankyn she reports in her *Prologue*. In both she "confesses" sincerely to what she acknowledges about herself and what she does not. Since this dream was, she tells us, constructed, we can consider its rhetorical purposes. In order to account for the rhetoric of the dream, one has to posit the personhood of the Wife, regard her as a conscious agent with plans and simultaneously a discloser of her inner life. She tells the other pilgrims what she would not have told Jankyn: that she had designs on him, that her mother (or mentor) had taught her how to make a man think about her erotically, that she actually had not dreamed the dream, but had made it up ("and al was fals; I dremed of it right naught" [III.582]). As she presents it to Jankyn it seems a sexual rather than a violent sequence, but, nonetheless, features him as the powerful spiller of blood in Alisoun's bed (either hymeneal blood or semen),[57] thereby suggesting a fantasy which could enhance his calculation that marrying a rich widow might not be a bad idea. (Note that even on this storytelling level, I have to posit an inner life for Jankyn in order to make Alisoun's declared motive work.) When the Wife supplies the blood-as-gold transformation, therefore, Jankyn can seize on the allegorical system he (as a clerk) has always ready, hiding his materialistic motives from himself.

Freud writes, "Most of the artificial dreams constructed by imaginative writers are designed for a symbolic interpretation of this sort: they reproduce the writer's thoughts under a disguise which is regarded as harmonizing with the recognized characteristics of dreams."[58] Although I would not want to argue that Alisoun actually did dream this dream herself, as Leicester does,[59] I do want to insist on how fully she must be seen as understanding unconscious processes in designing the dream, and how large a role her own desires play in it. She becomes so emotionally involved with this pseudodream that she loses her train of thought as she rehearses it for the pilgrims ("lat me se what I shal seyn" [III.585]). Freud is clear: *a dream is a (disguised) fulfillment of a (suppressed or repressed) wish.* Considered as a sexual dream, it restates a wish about which readers already know: the wish that "he, / If I were wydwe, sholde wed me" (567–68). But the manifest content—the image of the stabbing and the bloody bed—could be seen to function as both a screen for the sex in the dream and a punishment accompanying her wish for a replacement husband.[60]

In some ways it is also a prophetic dream. It may be taken to foreshadow the fight over the book in which Jankyn almost does kill Alisoun. It also seems an acknowledgement of Alisoun's "ego theme" of entwined sex and combat (Venus and Mars, her constitutional makeup) and, therefore, prophetic in that it discloses the intricacies of her personal history. As Freud puts it at the end of *The Interpretation of Dreams*, "this future, which the dream pictures as present, has been moulded by his [the dreamer's] indestructible wish into a perfect likeness of the past." The ploy, then, can be read in medieval systems of prophesy, astrology, and truth-to-type moral wandering, but equally well in modern psychoanalytic terms. I want now to return to Hayden White's strong analogy between Freud's description of the role of the dreamwork and the trope of allegory, especially in the way both use personal and cultural images to screen as well as present thoughts. Spearing comes to the same analogy through Macrobius, whose terms imply "dreams are 'natural' equivalents to the artifice of allegory.... Unlike Freud, Macrobius does not suggest any reason why dreams should conceal their true meaning and need interpretation."[61] In other words, the connection between dreams and storytelling with an allegorical bent was understood long before Chaucer or Freud.

The Wife's ingenuity and willfulness are indicated by the fact that she both creates the dream and interprets it, stressing again the role of exegete she assigned herself earlier in her prologue. But none of this explains why she told the pilgrims about this episode. How are her present rhetorical purposes being served? In an intricate weaving together of inadvertent confession and self-presentation, Alisoun brags about her cleverness (as she had when speaking of her old husbands) while, at the same time showing her mendacity and opportunism to a group to whom she had earlier offered readings of the sacred text. Not every contradictory gesture in fiction is readable as psychological complexity, but this one is. She wants to be *regarded*, to be taken seriously, and this seems to her to require a "true" confession, a confession that expresses both the beauties and triumphs of her life and the compromised means by which her victories were won.

Criseyde's Dream of the Eagle

A different aspect of Freudian dream theory is relevant to Criseyde's dream in Book II. After her interview with Pandarus, Criseyde dreamed:

> How that an egle, fethered whit as bon,
> Under hire brest his longe clawes sette,
> And out hire herte he rente, and that anon,
> And dide his herte into hire brest to gon—
> Of which she nought agroos, ne nothyng smerte
> And forth he fleigh, with herte left for herte.
> (II.926–31)

The most striking thing about this dream is that Criseyde, in waking life "the ferfulleste wight / That myght be" (II. 450–51) felt neither fear of the long claws nor pain in the exchange of hearts. Freud's comment would seem to apply: in dreams, "the ideational content is not accompanied by the affective consequences that we should regard as inevitable in waking thought.... In a dream I may be in a horrible, dangerous and disgusting situation without feeling any fear or repulsion." In some dreams the ideational content of the dream controls the affect, while the image in the manifest content is passed over.[62] The chain of associations in dreams, as I have claimed earlier, is always both personal and cultural. What this might mean in Criseyde's case is that the raptor she would have feared in "real-life" is in the ideation of the dream associated with majesty, power, and probably either Cupid or Troilus himself. These are, of course, cultural associations and so is the "allegory" they produce as narrative (the "exchange of hearts" common in love poetry and romance). The fact that the ideational level is experienced as pleasant rather than threatening must mean, then, that Criseyde has already begun to regard Troilus with favor, to embody his dream-image as powerful dignity, and submit to it without fear or pain. Most readers of the poem do interpret the dream as Criseyde's entry into love. My point is that the conventions used to mark that emotional event may also be taken to signal the text's awareness of the specificities of inner life, as Freudian systems would much later come to explain them.

Varieties of Luminous Detail

Equally interesting are those pilgrims who disclose their inner lives without seeming to intend to, among them the Knight, the Prioress, Franklin, and Clerk. In each of these cases, I want to stress a particular moment in and through which personhood appears suddenly and inflects the whole tale with its *claritas*, illuminating an additional element of particularity to the characterization of the pilgrim-tellers through their involvement with fictional personages of their making.

Theseus Revealed

The Knight represents himself in the tale through Theseus, who is wise almost to imperturbability. Chaucer's accounts of the Knight and Theseus do not seem to suggest lurking complexities of personality. But, near the end of *pars secunda*—when he finds his escaped political prisoners fighting in the woods—Theseus has a private conversation with himself in the middle of a public, in fact a judicial, occasion. Palamon has confessed that both men deserve death for their escape and unauthorized duel, and Theseus takes his words as a confession that he will submit to execution without a trial involving torture (I.1744–47). The women weep until "aslaked was his mood" and the poem presents a series of the arguments that had (presumably) changed Theseus's mind (1748–71). But, then, Theseus addresses *himself* directly in an internal monologue: "And softe unto hymself he seyde" (1773). The contents of this inner speech do not continue his thoughts about the naturalness of escaping from prison if one can or of the derring-do produced by love, but look inward at the kind of ruler Theseus wants to believe himself to be. He scorns the undiscriminating cruelty that would punish the contrite as harshly as the defiant; such a one would be less than human ("a leon, bothe in word and deed" 1775), in short, a tyrant. But when he resumes his public guise by speaking "on highte" (aloud), he does not announce those thoughts, but returns to "the things we do for love."

In this judgment scene, two cases are argued: aloud, how the escaped prisoner should be dealt with and internally, how a civilized (*gentil*) ruler should behave toward those who fall under his power. I propose the internal monologue as a luminous detail that both confers intellectual and emotional depth on the Knight and his character Theseus and organizes other features of the *Knight's Tale* into a more coherent shape. Although it is true that Theseus addresses himself rather formally, his manner seems far more internalized than Chrétien's Lancelot (who mentally attends to a debate between Reason and Love), and its formality suits the communal genres of epic and chronicle while insisting on the importance of inner life. It is not historically irresponsible to read in it both Theseus's and the Knight's "secret" worries about the way the sanctioned term "chivalry" masks the involvement of battle with cruelty and tyranny. Such a reading would not fall outside a medieval horizon of understanding: Henry of Lancaster's penitential *Livre de Seintz Medicines* (1354) shows an awareness of the temptations to tyrannical behavior (pride and wrath, since his scheme is the seven deadly sins) experienced by those in military command.[63]

Although we usually assume that revealing someone's secrets will embarrass them, the Knight's description in the *General Prologue* is not sullied by the nuanced doubts revealed by the implications of Theseus's monologue. It rather contributes another layer of specification to the character of both Theseus and the Knight himself, illuminating and specifying the phrasing "And though that he were worthy, he was wys" (I.68) in its implication that military worth would not normally imply complex thinking. *His* "worthiness" includes wisdom, and what that wisdom includes is his "secret" doubts about his estate, the estate that fights and rules.

In his distanced, dignified, slowly unfolding narrative, the Knight seems to replicate and enhance the secular historical record of the ancient world—although highly Christianized, it seems designed to avoid competing with the clerics on the pilgrimage. But as a man of "real" wars, the Knight cannot let the description of Theseus's "pleyn bataille" against Creon pass without a look at the grisly "taas of bodyes" in which the cousins were found half dead. The decoration of Mars' temple makes the same point: war does not leave the soldier with images of straightforward male competitiveness alone; there is also the "symlere with the knyf under the cloke...the sow freten the child right in the cradel" (I.1999 and 2019) together with all manner of bizarre accidents. (Our composed Knight sounds here a little like Berthold Brecht in *Mother Courage*.) The internal monologue in which Theseus considers and rejects tyranny, formalized as it is, illuminates why these melodramatic details surface in the Knight's imagination cloaked as artist's depictions of Mars. That preoccupation, in turn, adds weight to the interpretation of the genre of the tale as an epic of establishing a civilized polis.

Prioress

The Prioress is not a small woman—"she was nat undergrowe" (I.156)—but she tries to deflect attention from any unseemly self-disclosure by presenting a prologue and tale closely associated with the Virgin Mary (in the Prologue Psalm 8, an office of the Virgin, and in the tale, a miracle of the Virgin) and with the role of nuns in teaching the young. Her constant attention to what is little, scantily informed, and not normally held responsible, suggests a selfhood not quite comfortable with the cloister and the relationship with children it mandates. Her "conflict" is her simultaneous attraction to the small, suggesting her desire to nurture children and her desire to *be* small, nonaccountable—to disappear from the moral demands of adult life. Her mindset conflates acting *on behalf of* a child with acting *like* a child. The luminous detail that organizes these small fissures in her self-protective strategy is the tale's three-stanza account of the grieving mother, distracted, but emboldened by fear to importune the Jews (VII.586–604). This seems to me an instance of a brief scene suddenly deepening the emotional stakes, "the precise instant when a thing outward and objective transforms itself, or darts into a thing inward and subjective," as Ezra Pound wrote concerning his poem "In A Station of the Metro."[64] In this passage the Prioress's imagination is represented as kindled, in contrast with the surrounding more or less predictable stanzas, bespeaking her investment in the mother-child bond. Her intense empathy with the mother—her all-night vigil, her paleness as the light of the next day dawns, her "bisy thought," her hatred of the Jews overcome by her need to inquire among them, her sudden "inwith" intuition that took her near her murdered child—is rendered with an intensity missing in the traditional phrasing of the rest of the tale. The passage reveals the Prioress's inner life as deeply invested in motherhood, which her vocation has permanently denied her, and organizes hints of her fascination with smallness.

Her empathy with the mother also stands in marked contrast to her gloating equanimity at the torture and execution of an unspecified number of Jews who merely "wiste of" the murder of the boy. Here she eschews the chance to describe a process of trial and judgment, evading the adult responsibility to end her tale with a satisfying sense of justice. The Knight's Theseus paused to temper his anger when he found offenders in his power, but the Prioress's imagination at a similar moment is not touched with the need for reflection. She is like her clergeon, aware only of polarized meanings—honor to Mary, death to the Jews. After a beginning in which she dons a cloak of invisibility, at the end, she becomes imposing, even intimidating, "nat undergrowe."

Dorigen's Promises

In the previous chapter, I made a case for the individualization of both Dorigen and Arveragus in the *Franklin's Tale*, and here I want to return to Dorigen and her promises. It is the first promise, the one she makes to Arveragus rather than her later promise to Aurelius that seems to me the really luminous detail. The Franklin presents the contract the couple arrives at as the tale opens as entirely private (V.738–60): she "pryvely" agreed to marry him and submit to his lordship, he "of his free wyl" offers to obey her as his lady. To keep this bargain, both of them will have to live as "split subjects," and, as we might begin to suspect, the plot will test their ingenuity and stamina in doing so. The Franklin's wise excursus on patience (761–90) provides good council for meeting the requirements of daily domestic life, but the next few lines stress again the contradictory nature of the relationship: "servant in love, and lord in mariage...his lady and his love" (793, 796). The narrator's return to this formulation signals it as a problem (suggesting that it is an unresolved issue for the Franklin), although his characters experience it (at this time) as a solution.

A rash promise is often the precipitating factor in the plots of fictions of this lineage: Mark's promise to Gandin in the various versions of the Tristan story is typical. What is striking about this tale is that the rash promise is not made publicly or by a king. Both of Dorigen's promises are privately sworn, and Arveragus, at great cost, acknowledges that a woman's promise is as much a part of the social contract as a man's. Richard Firth Green argues that Chaucer managed the effects of this tale to acknowledge that any code of honor in promise keeping that excludes women and erotic life would amount to a "denial of women's essential humanity."[65] Dorigen's "trouthe," unlike the king's public promise, is to an inner integrity alone. Her sense of herself is, therefore, somewhat stranded, cut off from the daily counsels that bind fellow citizens in a common culture, which may account for the extravagance of her despair and contemplation of suicide. Dorigen's questioning of God's "purveiaunce" (V.865–94) has been adduced as evidence of her un-Christian confusion, but I take her stance as the painful doubting of an intelligent, serious woman with some pretty good theology at her beck, not to mention eloquence about her existential angst, which the "argumentz" of clerks do not dissipate. Her attempt to use the past looks very much like that of Heloise featuring herself as Cornelia in Lucan's *Pharsalia* (for further discussion of which, see p. 151 below). Like Bunyan and Kierkegaard, she is shown reasoning with God. This is where memory and authority come in—the long recital of suicides to prevent sexual taint may have seemed a "natural" way to explore her isolated situation to medieval people whose own memories were stocked with such stories. My argument is not that Dorigen's situation is a perfect match for the stories she cites (Heloise's is not either), but that she is examining precedents for ways to understand her predicament. Although it seems to violate the principles of proportion and thrift (presenting more cases than necessary to satisfy epistemic hunger), one could see Dorigen's long soliloquy as an overdetermined feature of her inner conflict and responsibility to past models of behavior, a veritable parsimony for which no quicker narrative solution would serve. Throughout her story, Dorigen is surrounded with words, as Griselda is not. The Franklin takes pains to create a specific discursive mode for Dorigen, revealing his regard for a woman's personhood.

Griselda's Telling Gesture

Griselda's is a tale that depends on the nearly successful withholding of inner life. The Clerk is just the man to tell the tale, since he also keeps his own counsel—he has seemed to the Host "stille as a mayde newe spoused" (IV.2–3). He depicts a woman behaving with remarkable restraint, even while he marvels at it and forebears to announce the allegorical point until the whole tale has been related. It is not only her lack of speech that occludes Griselda's inner life, but her serene, even cheerful, countenance throughout her sufferings, several times insisted on by the Clerk as her own will. J. A. Burrow stresses her unchanging demeanor and asks, "What is the reader to make of such insistence?"[66] Is she dissembling or is she to be taken as having no undisclosed life at all? The question is ultimately answered, in my view, by the telling gesture of her swoon on finding her children alive during the supposed wedding banquet.[67] Susan Crane argues for the dual role of gestures of self-performance as both assertion and enigma; Chaucer's version of the Griselda story "assumes that she is capable of hidden thoughts and secret desires, but locates her virtue as a wife in her perfect visibility."[68] Crane sees Griselda's "self-objectification" as alluding to both the Christian allegory and current marriage practices that value "the visible, palpable creation of identity in rhetorical and material performance." Griselda (and real-world women like her) negotiate their identities through overt actions that to some extent reconcile exemplarity with psychological realism.[69] In my scheme, this aspect problem is related to the duck/rabbit bifurcation of genre the tale as a whole exhibits. The sense of wonder the tale evokes is in part a result of the unsettling effect of this impasse in aspect recognition.

All along Griselda has avoided Walter's attempts to pierce her inwardness, and the tight control the Clerk has exercised over the narrative voice has not let readers see it either. He kept secret (or at least uncertain) *her* private imaginings until she expresses them out loud—"Youre woful mooder wende stedfastly / That crueel houndes or som foul vermin" had been eating the children's corpses (IV.1094–95). Her first swoon might be attributed to surprise, but the second follows this disclosure of her earlier fears, testifying to the strength of the emotion generated by the images that have apparently haunted her for years. Yet at the time of her children's abductions, Griselda's was a life so inward that it almost escaped detection through readable signs. The Clerk has here indicated that he is able to imagine the central figure of his allegory as a whole person, and that he, to some extent, let himself fall under the spell of her humanity, signaling his sympathy with her by repeatedly criticizing Walter (IV. 449–62, 616–23, 701–7, and 785–91). On the "estates" side, one might say that in portraying his cleverness and subtlety, Chaucer's account of him is merely filling out the positive stereotype of a diligent cleric and Oxford Aristotelian, but the Clerk's involvements with his characters suggest as well a man of warm egalitarian feelings who refashions Petrarch's allegory toward realism and eschews its flattened effects.[70] His poetic gestures betray an uneasy teller, disturbed by the various implications his story might bear, rather than an otherworldly allegorist given to serene abstraction. The ordered complexity of the tale evades easy conceptualization, and its sudden flashes of formal coherence, both allegorical and realistic, produce its powerful aesthetic effects.

Regarding Criseyde

The narrator in *Troilus and Criseyde* lavishes concern on the gestures that signal Criseyde's inner life, as they occur in the story. His "regard" for her, to return to Witmore's formulation, "confers value...signals interest, awareness, deference and even obligation."[71] Criseyde's is a striking figure in any reading, but descriptions of her throughout the poem contrast sharply with traditional modes of positing female comeliness, even in Chaucer's work, where descriptions of Custance, Griselda, Emelye, Alison in the *Miller's Tale*, May, and even Pertelote get more wholehearted blazons. The poem maintains a kind of intimacy about Criseyde's beauty; she has no other suitors during Troilus's courtship, nor does she seem to excite lascivious thoughts wherever she goes, as some medieval romance heroines (including Chaucer's Custance) predictably do. Her beauty seems manifested particularly for Troilus, the narrator, and the reader. The narrator presents her as a specific woman, represented minutely and "realistically," and whose particular qualities of person and character have worked a subtler magic than heroines identified starkly as the most beautiful woman living.

The intimacy of Criseyde's portrait is fullest in Book II. I will argue in chapter 4 that such nuance is itself a contribution to the design of the poem, one which cannot without loss be passed over in order to arrive at the Boethian struggle of rectitude with the seductions of Fortune.

Contemporary painting, which Chaucer might have seen in Italy, had begun to portray specific, observable details in minute mimesis of secular scenes, for example, the city of Siena in Ambrogio's "Effects of Good Government" (1340).[72] This emergent style heralds the depiction of persons in terms of small gestures, those not immediately readable in terms of the traditional symbolic meanings of a scene, during the next century. Especially striking is the direction of a glance, as in Leonardo da Vinci's "Virgin of the Rocks." The viewer's attention follows the way Mary looks at John who in turn glances at the baby Jesus. This technique contrasts with the more obvious gestures and stances of the Holy Family like the baby extending two fingers in benediction (although he does so here too), or the Virgin gazing at the heavens. The glances, and all the tenderness or wonder that can (must?) be seen in them, retell a familiar story with an added element of a human investment that includes suppositions about the figures in the painting and the viewer's connection with them.[73]

Burrow has discussed this late medieval interest in gesture and glance in terms of textual representation, and his readings of the ways in which both deliberate "speaking looks" and involuntary facial and gestural reactions "offer meanings to be read by an observer" (either a character within the fiction and a reader outside it). His interpretations of the small gestures made by Pandarus and Troilus are firmly tied to a recognition of the cultural patterns that reflect caste relations and proprieties, and I find them very convincing. His description of the nuances involved in Troilus's first reaction to seeing Criseyde, with all the subtle clues to her "womanly noblesse" he is able to find in her deportment suggests the care with which Chaucer has mobilized nonverbal clues, successfully refuting Robertson's imputation of mere lust to Troilus's reaction upon seeing Criseyde for the first time.[74]

Book II involves a similarly nuanced account of Criseyde's actions but, I think, a somewhat more elusive sense of their "meanings." The narrator invests external gestures, even slight ones, with remarkable suggestive power, but not the monologic allusiveness dictated by medieval iconography (Heracles in a lion skin, Jerome in the wilderness with a book) or even the socially meaningful signs of deference and aloofness interpreted by Burrow. The sudden and decisive looks and gestures accompanying Troilus's first look at Criseyde contrast sharply both with her reactions and with the way her gestures are presented in the long middle scene of Book II. There the reader must observe Criseyde's reactions in what we now call "real time," minute by minute rather than in summary. The delicacy and variety of these gestures resembles little in previous medieval narrative strategy, but much in recent novel and film. (This technique seems a direct challenge to the "iconic" school of thought as a way of reading, but it does not seem to me to nullify arguments for Criseyde as Fortune or Nature when seen from the eighth sphere.) To see Book II in this way for Chaucer's generation, we must posit a "learning subject," an audience being taught by hearing or reading this text to attend to subtle gestures unfixed by iconography or culture as clues to the emotional contours of the story. This is exactly what Robertson asserts is impossible for medieval readers, accustomed to "rigorously nonpsychological" (as opposed to "romantic or modern") literary art, and what Alan Singer posits as characteristic of art of all kinds.[75] For others who accept the overall Boethian or Augustinian outcome of the poem, these gestures are impressive and readable, but ultimately overwhelmed by typology.[76]

What is remarkable about Book II is its sheer density of intimate gestures, most of them Criseyde's. In 142, she casts down her eyes; in 215, the others note that she and Pandarus need privacy; in 252, she looks down again, and Pandarus coughs; in 275, she is aware that her uncle is studying her face (as he had in 265, "inwardly"); in 302–3, Pandarus notes that she trembles and blushes; in 408, she weeps; in 428, she sighs; in 448, she reaches out for the "lappe" in his garment; in 652, she blushes at her own thought: in 689, she hangs her head; in 1197, she both blushes and hums; and in 1470, she blushes again. Pandarus (253, 265, 408, 505) and Troilus (645, 1086, 1256) are also described in terms of these small gestures in Book II and contribute to my argument about its "realism" and intimacy, but it is Criseyde's subjectivity that is in focus most consistently in this long middle scene. Daniel Dennett would classify these signs as "expressing mental states," which may be intentional or not, as opposed to "reporting" them, in her internal monologues, for example, which is always intentional.[77] Chaucer presents both expressions and reports. The unsettled nature of her thoughts and feelings is reported by the narrator in a sustained metaphor of sun, clouds, and wind (763–70) that seems to account for the heightened and shifting picture we are seeing, and the terms of the metaphor are repeated in an interior monologue given in Criseyde's voice (778–84).[78]

My first point is that these minute gestures and the dream are presented to evoke Criseyde's inner state without specifying an iconographic or generally understood meaning for each or for all considered together. Their function seems instead to be mimetic: this is what it may be like to be faced with the secret Pandarus has come to tell Criseyde. Emotion (curiosity, fear, doubt, hope "now hoot, now cold") and cognition (some commonplace thoughts, some particular to her) are both represented. I find it hard to withhold the term "psychological" from a sequence like this, but by that term I do not mean to say that Criseyde's interior life can be captured by a psychological concept. Instead, what these gestures tells us is what the narrator can see and we must interpret, just as we must interpret Mr. Darcy's discomfiture in Elizabeth Bennett's presence or the behavior of people we watch in "real-life." C. David Benson implies that the narrator is holding out on us: "Like a good semiologist, the narrator examines the signs provided by other accounts, but he admits that he has no authoritative access to her deepest feelings."[79] I think that is exactly the game, especially in Book II—we are being asked to imagine this particular woman in this particular situation; neither we nor the narrator can know more than the "signs" by which inner states are suggested.

We will not all read those signs in the same way. When Hero blushes at being accused in *Much Ado about Nothing*, Claudio interprets her blush by acknowledging what onlookers are thinking, "Comes not that blood, as modest evidence, / To witness simple virtue?" but concludes "Her blush is guiltiness, not modesty" (IV.i.36–37, 41). The gesture itself can mean either. I have thought that Criseyde's downcast eyes, when Pandarus offers to tell the secret, indicated a kind of anxious modesty, and his cough is meant to make her look up (II.252–53), but Sheila Delany finds it "conscious self-presentation" which overplays her feminine role.[80] The point is that such gestures are readable, but not through a fixed code. They provide a particularly strong case for reflection by the reader as an ingredient of aesthetic pleasure, which is acknowledged in Christian thought as early as Augustine's account of his delight in the difficult similitudes of Scripture in *On Christian Doctrine*.

Secondly, I want to stress the deployment of time Chaucer has suggested for this book. The audience finds out about Pandarus's visit in so much detail that the scene takes as much time to read as for the events to occur, seeing every change in facial expression, hearing every cough. They are being asked to think and feel with Criseyde. This slow, detailed unfolding looks forward to the pictorial art of the coming century and the verbal art often claimed to appear first in *Hamlet* or *Pamela*. It does not resemble the summary assertion—"his strength was renewed because of her love"—or the often-lovely figures—Perceval staring at the red blood on the white snow—of the romances.[81]

A new kind of attention must be paid to it. Whether or not the epilogue eventually discloses the "real meaning" of *Troilus and Criseyde* at this early point in the poem, audiences must struggle to impose a pattern on familiar, but uncoded, signs which seem continuous with ordinary lives (I am assuming that medieval people did glance and blush and cough). After Criseyde has read Troilus's letter, she responds to Pandarus's questions about it by turning red and humming. I have never read about any other medieval hums or any commentary on what humming means. One might think that Criseyde was feeling pleased with the letter and flattered by it, or that she hummed to avoid answering immediately, or that she was already forming a devious plan to use Troilus's declared homage for selfish ends. Chaucer is teaching his readers new tricks, which demand altered structures of feeling, in the presence of texts and ultimately of real-world situations. For readers who learn those tricks, his treatment of Criseyde's inner life produces a more capacious regard for persons, women in particular.

It seems to me that Chaucer found persons beautiful—not always agreeable, but beautiful—that in imagining and understanding his images of their inner lives and external actions he brought his own mental powers into play and challenged those of his audiences to think with him. The Chaucerian representation of Criseyde, for example, eagerly "devised" and yet found enigmatic by the narrator ("men seyn—I not—that she yaf hym hire herte"), stands at the individualizing pole among the medieval modes of characterization, along with the Wife of Bath, the Pardoner, and the Knight. Her image also figures in Chaucer's struggle with the problem of female allure and its value. This chapter has inquired into aesthetic features of her psychological realism; the next will conclude with a consideration of her beauty (both her imputed beauty as a female character and the formal beauty of Chaucer's presentation of her) and the beauty of the poem in which she plays so central a role.

CHAPTER 5

THE BEAUTY OF WOMEN

Look not upon a woman's beauty, and desire not a woman for beauty.

Ecclesiasticus 25:28

to be frank, a beautiful woman, that's what beauty is!

Plato, *Greater Hippias*

There Is No Maid
Good, bad, old, young, religious, secular—
Not even a nun, chaste in both body and soul—
Who'll not delight to hear her beauty praised.

Jean de Meun, *Romance of the Rose*

Nowhere in medieval thought are the contradictions of aesthetic attitudes more obvious than in dealing with beauty in women. Biblical and classical traditions flow together to create a fund of long-standing common wisdom, both very loud and perfectly schizophrenic. On the one hand, female beauty is always already complicit in the descent of man into sinful lust. The pit into which the man falls to his damnation is opened by the mere sight of a woman's beauties, whether or not the woman in question is aware of his gaze. In a remarkable application of Exodus 21, the writer to anchoresses concludes that the penalty must be paid by the one who uncovers the pit, not he who falls into it.[1] On the other hand, the visually apprehended beauty of the Bride of the Canticles, the Virgin Mary, Beatrice, the Pearl, and many other prominent female presences is a sign of their merit. Medieval romances typically move, as Joan Ferrante says, toward the union of prowess with beauty,[2] and this formulation would seem to be corroborated by tales of military contests offering the winner the hand of a beautiful princess and by somewhat soberer stories from historical sources. This contour figures the new society as one in which the weak are protected and the strong are civilized by the radiance emanating from the beautiful.

In Prudentius's *Psychomachia*, both the Virtues and the Vices are personified in female form, but their warfare is waged for the "mansoul," the male human subject. Saint Jerome avers that any woman who "wishes to serve Christ more than the world...will cease to be a woman, and will be called man."[3] The generalization that the Middle Ages, like Alanus in Joan Ferrante's remark, "rejected women morally but accepted them philosophically, as abstractions"[4] seems only a partial truth (although the Bride and the Pearl may be regarded as ideas), but that doesn't solve the problem of how to read the tangled antifeminism and woman-worship presented in many fictional female figures. Chaucer's practice, in this as in other matters, plays various complex language games calling on components from both sides of the schism. Attention to the aesthetic effects of this complexity, that is, allowing imagination and understanding to be pleasurefully "quickened" (*CJ*, p. 60), undermines the single-minded project of ideology critique to reduce the *Canterbury Tales* or *Troilus and Criseyde* to concepts about women.

The beauty of women and the study of art—both as inspiration for good and seduction to perdition—are connected across a long history. Beauty here has two quite different senses: women presented as beautiful and women beautifully presented. Aesthetic effects in art are produced by good construction (as Bonaventure and Aquinas argued), not by choosing beautiful objects to depict, and the idea that beautiful images may be troubling rather than decorative is a well-nigh consensus view in contemporary aesthetics as well. In this chapter, however, the concept of "the beauty of women" tends to entwine the two senses, especially in moral terms. For both medieval and contemporary thought, the subject is further complicated by the way debates about the value of feminine beauty are meshed with the feminization of the philosophical domain called aesthetics.

Beauty seems too "good-hearted" (in Elaine Scarry's term) for the tough-minded positivism of the current human sciences, as I argued earlier. Even in circles that still discuss aesthetic effects, the sublime, especially the transgressive or scandalous, has more cache than life-enhancing beauty, although Kant's treatise puts them on an equal footing. A neat analogy can be detected between medieval anxiety over women and contemporary critical theory's anxiety over "the aesthetic" (when it is not sublime): it is sometimes rejected *in toto* because of its nature (like the medieval woman) and sometimes blamed in particular cases for presenting some human travesty appealingly "astheticized." Alexander Baumgarten, usually identified as the earliest writer to use the term aesthetics, posited it as a "feminine analogue of reason," as Terry Eagleton points out.[5] In her rejoinder to Eagleton's attack on "the aesthetic" as a mere tool of hegemony, Isobel Armstrong shows him similarly referring to aesthetics as feminine. In Eagleton's view, she writes, "because ideology requires a scene of seduction in which the fierceness of power and the brutality of capital can be disguised, hegemony brings on the dancing girls. The aesthetic is a woman. That is the second thing wrong with it."[6]

Since the images in art are hypothetical (Sidney, Kant) and therefore self-referential rather than deliberative, artistically derived knowledge is not amenable to ordinary reality testing. Hence aesthetics has become the counterterm to empirical science, with its long-standing male-inflected tradition in Western thought. Mary Wollstonecraft (responding to Edmund Burke specifically, but to a broad-based cultural discourse at the same time) argues that in "aestheticizing women's bodies," directing their activity to "novels, music, poetry, and gallantry," and denying them equality in the economic sector, society has used their male-defined beauty and discrimination of the beautiful as a trap. Women must appear beautiful to marry well and must marry well to indulge their elevated aesthetic tastes.[7] The work that aesthetics performs in gender ideology is thus to overemphasize (fetishize) female attributes as beautiful, giving some women a certain kind of power in the big world (the power to "marry up"), but separating aesthetics from both ordered knowledge and economic productivity. All these arguments link aesthetics with a vaguely erotic form of desire. Perhaps medieval positions that warned against the snares of beauty are not so far from Eagleton's warning that aesthetic responses merely drive "social power more deeply into the very bodies of those it subjugates."[8]

The aesthetic has also been seen, at least since Schiller, as the locus of freedom from hegemonic pressures, and it still is (see chapter 1). Raymond Williams posits effects that cannot be reduced to ideology as "specific alterations of physical rhythms and the like...more varied and more intricate than any general naming can indicate"; although he declines to give the name of beauty to this power to move us, most people would.[9] What is important about Williams's position here is that such effects, whether one calls them "beauty" or not, cannot be ignored, assimilated to the instrumentalities of ideology, or denied their potential for emergent modes of thinking. Herbert Marcuse notes the recurrence of the "idea of Beauty...in progressive movements, as an aspect of the reconstruction of nature and society,[10] just as, according to Joan Ferrante, the beautiful lady of the medieval romances 'intrudes upon' the lover's life, awakens him, and separates him from an aimless immersion in the world."[11] It is my hypothesis in this chapter that textual beauties may also have the power to awaken sensibilities and focus intellectual acuity.

The slightly metaphoric term "awakens" suggests that something of value (perhaps knowledge of the good) may be gained in our attraction to beauty, weighing against its sinister seductiveness.[12] Bonaventure's *Mind's Road to God* passes through the world of sense apprehending, delighting, and judging the "traces [*vestigia*] in which we can see the reflection of our God."[13] In Bonaventura's account especially, beauty is said to instruct us to love the world. But too much insistence on the instructive role of literary beauty runs into a problem described by Alan Singer: "what preserves the authority of art," its self-referentiality, its deferral of assertion, its perfect unity "atrophies its connection to life."[14] The everyday activity of intellect is to affirm and deny things, but Sidney saves the poet from the charge of lying by saying he "nothing affirmeth." That position cannot help but weaken Marcuse's claim of "radical potential."[15] I want to stipulate that formal textual beauties sometimes do cooperate with a prevailing hegemony (and in such cases are like the female principle of following Fortune in the *Knight's Tale* by not awakening new social perspectives), but also that this cooperation is by no means inevitable.

Chaucer's major texts do not evade the association between women and beauty; nearly all their overt references to beauty allude to women (in the *Canterbury Tales*, thirty of forty instances; in *Troilus and Criseyde*, fifteen of fifteen instances). Nearly all the women in these fictions are described in terms of their beauty, or lack of it. This chapter will attempt to look into the complexities of Chaucer's beautiful females as they become intelligible, readable as moral and intellectual forces within the *Tales* and *Troilus and Criseyde*, and of his construction of beautiful fictions about them. To begin with, I will consider some of the most obvious and conventional cases—those in which *mulier est hominis confusio*—then the equally seductive pathos of females who suffer on account of their beauty, and, third, women whose beauty inspires civilized virtues. The chapter concludes with the most vexed case, that of Criseyde, which evokes all three types in an unstable mix. Criseyde's case in particular requires a vigorous application of the hermeneutic circle, since the various parts of the narrative invite different versions of what to see her *as*.

Seductress

In Chaucerian texts, this first category is slimmer than might be expected. The tradition associated with Prudentius shows Indulgence (*Luxuria*) throwing violets on the battlefield "as if in sport," instead of wielding arms, enchanting her adversaries the Virtues, "softening their iron-clad muscles and crushing their strength."[16] Dalida's role in the Monk's rendition of Sampson's fall would have served this scheme as Exhibit A from the *Canterbury Tales*, except that the Monk diverts the moral from a general distrust of women to a warning not to trust wives with important secrets. The unequivocal seductress in the *Monk's Tale* is Lady Fortune: "for whan that Fortune list to glose, / Thanne wayteth she her man to overthrowe / By swich a wey as he wolde leest suppose" (VII.2140–42). The Elf-Queen in *Sir Thopas* enervates her admirer, but she never actually shows up in this incomplete tale, so she may be just a figment of Thopas's fancy. (As an idea, she could still be a destructive force, of course, but the poem does not even hint at that possibility.) Pertelote gives Chantecleer bad advice (as things turn out) in telling him to take a laxative and ignore the prophetic potential of dreams, and it is her beauty that distracts him from his fear, but again the expected warning against women changes course, indicting the cock himself as victim of the clever fox's flattery. The turn in the plot that allows Chantecleer to escape is based on his having learned not to listen to flatterers, bypassing Pertolote's homelier role altogether. Certainly Emelye's beauty causes the cousins in the *Knight's Tale* much suffering, but aspiring to win her is never clearly presented as an evil. The closest hint is that women commonly "folwen alle the favor of Fortune" (I.2681), who really is, as the Monk says, a seductress. The tale is divided between romance, epic, and *consolatione* in its conformities to genre. As a romance heroine should, Emelye awakens Arcite and Palamon to new goals and feats of courage, and eventually conduces to the public good. Even in the mode of philosophical fable, their contest is eventually read as providential by Theseus (voicing Boethius).

The Miller's young wife Alison is presented as a charming image of rural nature conniving with feminine archness that does seduce all three of the men in the story, each to a separate sort of fall. The starkness of this narrative shape is softened by its being crisscrossed by several other prototypes: the jealous husband of the fabliau, who overreaches in thinking he can tame forces of nature; the overfastidious Absolon, who is too trustful of the stratagems of courtly fashion; and the clever-proud Nicholas, who outsmarts himself. Alison is certainly a danger to all these men, but her seductive power is only one feature of the comic disaster. The *Miller's Tale* provides, therefore, a much-weakened version of the "innocent man seduced" pattern.

May in the *Merchant's Tale* is in some ways a fuller example of seductive power. This tale foregrounds both the idea of female desirability and its incarnation as a particular woman. January sets out to be seduced, or one might say is already seduced by the idea he has formed of a beautiful young sex object who, as his wife, will not jeopardize his soul. He is looking for trouble, and the real-life May does not, it would seem, do more than live in town in order to attract him. The mirror metaphor (it is a metaphor—"As whoso took a mirror" [IV.1582]) is a brilliant reduction of the conceit used by Bonaventure and others of the mind as a reflection of the idea of God. First his mirror shows all sorts of fantasized beauty, then "Gan January within his thoght devyse / Of maydens whiche that dwelten hym bisyde" (1586–87). May's motives for marrying are obscured by a longish *occupatio* in which legal and clerical arrangements take place without mention of her predilections in the matter (1691–1708). At the wedding banquet, May is as meek as Esther, which leaves her intent as seductress ambiguous and prepares for the ironies to follow. Esther's meekness was itself a moral good in that it allowed her an epic, nation-saving role in the Bible, and yet it proved a seductive trap for Ahasuerus, leading to his defeat. The *Merchant's Tale* is perfectly clear that May is not trying to enchant January—he is already "ravished in a trance" (1750)—nor does she seem to be setting traps for anyone else. January's calculated resort to aphrodisiacs and his ridiculous overestimate of his sexual powers seem again to exonerate May and to dramatize her disgust with his attentions and his limits on her freedom. She does not exactly seduce Damyan either, since he only saw her in her subdued meekness at the wedding banquet. Her marital lapse, then, is readable as lust certainly, but also as desire for freedom and opposition to January's "hond on hire alway" (2091). The apostrophe that explicitly castigates infidelity is addressed to Fortune—"O sweet venym queynte!" (2061)—contains the suggestion of sexual betrayal before May has had a chance to commit it.[17] May's *beauty* (however blameworthy her behavior) is not easily intelligible as the culprit.

All these cases seem the obverse of Ferrante's maxim that allegorical women may be good while real women are not. Fortune is the allegorical female, and the trajectory of her narrative is always the same: she lies in wait to overthrow men in some unexpected way. No matter how much trouble the specific females in the *Tales* may cause men, the betrayal of male innocence is not the outline of their story. No matter how tellingly some of them can be seen as features of male psychomachia, Chaucer's females seem to be cast as moral agents, some for good, some not, with problems of their own.

Virginia's beauty disrupts the lives of all the men in the *Physician's Tale*. It begins with Apius: "So was he *caught* with beautee of this mayde.... Anon the feend into his herte ran" (VI.127 and 130). Claudius's integrity is destroyed and Virginius must (as he sees things) kill what he loves most. Harry Bailey thinks her beauty caused all this, including her death (291–319); it seemed to him "deere boughte," as if she had decided to acquire it. She did not, of course, and she was a good example of Hamlet's "chaste as ice, thou canst not escape calumny." Her story belongs in the next section.

Victim

The Host's misreading of Virginia's agency is surely marked as misreading, but he is right about the emotional impact of the tale—it is addressed to outrage against Apius and pathos toward Virginia, especially the latter. Pathos figures heavily in medieval stories about women, and medieval people apparently became deeply engrossed in them, as Harry does. The Monk is so engrossed; he finds Nero's ruthless denial of tears of pity for his mother's "dede beauty" and his cool "A fair woman was she!" (VII.2488) outrageous. Michael Stugrin writes: "what we know of medieval emotionalism and taste for pathos suggests a willingness to participate in the common experience of a pathetic spectacle (the Passion Play, for example) or tales of suffering (the innumerable saints' legends and devotional texts like the *Meditationes Vitae Christi*)."[18] Even the young Augustine delighted in weeping at theatrical productions in Carthage, though later he regretted having fallen so deeply under the spell of art.[19] What Northrop Frye calls "low mimetic tragedy" does not purge pity, but transforms it into sensation,[20] which sounds like what the Host and Augustine are both testifying to. The positive effects of pity turned to sensation can contribute to the seductiveness of medieval romance heroines, who must be saved by the true lover from predators or unwelcome suitors. In Arthurian tales, the lover's response is pity, a softening of the heart that ultimately counts as justice and a noble protection of the weak. In Chaucer's work, pity rarely becomes a motive for erotic action (although Nicholas's "protection" of Alison from both John and Absolon may be a comic distortion of that motif), but it does retain its aura of civilizing the warlike man, as when Theseus listens to the Theban women.

As far as number and measure (proportionality in the telling) are concerned, the *Physician's Tale* spends itself praising Virginia's beauty and modesty with the result that it cannot become tragedy in our sense—nothing she has done has precipitated the pitiable outcome of the tale. Chaucer frequently appeals to pity by using vivid particulars. Quintillian defends the practice, using Cicero: "*illumination* and *actuality*. . .makes us seem not so much to narrate as to exhibit the actual scene, while our emotions will be no less actively stirred than if we were present at the actual occurrence."[21] Augustine would ask, stirred toward what? "Where does it [our pity] flow?" Love for feigned sorrow cannot lead to merciful acts, but only to the spectator's emotional indulgence.[22] Frye's further point that "pathos is increased by the inarticulateness of the victim"[23] is clearly appropriate to Virginia—her father does almost all the talking and her complaint against her death goes unspoken, which means that the girl herself is not the one asking for our pity.

Howard Bloch argues that the many inconsistencies of the surface of the tale indicate that it has "renounced the pretense to historical or biographical accuracy" and is therefore best read as an allegory of the contradictions involved in the medieval concept of virginity.[24] The usual suspects—Jerome, Ambrose, Origen, Tertullian, Cyprian, Chrysostom—are turned out to produce this sequence: a virgin has not slept with a man, has not desired to sleep with a man, has not been desired by a man, has not been seen by a man, has not entered the thoughts of a man, and has not adorned herself, has transcended the corporeal—QED: the only true virgin is a dead virgin. Since clothing an idea in language is like adorning a virgin body, Chaucer has violated Virginia's purity by praising it. So, contrary to her last words, she does not in fact "dye a mayde" (VI.245). Two assumptions underlie Bloch's analysis: that the patristic tradition he evokes is univocal and binding on late medieval discourse, and that the particulars of this tale cannot be accounted for without resorting to a rarified level of abstraction. On the first point, I would object that the righteous woman, including the virgin, is *also* urged by scriptural and patristic authority to let herself be seen: Matthew reports Jesus as saying: "Let your light so shine before men that they see your good works and glorify your Father who is in heaven (5:16). The logic of this kind of regard is described thus by Elaine Scarry: beautiful things attract attention to other things in similar categories (lateral regard) and they "carry greetings from other worlds within them"—otherwise they would be too fragile "to support the gravity of our immense regard."[25] The logical contradiction Bloch cites is produced by his method of selecting and splicing his authorities, and by ignoring counterevidence from Chaucer's contemporaries, where the gaze does not always destroy purity, but often inspires moral good. Even in well-known tales of virgin martyrs, the attention women attract serves to spread the Christian message, as Ruth Evans has argued.[26] Chaucer's own Cecilia in the "Second Nun's Tale" is an obvious example, and Evans deals with several more.

On the issue of necessary allegorization, the inconsistencies the tale admittedly contains are better explained in terms of a fable closer to social reality. The tale spends a good deal of its time (ll. 5–118) discussing the factors responsible for Virginia's excellence—Nature and upbringing together. Then Apius claims her because he has seen her and he is a socially powerful man, and Virginius asserts the prior and superior counterclaim of his fatherhood. Virginia's obvious nonagency may very well be the point of an only slightly allegorized comment on the patriarchal ownership of women. Apius's obsession with the girl may be extreme, but only slightly more improbable than Walter's with Griselda or the Sultan's mother's with Custance. Virginius, too, is an extreme case, but surely readable in terms of the desire of most wellborn fathers in the Middle Ages to control their daughters' sexual careers.[27] The other issue the tale highlights is that of pathos itself. Everything said about Virginia—her beauty, her continence, her modesty, her unassertiveness—echoes the sacrifice Abraham was asked to make of Isaac, a biblical episode performed and loved as a mystery play. Indulging the sensationalism of seeing innocence sacrificed goes all the way to the death in Virginia's case, no angel at the last minute. But the *subject* of pity comes up again at the very end of the tale, when Virginius forgives Claudius. Perhaps the fable wants us to notice its lapse of psychological meticulousness in making Virginius stoically set on his daughter's death and yet moved to pity toward the betrayer of their family. Perhaps, in other words, the poet is displaying the Physician failure to tell an aesthetically satisfying story: his tale indulges emotion rather than using it up, and then allows a misguided pathos to close it.

Custance in the *Man of Law's Tale* is also made to suffer for her beauty and she is just as blameless—"in hire is heigh beautee, withouten pride" (II.162)—as Virginia was. Apius saw Virginia with his own eyes, but the Sultan only heard about Custance from merchants. Her *image* in his mind provoked a desire so irresistible that he agreed to be baptized—Custance was not even looked at. Dorothy Guerin notes that Custance is presented as more passive, less literate, and less vocal in Chaucer than in Trivet, his primary source.[28] This is particularly notable in a story that positions her as the emissary/sacrifice given to convert the Sultan and his people—the successful emissary, when she is given half a chance. Her counterfigure in the *Canterbury Tales* is the equally evangelical Saint Cecilia, whose discourse, rather than her suffering, is foregrounded, and whose story disturbs the gender binary active male/passive female.

The narrator does not like Custance's being sent to Asia and he expresses himself freely on this and other points.[29] This self-conscious narrator—whose habits of presentation may be based on the fact that the Man of Law himself holds the legal office of "narrator"[30]—creates some striking rhetorical effects, among them the denunciation of the Sultaness (II.358–71) and the identification of Custance with Daniel and with Mary the Egyptian 469–504). Custance's dialogue, while not completely absent, is overshadowed by his. Her image is present visually—her virtuous beauty reported, her pale face as she stands before Alla (645), her motherly gesture in covering her baby's face with a handkerchief

(837), and the beauty her son inherits from her and displays for his father (1031–32). It is also present through the impression made by her life—her diligence in the constable's household (530), the "perfeccioun" that attracts the accuser knight (582), and her blameless life with the senator's family.

Although she does have one moving speech, phrased as a prayer to Mary (II.841–61), Custance's silence about her adventures is one of the most notable things about her. She was so "mazed" by her first sea voyage that she "forgat her mynde" (526–27), but apparently she did not tell her story to the constable later either. When the senator's ship rescues her from her second voyage adrift, she once again remains silent, even though she is returning to a home she left most reluctantly—"ne she nyl seye / Of hire estaat, althogh she sholde deye" (972–73). She stood "dumb as stant a tree" when brought before Alla, her heart "shet in hire distresse" (1055–56). Although her good works are continually referred to, they are not described (except the restored eyesight in Part II, and even that is passed over very quickly), and they do not include any efforts to protect herself. The active agent in Custance's escape from perils is, of course, God, sometimes acting through Mary. Three times her deliverance is credited to miracles: her first survival on the sea (477), the striking death of her accuser (636 and 683), and her second survival (950–52). The narrator seems impressed by each of these events, and records his awe at some length, but Custance herself has nothing to say about them. Her silence on her own behalf seems to me to strengthen the claims for pathos in the tale, since, as Frye argues, pathos must avoid highly articulate appeals to pity lest they become mere "tear jerking."[31]

All the characters in this tale, except the two wicked mothers-in-law, weep. The people weep when Custance is sent to the ultan (II.288); the constable weeps when he finds her in the steerless boat (529); Alla weeps when she stands before him in judgment (660), when he replies to the false news of his son's deformity (768), when he realizes he has been lied to (897), and when he and Custance find each other again (1065–67); Alla's people weep when she is consigned once again to her boat (820); Mauricius weeps as a baby (834) and when the would-be rapist boards the ship (919); and Custance weeps at each of these points. Her pity goes out even to her lecherous accuser struck down by God Himself (689). The narrator outdoes all of them in expressing and evoking pity. My argument is that his fully articulated emotional outbursts—outrage at injustice and pity for innocent suffering—relieves Custance from arguing her own case. It saves her figure from self-pity while indulging the pathos of her situation at every turn. Her feminine unassertiveness is countered by the hyperbolically evil mothers-in-law, but their ruthlessness is not identified as female. The "Sowdanesse" is called a virago, a "serpent under femynynytee," and a "feyned womman" (359–62), and Donegild is "mannysh" (782). In presenting these contrasts so baldly—good/evil, passive/aggressive—Chaucer represents the Man of Law as rhetorically overbearing without rendering the tale aesthetically cheap for moderns.

Griselda is also nearly silent; the Clerk's presentation of her silence is strategic in that she herself makes no bid for the audience's pity. She is another beautiful woman whose story is told with the effect of irresistible pathos, a motherly woman whose children are threatened, a doer of good works among the people, and a sufferer who does not seem to defend herself. Pathos is an important component of the *Clerk's Tale* and the tale is not rightly experienced without it. As John Hill argues, "The prudent reader can avoid being abused by feeling but cannot avoid knowing feelingly; a softened heart is essential for right understanding of a humanly complex issue."[32] Yet Griselda is not ultimately a victim; the stronger thrust of her legend presses her agency. Late in her story we see her under a new aspect, see that she must be numbered among those whose beauty is a sign of her wisdom and her wisdom-enabling life.

Inspiration

Like Virginia and Custance, Griselda is a woman whose beauty attracts a man's attention and who is subjected to bitter suffering as a consequence. The text presents Walter's attraction, though, with a difference: "His eyen he caste on hire, but in sad wyse.... Commendynge in his herte hir wommanhede, / And eek hir virtu" (IV.237 and 239–40). Apius and the Sultan considered Virginia's and Custance's virtue as an impediment to their desires, but Walter desires Griselda's hand because he sees that she is virtuous. As soon as she is seen by the Clerk's narrative, her beauty is associated with both the natural, because of the temperance of her habits, and the sacred because "hye God sometyme senden kan / His grace into a litel oxes stall" (206–7). Her being seen is not presented as a pit the gazer falls into, but as a proof-text for the egalitarian speech Walter had made to his people. If Walter had been more certain of his ground, we could have skipped from the end of *secunda pars* to the prosperity and happiness of the closing lines (1130–38). Kathryn Lynch argues that we should set Walter's uncertainty in the context of late medieval debates over rational or empirical standards for certainty; he becomes the man "who must plunge his hand into the fire to certify that it truly burns."[33] This is, of course, a neurotic (even criminal) overreaction to the problems raised by the philosophical currents of the day, but it is not beyond the Clerk's ken to be pondering it. In the end, by proving to himself that Griselda has been "translated," he offers his realm a new mode of wisdom, one that issues from the poorest household in the village, but governs by promoting the "commune profit" (431).

Griselda's beauty functions in this reading as a sign of her wisdom, and her behavior teaches Walter and resolves his philosophical anxieties. She may be numbered, then, among the figures of grounded, steadfast Lady Philosophy rather than the deceitful and destructive Lady Fortune. In my reading of this interpretive line, Walter's appears as the selfish, restless Western male quest for validation that is willing to subject natural and sacred truths to cruel extremes of analysis. Yet Walter must also be numbered among those saved by finally understanding the implications of his wife's beautiful nature. Griselda's role in her story confirms the overarching medieval construal of beauty as representing and teaching goodness.

There are several other representations of the wise female in Chaucer's major works—the Monk's Cenobia and Croeses's daughter come to mind, the former for her prudent management of her kingdom and the latter for her bold insight into her father's dream. Cassandra is also a figure for grounded wisdom, as interpreter of Troilus's dream from historical knowledge and informed dream-lore. Canasee's wisdom is mediated by the special powers accorded her by the magic ring, which allows her to understand the animals, but her wise kindness to the injured falcon is not magical. Saint Cecilia, whose physical beauty is nowhere stressed—"Faire Cecilie the white" [VII.115] is as close as we come to a description of her—teaches Almachius first principles, like Lady Philosophy herself, and more courageously since she is treated as an historical rather than an allegorical figure and will eventually die for her forthrightness. Exhibit A, though, has to be Melibee's wife, Dame Prudence.

David Wallace claims that wifely eloquence "will prove to be the most distinctive feature of Chaucerian polity."[34] Such council works for peace within and between the communities of the day, tempering the male egotism that fueled medieval conflicts. Few commentators would argue that Prudence is wrong in her pronouncements of scriptural and classical wisdom, but not many would argue that she and her tale are beautiful. In this "tale" the divide between intellectual validity and aesthetic impressiveness looms large. Intellectual truths can indeed strike us with aesthetic power—"Euclid alone has looked on Beauty bare," writes Edna St. Vincent Millay. The element of surprise is present when one *sees* rather than *works out* the necessity of certain formulations in geometry or mathematics. (Of course, there is a wide variation in how different people intuit such matters. Douglas Hofstadter recounts the story of Srinivasa Ramanujan's rare "friendship with the integers," which enabled him to have immediate reactions like "it is the smallest number expressible as a sum of two cubes in two different ways" to the remark that the taxi his friend had taken to see him was number 1729.)[35] The rightness of Dame Prudence's logical sequence may strike the reader eventually, but it cannot impress him immediately. Number and measure are involved. John Hill remarks that *Melibee* "may have appealed to a medieval taste for *copia* and compendium"[36] and if so, the divide between medieval people and ourselves is large indeed in this age of the sound-bite. The *Knight's Tale* also takes a while to unfold, but the revelation that each cousin has received what he asked of the gods nonetheless produces a flash of insight, while Prudence moves from point to point with a relentlessness and prolixity that we are unlikely to experience in that way, however *true* we think Chaucer's early audiences may have felt the ideas of the tale to be.

Melibee enacts a rejection of pathos by prudence. What is remarkable about this is the reversal of gender roles: it is Melibee who is presented as suffering pity for the attack on his women and outrage against his enemies, while Sophie's position is unrepresented, and Prudence seems bent on constraining these feelings by subordinating them to dispassionate reason. Her relentless reasonableness opposes the association between women and sentiment that most medieval formulations took for granted. She is without other specific traits, the only one of Chaucer's characters, I think, who is entirely allegorical in conception, very like Lady Philosophy in asking that the particular situation Melibee inhabits be supplanted by the general wisdom of the ages. Another Canterbury pilgrim, also female, had made that argument earlier in the journey.

I mean, of course, Alisoun of Bath. The knight in her tale wallows in bed to avoid her on their wedding night, consumed with self-pity. Like Melibee, he was subjected to a longish, although more pointed, curtain lecture on the general issue of true worth, and, like Melibee, he was slow to yield to it. It has never been completely clear to me whether the knight, once he allows his wife to choose, sees a beautiful woman or sees his new wife *as* a beautiful woman. Whichever tack is taken, though, the conclusion does have that shock of surprise and enlightenment that unites the cognitive and the emotive without the labor of stepwise consideration. This distinctively aesthetic pleasure is enriched and complicated by the fact that Alisoun is not the pilgrim by whom we expected to be reminded of these important truths.

So far we have three patterns before us for Chaucer's presentation of female beauty: as the "bait, on purpose laid to make the taker mad," as the likely-to-be-victimized "accident" (as both "surface feature as opposed to substance" and modern "contingency") that intensifies pity, and as the outer sign of an inner gift capable of instructing and civilizing men. The inclusiveness, variety, and force of the images in the *Canterbury Tales* that explore relations between beauty, femininity, and rectitude create an aesthetic of complexity and nuance reaching from the opposition between Lady Fortune (the betrayer) and Lady Philosophy to the complexities of May and Dorigen and in all sorts of tones and registers. This brings readerly imagination and understanding into full activity, which is Kant's touchstone for beauty (*CJ*, p. 60). Chaucer's most extensive and complex figure for female attractiveness is of course Criseyde.

Devising Criseyde's Beauty

The image of Criseyde is so engaging and complex that it takes an effort to regard it as a created object. The poem introduces her image in breathless wonderment, at once natural and transcendent. God's creations have an immediate aesthetic force—the rainbow is Philip Fisher's example—which may or may not be investigated further, but human creations are necessarily attended by meditative cognition. Much of the pleasure taken from art involves reflecting on it, and that reflective pleasure depends on grasping the work *as something*. Consequently, both interpretive theory and aesthetics are implicated in an inquiry into the beauty of Criseyde and of *Troilus and Criseyde*. Many construals of the design of Criseyde's image are possible. She has been seen as an allegorical figure for Fortune or Nature, or as the virtual portrait of a human person whose story testifies either for female agency or for the recognition of constraints on female agency. Which aspect of Criseyde's complicated image we take as the key to the larger design of the poem will depend, of course, on the fore-conceptions (especially the ideological commitments to theories of history and gender politics) with which readers, including medieval scribes and glossators, approach it in the first place.[37] These fore-conceptions in turn are subject to the changing currents of social and cultural history that inflect readers' ideological conditions of understanding. As Gadamer argues, we should not, and perhaps cannot, escape these conceptions (some of them not fully recognized), but we can inquire into the ways various critical responses arrange the details of the narrative around them to make the poem coherent. The fact that it can seem coherent by placing Criseyde as seductress, victim, or inspiration is itself a testimony to the protean inclusiveness and simultaneously its hold on imagination. But beauty requires luminosity as well as coherence. Therefore, I begin with the radiant vision of Criseyde, inside the poem for Troilus and the narrator, and outside it for a good deal of the history of criticism.

Criseyde the Vision

Troilus thinks Criseyde is beautiful, and so does the narrator of the poem. Her person is described by the narrator before Troilus sees her:

> Nas non so fair, forpassynge every wight,
> So aungelik was her natif beaute,
> That lik a thing immortal semed she,
> As doth an hevenyssh perfit creature,
> That down were sent in scorning of nature.
> (I.101–5)

If it seems to veer close to contradiction in referring to Criseyde's beauty as "natif" presumably meaning "inborn, natural" and yet "immortal," "aungelik," "hevenyssh," and "scorning of nature," this description is nonetheless deeply tuned to a medieval aesthetic which blended scriptural with Platonic notions. Such an aesthetic ascribed beauty both to the "number, weight, and measure" according to which God had brought the natural world into being, and to the Platonic idea that living creatures are "made in the likeness of the intelligible and embracing all the visual."[38] The poem's praise for Criseyde is extravagant, of course, but it is coded to signal a particular kind of excellence, very different from the specific this-worldliness of, for example, the Miller's description of Alison. In this passage Criseyde's beauty is intelligible, able to be read, and it is phrased to signal value, born of nature but asserting as well a transcendence of the merely natural. Here the poem sets up both a fusion and a tension between the sensible and the intelligible regarding Criseyde. Her beauty is presented not as something to be apprehended simply, like the beauty of a flower, but something to be pondered over, something "in scorning of nature," which must be understood *as something* the meaning of which is warranted elsewhere.

The pattern of immediate delight and anxious pondering is replayed in Troilus's reaction to seeing her. The deep impression Criseyde makes on Troilus is described in terms of *his* astonished reactions rather than the specific features of her beauty that inspire them, the narrator adding some traits of character that "men might in her gesse":

> And upon a cas bifel that thorugh a route
> His eye percede, and so depe it wente
> Til on Criseyde it smot, and ther it stente.
> And sodeynly he wax therwith astoned,
> And gan hir bet biholde in thrifty wise.
> "O mercy, God," thoughte he, "wher hastow woned,
> That are so feyr and goodly to devise?"
> (I.271–77)

Troilus's response to Criseyde's fairness conveys a sense of wonder, the radiance (*claritas*) of Criseyde's outward form astonishing and awakening Troilus. In this passage, Wittgenstein's account of aspect, which I have been using mainly to inform a modern sense of *integritas*, seems to "dawn on" Troilus with an all but supernatural luminousness.[39] But *devise* in Chaucer's lexicon also means to "explain" or "construct"—"astoned" as he is, his understanding is also awakened.[40] He is having an intense aesthetic experience. His attention is deeply engaged by the glance "somdel deignous" by which she seemed to say, "What, may I nat stonden here?" followed by a brightened expression. Here Troilus is shown as attracted (in terms of both desire and affection) to a sign of independence rather than flirtatiousness. The narrator's description of Criseyde is closely echoed in Troilus's reaction to her. He wonders where she has dwelt (since she was sent down in scorn of nature); her feminine figure strikes him as well-proportioned (number and measure); he shrinks in his horns because her image abashes him as a vision of heaven might. This reaction also seems to call up Bonaventure's three-part reaction to beauty: apprehension, delight, and finally judgment. In these passages, the poem presents Criseyde's particular style of beauty as a given of the poem.

Through most of the poem, the details of Criseyde's physical beauty are evoked largely through abstract and generalized language in which it is hard to see an ironic shading. In Book III, her beautiful flesh, its delicacy, its whiteness inspire Troilus to apostrophize Love, Charity, Citheria, and Imeneus (Hymen), as well as to caress his lady, in keeping with a medieval understanding that sight both "articulates the desires of the flesh" and also serves as "the handmaiden of an embodied mind," in Suzannah Biernoff's phrasing.[41] Furthermore, her love has good effects on him. The elevation of his deportment appears in more than just courtly manners for he flees Pride, Envye, Ire, and Avarice, the most serious of the deadly sins—to mention all seven might have seemed to work against Chaucer's attempt to suggest a pre-Christian setting. In other words, the immediate delight and the cognitive judgment do not seem to be pulling in different directions. Loving Criseyde makes him love the world (lateral regard). It is not until Book V that the most specific thing we know about Criseyde's looks is presented in a formal blazon, sandwiched between portraits of Diomede and Troilus. Only then do we find out that her eyebrows met in the middle, a questionable feature of beauty, as the narrator himself signals (save *that*, there was no lack [V.813–14]). As if to temper the list of her praiseworthy nonphysical qualities, the narrator slips in "slydyng of corage," as though it followed from tenderheartedness (825). This succession of registers in which Criseyde's beauty is represented follows the trajectory of the story, which moves from idealization to consummated union and then to the encroachment of the external world on the lovers' story. The aspect under which one sees the beauty of Criseyde's face "lik of Paradys the ymage" was, in book IV, "al ychaunged in another kynde" (864–65).[42]

But of course the vision is not of Criseyde's figure alone, but of her story. Can her behavior be read as beautiful in either a medieval or a contemporary system of valuation? Surely her acceptance of Diomede and unfaithfulness to Troilus would have to have been and would still appear as ugly.[43] Bonaventure's two tests for art—good construction and faithfulness to the reality that lay behind it—are relevant here. On the principle of good construction, the figure of Criseyde could be admired for the detailed and subtle way her character is delineated throughout this long poem, how each step in her history has been accounted for, in short, its intelligibility.[44] On the second point, that of verisimilitude to extant models, one might stress either her idiosyncrasy and particularity or the way her image "accurately" represents female intransigence in general. Her capacity to *represent* femininity is, of course, how Robertson will argue for admiration of the poem and simultaneously execration of its heroine and all she represents. That iconic role is also what Criseyde herself fears in Book V, when she laments that she may be rolled on many a tongue "unto the worldes ende."

Criseyde's concern for the history she will create suggests one aspect of medieval reading practice, the one that authorizes Robertson's assessment of Criseyde and of the poem. Paul Strohm posits a wider range of such practices by examining the many and shifting ways the narrator addresses his audience, concluding that:

> Chaucer's poem presupposes an audience capable of embracing a mixture of styles and tones of voice and of managing abrupt transitions between them. It presupposes an audience able to both inhabit and stand outside a particular point of view.... It presupposes an audience of some literary sophistication, which shares literary expectations formed not only by the experience of the work at hand but also by acquaintance with other major texts and genres of antiquity and the newly flourishing vernaculars.[45]

Note that, particularly on the point of acquaintance with old and new texts, Strohm agrees with Robertson that Chaucer's audiences knew a good deal about how to read, including how to read exegetically (and so, from a different vantage point does Evans),[46] but he comes to non-Robertsonian conclusions about the limiting nature of their horizon of expectations. With Strohm's suggestion to watch for "mixtures," we might consider the various aspects under which Criseyde is presented: snare, victim, *and* inspiration.

Criseyde the Seductress Fortuna

The acknowledgment that Chaucer's nuanced fictional strategies suggest some sort of "realism" has not precluded construals of Criseyde as a figure in a sustained allegorical design. Hugh of St. Victor regarded the "ornamental" layer—the literal or historical details of a work—as providing a "relatively harmless" pleasure, while the timeless ideal it clothes, the "norm...which is continually repeated throughout the variety of incarnations," remains in mind when the outer layer is discarded.[47] The beauty of Criseyde occupies two completely different places in this scheme. (1) It would be pleasurable to contemplate the creaturely appeal of a lovely, fragile, and generous woman; this would not be wrong, but it would be intellectually meaningless, like admiring the fragrance of a flower. (2) To see Criseyde's function in the design of the poem—to see her as the temptation to enjoy the world without seeking out the substance behind its appearances—would be pleasurable in a deeper, higher, and more stable logic. There her moral failings would be grasped as features of the design, in the way that monsters depicted well are called beautiful. If she is represented as we can believe she truly is, even the seeming realism of her portrait can be put to work in the cause of didactic allegory. Its explicit moralization at the end—Troilus's detachment from the world and the address to "yonge fresshe folkes, he or she" (V.1835)—seems not simply a warning against seductive women, but against the unstable world of contingency. Especially untrustworthy is the sensibly beautiful part of that world that incites aesthetic rapture. Seen this way, the poem is an argument against taking beauty too seriously.

Robertson's view (the most thoroughgoing and influential of such perspectives) is that the medieval horizon of understanding was bounded by the work of Boethius, "widely regarded as a saint" and impossible for Chaucer to see around or beyond—any doubt he might have on this issue would be "strange indeed" in the fourteenth century.[48] Furthermore, no one reminded of Fortune while reading the poem (and of course the poem does refer to Fortune remarkably often) "could possibly regard passionate regard for a fickle woman with anything but disfavor" (p. 472). Robertson's method of historicizing this text is based on a very strong version of what we might now call ideological situatedness: what Chaucer says in *Troilus and Criseyde* is what he always says and what all the "major allegories" including the Bible always say. "It is his 'o sentence'" (p. 501). Robertson's famous passage on "Troilus and Criseyde" in *A Preface to Chaucer* makes the full case for a Boethian backdrop which immediately signals the poem's design as an account of the fall from virtue into the hands of Fortune, and, therefore, a tragedy in the medieval, rather than the modern or Aristotelian, sense (pp. 472–504). The fall into Fortune's uncertain world is presented in the poem as the world of sexual affections inflamed and disguised by a veneer of civility conferred by "courtly love." Troilus is "man," tempted by the seeming beauty of Criseyde as "woman," who stands for sensuality and betrayal long before she takes up with Diomede. In Book III, rather than enjoying a heavenly union, Troilus is merely resigning his manly higher reason to his "idolatrous lust" (p. 493). Chaucer's narrative strategies signal at every turn that Criseyde is not a beautiful or loveable creature, but both a specific instance of deceptive femininity and an icon for the falseness of the seemingly beautiful world. These signals were binding on his first readers and on us if we aspire to read "historically," in Robertson's view. These fore-conceptions—that the poem is tragic in a fully known medieval sense defined by the Canterbury Monk, that theological tenets underwrite all medieval structures of feeling—allow the *integritas* and proportionality of the poem to be seen in rigorous conceptual terms. They are entirely congruent with Augustine's use of *caritas*, which explains the surface features of the scriptural text, but is not subject to the modifications predicted by the Gadamerian hermeneutic circle. They do not allow for the sudden radiance with which Troilus and the narrator regard Criseyde.

Not all who stress the poem's allegorical and admonitory dimension begin with Robertson's fore-conception of a strictly Boethian medieval horizon. Some critics who stress the intelligibility of the poem see it as a talisman against the vogue for the genre romance and the practices (if there were any outside fiction) of "courtly love," with their apparently strong assault on medieval imaginations. Alexander Denomy, C.S.B., for example, argues that the idea of the irresistibility of sexual love and even of its ennobling potentialities, would have been familiar in the late fourteenth century and that Chaucer's readers, including officers of the Church, were *able* to read the poem as a love story and might have done so if Chaucer had not added such pointers as the "Palinode" at the end of the poem and the pretended authority of Lollius. In his view, the detail and specificity found in Archbishop Tempier's condemnations of "courtly love" suggests that something *in mind* or *in practice* needed to be refuted.[49] Like Robertson, Denomy regards the poem as condemning the love affair, but he does not regard either its production as inevitably condemnatory or its readership as bound to Boethius or even Christian doctrine on this point. His analysis stresses the stratagems Chaucer finds to defeat what Robertson calls a "romantic" reading, and, therefore, reasons that such an interpretation was available for fourteenth-century audiences of the poem. Both these critics, needless to say, are reading history—in fact, both are reading the fully stated historical records of theology, biblical exegesis, and ecclesiastical edict (big History)—but they use what they find to suggest very different reading publics.

From yet another vantage point, Sheila Delany construes what early readers did by pointing out passages that force "an intellectual perspective," breaking into any incipient identification with the characters by foregrounding the author's shaping consciousness. She writes that the poem makes use of an alienation effect (like that defined by Berthold Brecht) to disrupt the normal "romance" cues (like Denomy, she assumes their familiarity to Chaucer's audience), eliciting an understanding of the work "through an act of conscious will"; not "a passionate swoon, but a passionately correct esthetic and moral judgment."[50] These textual moments show Chaucer's work subversive of the conventional poetic form of romance and conservative in the ideological aims of his design. Unlike Robertson, Delany finds the Augustinian ideological bent outdated even in Chaucer's time, but she admires the force and subtlety of the poem's forward-looking aesthetic.[51]

In what sense is Criseyde beautiful in these allegorical readings? Her role in the fiction is to stand for the enticements of moral evil, including sensuous beauty and female sexual responsiveness; her character is that of uncommitted Fortuna. Hence, the sensible image may be responded to as *beautiful only until it becomes intelligible*. But even then, although her conduct is not beautiful, Criseyde might be seen as beautifully embodying her role in the misogynous fable (that role "well constructed," in Bonaventure's scheme). The poem, however, *is* beautiful: Robertson calls it "one of the most moving exemplifications of Boethian ideas ever written."[52] Its beauty is predicated on its insistence that Criseyde's beauty is demystified. Alertness to allegorical potentialities is surely a feature of medieval structures of feeling. By Chaucer's time, elaborate justifications for treating the animals and minerals as representing features of moral and social life (the pelican as nurturing and Christ-like, for example) became increasingly fixed and institutionalized on the one hand and increasingly complex and shifting ("a polyphony of symbols," as Eco puts it)[53] on the other—but either way an ever-present force. In large part, the cognitive dimension of art was served by the habit of approaching a story as an enigma in which the literal could reveal those "higher" disclosures worthy of meditation when the "accidental" details of the narrative had faded. There is, in other words, a measure of historical accuracy in approaching the poem with these fore-conceptions, but there is also a loss of responsiveness to effects deemed central by other readers of the poem and the medieval world.

Criseyde the Victim of Misogyny

It is also historically accurate to see dominant discourse in Chaucer's world as deeply imbued with patriarchal authority. Carolyn Dinshaw stresses Criseyde's presentation as victim, seeing her story as an *unmasking* of the patriarchal control to which females were (are?) subjected in their quests for autonomy and happiness. Such control bleeds "naturally" into the well-attested practice of medieval Christian aesthetics in rendering a beautiful object witness to the timeless truths available through faith. She, therefore, levers her construal of Criseyde against both Robertsonian styles of allegorization and advocates of her "realism" and appeal (like E. Talbot Donaldson), arguing that both invoke "structures of [male] authority in order to order the disorder, to stop the restless desire represented in and enacted by their texts, to find rest."[54] In Dinshaw's reading, Troilus and the narrator resist this capitulation through most of the poem—they keep working lovingly on the enigma of Criseyde—but from the eighth sphere a "soothing and harmonious" ideology is finally invoked, though at a price. The price, of course is to banish Criseyde from the realm of the beautiful and the valuable. Modern accounts of tragedy do not so easily underwrite "soothing and harmonious" ideological comforts and nor do Aristotle's. Dinshaw reads with fore-conceptions that resist the male-inflected impetus for cosmic order and point out how women are victimized by the practical and ideological control men exert.

The key to Dinshaw's critique of the "authorized" reading that blames Criseyde for the tragic outcome of the poem is the necessity of the exchange of women.[55] Criseyde's disloyalty is inevitable not because women are fickle by nature or because the very specific woman Chaucer creates is, but because the patriarchal exchange of women is a practice more basic to Western culture than the delicacy of feeling and respect for female agency suggested by the "craft of love" as the courtly system portrayed it. When the exchange is enacted by parlement, everyone except Hector ("she nys no prisonere") seems to agree that it is within the city's prerogative to trade Criseyde for its supposed benefit. It is, of course, at this point that the emphasis on agency for both hero and heroine begins to erode. What appears in its place is stress on the larger structures of kinship and exchange that seemed less obtrusive when Pandarus promised Troilus his kinswoman, Criseyde, early in the poem. But perhaps even more telling than this first hint of women traded among men is the fact that Troilus, grateful for Pandarus's help, offered him any one of *his* sisters (III.406–13). Looking back over the slow wooing with its delicate nuances of reluctance and consent, we now see *in addition* the harsh outlines of social inevitability: men trade women for their advantage.

Rather than papering over the stern story of a woman traded by her uncle and then by her polis with fascinating psychological "realism," Chaucer's narrative line enables a critique of patriarchal control, highlighting the reading errors Troilus, Pandarus, and the narrator finally make. The fiction reveals that Criseyde has understood from the beginning the limitations of her agency, and knows that when Diomede offers her protection she must accept it. What society demands of her all along—a certain selflessness about being traded—she delivers. Untrue to Troilus, she is " 'trewe' to patriarchal society."[56] Chaucer has constructed the poem to enable a reading of it (and of literary and social practice) that does not naturalize patriarchal authority. The poem is therefore beautiful in manifesting a new potentiality for the deep structures of fiction, Chaucer's society, and much that has befuddled us since. Its aesthetic shape is, in this view, a fully realized tragic configuration in which an ironic universe turns the strivings of both major characters against their happiness, not because they are wrong to love, but because they are subject to history.

Dinshaw's reading evokes an historical profile of the social oppression of the Middle Ages at least as convincing as Robertson's profile of its philosophical unanimity. But the lynchpin of patriarchy's omnipresence can authorize quite different readings of the poem. Elaine Tuttle Hansen, for example, links feminist theory with linguistic slippage, finding the (male-authored) "intelligibility" of the figure of Criseyde to be the very figure of error and instability. Clues that pervade the poem and produce its outcome point to her as the scapegoat for all the failures and betrayals of individual men and the male-dominated society the poems depicts. She is the letter A, "In beauty first so stood she, makeles" (I.172); "alone she has no meaning...but as part of these larger units [words and texts] she means different things at different times."[57] Criseyde's individual beauty contributes to the design of the poem by making her a focal point for the allure of beautiful women who seduce men away from virtue and of beautiful texts which mask the workings of masculine ideological systems by manipulating language.[58] (In linking the beauty of texts with the beauty of women, Hansen's analysis returns us to Isobel Armstrong's objection to Eagleton's depiction of aesthetics [see note 6]). Both Chaucer and the narrator are like the Criseyde they present, but this is not a good thing, although the author, of course, is aware of his complicity with the power and slipperiness of language, while the lady seems caught in her own net.[59] In Hansen's reading it is not Christian doctrine but feminist hopes for a woman-friendly Chaucer (and medieval mindsets in general) that Criseyde's image betrays. *Troilus and Criseyde*, which presumes to say so much about "real" women, is actually patronizing; although it is seductive, it is not a beautiful or an admirable poem. Criseyde's is a figure whose "'final meaning' is fixed as both real and paradigmatic,"[60] and that very coherence is in cahoots with the patriarchal system which oppressed Criseyde and has oppressed real-world women for centuries. Instead of the "learning subject" posited by Dinshaw, Hansen sees dominant discourse, slightly disguised, but writ large.

Criseyde as Inspiration

If the "literary sophistication" (Strohm) of at least part of Chaucer's audience is taken into account, the ancient conception of tragic irony—the mysterious reversal of fortune and loss of good as opposed to the "medieval" sense of error punished—might be called into play. Such a fore-conception discloses the sad fact that no decision the lovers might have made in Book IV could have prevented some version of the disaster that was to befall them. Criseyde is usually blamed for not agreeing to elope and Troilus for not taking advantage of his male prerogative to carry her off. She blames herself in hindsight, regretting that she could not see the future (V.748–49) and wishing she had stolen away "with swich a oon" (V.740). But human beings do not see the future clearly—that is a basic ingredient of the tragic sense of life. Monica McAlpine argues that Criseyde's serious attention to the past—especially the example of Paris and Helen—leads her to her unselfish and civically responsible decision not to elope and qualifies her to be considered prudent.[61] An equally tragic outcome, though a different one, would surely have followed if one of Priam's sons had deserted Troy in response to the seductions of the daughter of Calkas. In one of the key moments of her gradually unfolding story, then, Criseyde inhabits the very ground granted to the hag in the *Wife's Tale* and Prudence in *Melibee*. Although she cannot be said to hold this ground steadily, we cannot "devise" her character without considering it.

Dispensing with Criseyde's self-declared falsehood as the complete and iconic meaning of her figure, allows attention its other aspects. After all, Troilus's "passionate regard" is not granted to "a fickle woman" (*PC*, p. 472) as the poem opens; Criseyde's betrayal occurs over 1,000 lines into Book V. David Aers considers Criseyde to be luminous (beautiful and illuminative) and interprets the love enacted in Book III as a brief release in which "[f]ulfilled Eros enables individuals to transcend social pressures, repressions and fears. Mutual love, involving the total person, is achieved, and in this mutuality we celebrate not only the triumph over adverse forces but the momentary and joyful abandonment of anxious selfhood."[62] Such a reading, if imputed to some members of Chaucer's early audiences, assents to Raymond Williams's proposition that new structures of feeling "cannot without loss be reduced to belief-systems," but are thought and felt as new and often recognized in their newness through art and literature.[63] In loving each other so fully, both hero and heroine leave the arena of socially imposed power relations between the sexes, especially those inscribed in patriarchal practices; they, therefore, put themselves at the mercy of unpredictable historical forces. Criseyde has taught Troilus (and possibly the audience for Chaucer's poem), to embrace, for a while, the uncertainty of a fellow creature's fate. Seen that way, the poem looks purposive without a defined purpose: very much like puzzling Aristotelian tragedy, very little like medieval *exemplum*.

Although it is true that Criseyde upsets Troilus's quest for certainty and stability, it need not be assumed that the quest is the ethical desideratum of the poem. (Boethius does not see it as attainable in earthly experience, which is where Troilus initially wants it.) Troilus exhibits the masculine will to settle the problem of free will and determinism and "devise" Criseyde and the world of the poem. Although his conduct is more appealing than Walter's and the "test" Criseyde undergoes is not one he designs, his struggle with unknowability participates in the male quest to banish uncertainty. The poem (and some of Chaucer's other work) seems to question the possibility of earthly certainties (Goddes pryvetee, the Miller calls them). Troilus has to give up on an abstract answer to the problem of the freedom of the will and so do we all. In Book III, both lovers overcome their fears (the Criseyde of Book II is at least as aware and fearful of uncertainty as Troilus, though in a different mode) and enact a private version of the "epic rashness" that marks much tragedy. And for a time, Criseyde turns her lover toward civility by loving him and enhancing his love for the world of experience. It is the worth of his love for her that impels him to seek certainty in love and philosophy. Hence, Aers' assertion that the couple's "joyful abandonment of anxious selfhood" is a triumph over oppressive forces may be understood as an aspect of Criseyde's characterization that successfully inspires (confers value), albeit impermanently, within the poem.

It seems to me that Criseyde's image may also be seen as inspiring in a quite different way. In contradistinction to medieval aesthetic theories that are said to privilege repetition and continuity, Alan Singer argues that if we are to regard art as contributing to self-realization, "It puts art potentially at odds with any abiding universalistic rationales, unsettling the protocols of intelligibility that legitimate those rationales."[64]

To regard the influence exerted by Criseyde's presentation as benign, it is not necessary, therefore, to posit that it teaches what medieval tradition already knows but needs to restate to itself. An aspect of *Troilus and Criseyde* particularly challenging to thoroughgoing exegetical reading habits is its insistent attention to minute gestures, especially Criseyde's, and especially in Book II. In chapter 4, I discussed the remarkable detail of the "real-time" account of Criseyde's falling in love. If Troilus's responses to her in Book I had the characteristics of a transcendent vision followed by contemplation, Criseyde's in Book II form a distinct contrast in that they are incremental and cognitive from the beginning (features also stressed in Dinshaw's analysis), with moments like the dream of the eagle and the sight of Troilus on his horse offered as "visionary" punctuation. Although plenty of detail is lavished on Troilus's actions and decisions, it is Criseyde's inner life that displays a protomodern complexity. Aers points to both the "diversity and fluidity" of Criseyde's "movements of consciousness" in Books II and V, and to Chaucer's choice of a female subject for presenting these new narrative strategies.[65] Chaucer's confidence that at least some in his audience would be inspired to grasp this narrative mode is another aspect of Strohm's assertion of medieval "literary sophistication," and of Singer's insistence that art is addressed to a "learning subject."

The "diversity and fluidity" of which Aers writes is more commonly associated with prose fiction, especially the novel.[66] Although Stephen Greenblatt credits Chaucer with extraordinary subtlety in creating *personae*, he points out that his corpus does not contain the word "fashion," much less suggest the *self* fashioning he finds prevalent ("though resolutely dialectal") after 1500, suggesting that certain thoughts about persons lay beyond Chaucer's horizons.[67] In my view, the term *devising* in Chaucer's lexicon performs work similar to "fashioning" in Greenblatt's. I have already argued that Troilus feels pressed to *devise*—explain or construct—Criseyde when he first sees her, and that readers must do so too in order to *see* her *as* occupying a particular role in the fiction. Here I am asserting something further: Book II shows Criseyde devising herself. She describes herself to Pandarus many times—for example, as a widow who should be reading saint's lives in a cave (II.18–19)—and to herself—currently her "owene womman" and happy with that state (750). Moreover, the second book opens with a description of her as a reader—a devisor of the "siege of Thebes." As many commentators on reading—from Augustine to Ricoeur—assert, "the interpretation of a text ends up in the self-interpretation of a [reading] subject."[68] Dieter Mehl regards her interior speech as Criseyde presenting herself to readers in "interior monologue or reported thought that hardly appears in

English fiction before Jane Austen."[69] What might have made internal "devising" available to fourteenth-century reception is confession, in which the penitent is urged to bring to mind an outwardly undisclosed mental life (see above, chapter 3). The many and detailed confessional manuals extant would be pointless if priest and people could not conceive of this style of self-reflection and potentially self-refashioning.

Criseyde is beautiful in this readings, and so is the poem—beautiful in representing a particular woman as readers could and can imagine her to be, producing her through complex, and ultimately coherent, details, and situating her story in a past detailed enough to allow our imagination of it, but resonant enough to suggest new knowledge and provide release from the "crude interpellations" of ideology. Seeing these effects as ideological—Aers aligns *Troilus and Criseyde* with a progressive social vision[70]—does not mean that their force cannot or has not been felt as aesthetic. He seems to be evoking something like Scarry's "lateral regard" when he thinks of Criseyde's personhood as creating respect for other female persons, then and perhaps even now. Bonaventure's standard of verisimilitude is also useful from a contemporary viewpoint in revealing an earlier age with impressive vividness and displaying an idea about the interpenetration of people's social selves with their most intimate internal "movements of consciousness." It is perhaps in the figure of Criseyde that Chaucer most fully engages Orhan Pamuk's speculation about whether "these two words can exist together: beautiful and real."

The figure of Criseyde is intelligible through both old and new generic and ideological lenses: for Robertson a warning against seductive Fortune, which cooperates with prevailing medieval hegemonies; for Dinshaw an unmasking of those hegemonies as oppressive patriarchy; and for Aers a moment of utopian hope for mutuality. All of these potential narrative shapes are convincing as argument; all of them "devise Criseyde" and her story. Yet the narrative that presents itself for aesthetic attention exceeds each of them and even all of them somehow superimposed. Although beauty may produce knowledge, it passes first through images of the sensible and, as a result, does not necessarily convey the same lesson for every reader. I have all along posited a divided audience for Chaucer's early readers: some of them grasping the Boethian or Augustinian point readily, some responding to the poem in terms of its delineation of new thoughts and feelings that resonate with their own inchoate intuitions. Insofar as all have value, all are also in play. The poem is not "finally" *about* stainless Troilus seduced, victimized Criseyde, or unselfish love; it is about all of these as well as conniving Pandarus and a tenderhearted narrator (who near the end flinches from *devising* Criseyde's traditional role in the story [V.1093–94]), an uncaring universe, and a great deal more—all circling about, competing for attention, exciting imagination, illuminating new structures of feeling.

The aesthetic in general has been and is still linked with the beauty of women; both are fragile, and the delight they provide can either fatally ensnare rectitude or inspire it. In Chaucerian images of feminine beauty and its effects—May, Emelye, Virginia, Custance, Griselda, and especially Criseyde—we see the remarkable and unsettled complexity of that linkage amply explored.

CHAPTER 6

THE AESTHETICS OF LAUGHTER

The game, one would like to say, has not only rules but also a point.

Ludwig Wittgenstein, *Philosophical Investigations*

Humour is a phenomenon caused by sudden pouring of culture into Barbary.

Ezra Pound, "*D'artagnan Twenty Years After*"

As speech is the culmination of a mental activity, laughter is a culmination of a feeling—the crest of a wave of felt vitality.

Susanne Langer, *Feeling and Form*

The world can never take a holiday from metaphysical first principles.
Even the raving, bolted in their cells, have not the files to file these chains away.

Gladys Schmitt, *Sonnets for an Analyst*

A man may seye ful sooth in game and pley.

Harry Bailly

Everyone knows that many of Chaucer's tales are funny; moreover, the frequent appearance of the paired terms "ernest and game" and "sentence and solace" suggests that their author knows that he and his created pilgrims are playing weighty and hilarious language games simultaneously. The presiding Host knows about the potential for "sooth" in "game and pley" and says so to the Cook (I.4355). Everyone also knows how complex the related, but not synonymous terms, laughter, humor, comedy, satire, and parody have been and still are. This chapter does not set out to untangle the scholarly debates about these categories, but looks instead at the breadth and inclusiveness of Chaucer's distinctive humor and the aesthetic effects it evokes. It deals only with the *Canterbury Tales* (and relatively few of them) because I want to concentrate on comic forms, and *Troilus and Criseyde,* although it can be characterized in several genres, does not seem to me to qualify as comic in its generic shape. Both it and nearly all the *Tales* are marked, of course, by sporadic humor. For example, Cecile, on the verge of martyrdom, answers Almachius with a zinger: your vaunted power over life and death is only the power to kill, not quicken (*Second Nun's Tale* [VIII.482–83]), which seems just the sudden swerve from normal expectation that identifies wit. Comment on these occasional sparks are also absent from this chapter—there are too many to do them proper justice.

Storytelling, funny or not, inevitably involves the "metaphysical," as Schmitt's poem suggests—"even the raving" are subject to the demands of intellect, and although I would not call any of Chaucer's narrators "raving," some of them are pretty riotous. What brings together the discipline of metaphysics and the outrageousness of wit is imaginative *play,* cultural play that suddenly pours its orderliness into "Barbary," as Pound says. Wittgenstein's conception of language games is particularly relevant to this chapter, and so are Freud's trenchant commentary in *Jokes and Their Relation to the Unconscious,* Henri Bergson's essay "Laughter," and Linda Hutcheon's *A Theory of Parody.* In the section on the fabliaux, I want to show how parody and satire (which predominate in that form) contribute to the coherence and shapeliness of both the individual tales and the unfolding frame tale. Antonio Damasio's *The Feeling of What Happens* makes a general case for the mind/body connection in a way that can be linked with Susanne Langer's "crest of a wave of felt vitality" in the presence of the comic. Daniel Dennett asserts that "luxuriant imagination" is central to fun[1] and much of what I want to say about Chaucerian fictions concerns such imaginative luxuriance: abundance of varied detail, pleasure, vigor, fertility, and profusion. It is perhaps Chaucer's most distinctive signature.

The *Critique of Judgement* turns up again because I am treating humor as a species of the aesthetic, as did Kant himself, along with Aquinas and Freud. All three stress the element of freedom from practical consequences characteristic of both aesthetic judgment and laughter. Aquinas frames it in terms of the fact that only humans experience both humor and beauty.[2] Freud characterizes both as "playful judgements," those which enjoy the object of attention rather than using it for a practical end,[3] in agreement with Kant. All three also assume the escape of beauty and laughter from the grip of specified concepts, without denying their address to intellect and shareability. Such assumptions license discussion of what has seemed the elusive and/or tedious business of "explaining jokes." Bergson begins his essay by calling laughter elusive and secretive, "a pert challenge flung at philosophic speculation."[4] Bergson, of course, took up that challenge, demonstrating that headway is not impossible, which should encourage Chaucerians to gloss and grope this secret region. What follows is a brief guide to six of the notions about beauty and humor that underlie my discussion of a few of Chaucer's comic tales.

1. Laughter involves both the sensible and the intelligible. The sensible is necessary for imagination to create a world and situation in which some laughably surprising thing happens. In the *Canterbury Tales*, this world is luxuriant in its range and abundance of detail. The sensible is also present in another sense: laughter comes straight from the text to a bodily reaction, which attests to a certain authenticity in that reaction. That authenticity impels the desire to think things through; the encounter with beauty impels, in Philip Fisher's phrase, "a drive toward intelligibility" (chapter 1, above). Walter Benjamin, not a writer usually noted for his appreciation of humor, agrees: "There is no better starting point for thought than laughter."[5] This sensible/intelligible nexus seems to me a fuller account of the experience of humor than Bergson's insistence on comedy as coldly intellectual, but that insistence calls attention to the intellectual craftedness of comedy, and, I will argue, of Chaucer's comic tales in particular.[6] Sudden intelligibility ("I get it") accounts for some immediate responses, of course, but the fullest effects of Chaucer's tales require the same sort of careful aesthetically oriented attention as is required to understand other beautiful objects. For textual objects, as Peter de Bolla asserts, hermeneutic desire for meaning accompanies an aesthetic response, in a sense precedes it.[7] In Chaucer's humor, the audience's hermeneutic impulse is particularly insistent: as we watch his characters outwit each other and/or themselves, we posit a coherent, though perhaps unfamiliar, world. In a broader sense, too, the intelligibility achieved in comic fictions enters the area of serious thought. Charles Muscatine claims that the *Miller's Tale* is so fully realized a fabliau that "the genre is virtually made philosophical" through "an assertion of the binding, practical sequentiality of events."[8] Comic effects are induced through sensible details, but completed by being rendered intelligible.

2. The usual censors operating in everyday life are circumvented by comedy's bribe of pleasure, producing imaginative freedom. Kant's stress on disinterestedness (as setting aside practical consequences) is an underlying condition for reacting to humor, but the major contribution to the mechanism by which laughter is released is of course Freud's. Freud maintains that jokes produce an economy in "psychical expenditure," that they

provide satisfactions and pleasures by finding sense in what seems senseless from an ordinary point of view. Those satisfactions are powerful enough to evade the censors that prevent direct references to sex or aggression, delivering the relief and pleasure of laughter before the censor can intervene to block it (*JRU*, p. 124 and 131). Word-centered jokes please because they replicate the childish pleasure of linguistic play not yet bound up with reasonable meanings and restricted by social decorum (p. 126). Hostile jokes evade societal prohibitions on aggressivity by delivering a burst of pleasure (p. 134). These observations reflect, of course, Freud's general theories of unconscious psychic mechanisms, but Bergson comes to similar conclusions about mental thrift, when he refers to humor as an "intellectual shortcut," a game played with ideas that relieves the "strain of thinking" (L, p. 182 and 187). This "relief" seems to me available only for the moment of "catching on"; many of Chaucer's jokes provide, even require, a lot of thinking before their full effects are felt. My point is that the particular bribe of pleasure offered by humor may be considered from either a psychoanalytic or a philosophical angle.[9] There are readers, D. W. Robertson, Jr. among them, who refuse this bribe, withholding their laughter and denying that the tales, when properly contextualized in medieval Christian thought, elicit it.[10] Robertson's work has elucidated many facets of Chaucerian practice, but in this matter he is surely wrong.[11] The comic tales have seemed funny to many generations of hearers and readers, including almost all the sondry folk on the pilgrimage.

3. The stimulus for laughter is unique to its object and not logically deducible; even when structures seem predictable, the joke produces a surprise. Tragic inevitability produces suspense by our knowing that fate will betray the protagonist, but not how it will happen. The suspense is not about the outcome, but about its precipitating causes. Comedy creates suspense about everything. John the Carpenter might discover the plot before his wife is "swyved" or not, Absolon might be *properly* kissed and led on toward any number of different humiliations, etc. This openness is a feature of all general accounts of humor, creating another likeness to aesthetic effects, since neither beauty nor humor is bound to rationally ordered concepts.[12] Comedy "greets" its audiences suddenly. Wittgenstein's duck suddenly comes into view when we thought we were looking at a rabbit. Ordinary logic fails; the "upside-down" idiosyncrasy of humor requires a new logic to be substituted for well-worn habits of mind, as Alan Singer has argued is the case for beauty. It is therefore expansive and fertile in its luxuriant growth; it inclines one to share it, to tell another funny story, or tell this one to someone else.

4. Weight, number, and measure are just as important in the aesthetic effects of comic fictions as of any other kind. The freedom and abundance

suggested by humor is widely acknowledged. Yet that freedom arises from and surprises us with laughter on account of its formal boundedness. Everyone has probably had the experience of failing to produce the crucial *form* for a joke and acknowledging the blank reactions of listeners with "I didn't tell it right." No matter how outrageously Chaucer departs from ordinary likelihood, the comic genres to be discussed in this chapter are not in fact disordered by their idiosyncrasies, but tightly ordered in unpredictable patterns. I hope to demonstrate that each of Chaucer's comic styles reflects both an internal form in which the parts cohere and in which a relationship to other tales produces further comic insights. The hermeneutic circle, with its mutually elucidating parts and wholes, applies as rigorously to comic genres as to others, and the artistic stakes are just as high.

5. Although jokes can be tendentious in intention, they can be laughed at with disinterest. In this contention, I have Bergson and Kant against me. Bergson's conclusion is that pleasure in laughter is not "exclusively esthetic or altogether disinterested" and is characterized by "secret intent" (L, p. 148). Like Matthew Arnold, Kant denies comedy, "a certain seriousness in its presentation" because its "interest" is in being agreeable. In my view, there probably are tendentious jokes and stories that cannot be grasped without "taking sides" (seeing them as concepts and identifying interests with or against them), but many others work by producing a kind of ambiguity about the "target" that allows or tricks one into laughter, even against firmly held practical interests. Just as beauty attracts without announcing its use, humor can amuse without identifying its target. Sometimes, too, the target of tendentious joking escapes unharmed by laughter. Laura Kendrick argues that deliberate irreverence may even become part of the renewal of the privilege enjoyed by the target object.[13] The reactions of the pilgrims, as reported in the links between their tales, suggest the validity of this observation, since the company collectively is induced by humor to admire the Miller's attack, apparently without damaging their respect for the Knight. Today we have even less at stake in whether millers are justified in disparaging reeve/carpenters or vice versa, but the jokes they tell about each other are still funny.[14]

6. Comedy is more likely to be context-dependent than other forms, and jokes are notoriously more topical and short-lived than other kinds of stories. The wonder is that Chaucer can still make us laugh, often at the same tale the next time we read it, when most jokes will only provide their intellectual and/or psychic shortcut once. I will attribute this effect to the complexity of some of his funniest tales, but I should say here that one source of the renewal of comic pleasure for us may be the result of our historical distance. We do not "get" the whole luxuriant joke the

first time. This is consistent with the necessity for hermeneutic attention discussed earlier. Scholarship regularly turns up new contexts, some of which may have been commonplace in late fourteenth-century England, others arcane even then. Many of these findings reveal new satiric or parodic targets for Chaucer's humor. As a result, his tales may be funnier now than they were to Dryden, Byron, or Skeat. One of the most important developments of this kind is surely V. A. Kolve's invaluable disclosure of the wealth of visual images that impinged on the imaginations of medieval English men and women. Equally instructive is his discussion of the way repeated images coalesce with the tradition as a whole, underscoring "the dignity and importance of the *mental image* for any discussion of literary affect."[15] These context-dependent insights recreate the *enargeia* or "imaginative vividness" of the medieval experience of Chaucer's work,[16] and they are nowhere more important than in the two major comic genres I will discuss in this chapter: fabliau and parody.

Fabliaux and parodies are not the only Chaucerian tales that induce laughter, but they are probably the kinds that lead to laughter most readily. Both forms require our imaginative fusing of historical horizons: the fabliau often produces satiric effects and, therefore, requires knowledge of the medieval context (specific housing styles and cartwheel designs) and parody demands acquaintance with some prior "coded texts" or stable textual forms for its full effects, as Linda Hutcheon argues.[17] These two forms are also the most deeply involved in the structural mode of the *Canterbury Tales*, since it consists of reported speech, albeit that of fictional characters. Fabliau allows those fictional characters to satirize one another or one another's *mysters* both in the tales and in the larger world; parody allows them to quote one another's lines ("Alone withouten any companye") or plot features (two suitors vie for the favors of a protected female). Fabliau satire connects us with the world of actions and practices outside the text, parody with other texts, thereby "inscribing continuity while permitting critical distance," as Hutcheon argues (*TP*, p. 20), but my purpose here is not to insist on entirely separate categories, only "family resemblances." The specific imagery involved in both genres is sometimes realistic, sometimes iconographic, and sometimes both at once.[18] There will, in any horizon of understanding, therefore, be an audience with greater or less appreciation for subtle comic effects—some people will recognize more of the icons and/or the coded texts than others will. Many medieval people would probably know that millers were reputed to have heavy thumbs, but not so many that the Virgin Mary had sometimes been associated with the weasel. The full effects of some of Chaucer's jokes depend on specialized knowledge, as does the

Nun's Priest's Tale on Geoffrey of Vinsauf's array of tropes, for example, but that tale produces a robust comic response even for the uninitiate.

"Right in His Cherles Termes Wol I Speke": Fabliau

The fabliau, when called by that name, is a distinctively medieval form often peopled by nonaristocratic, everyday characters surrounded by plausible, earthy details. Although the plots may turn on outrageous coincidences, fabliaux differ from fantasy and folklore forms in that their agents are human—usually presented as familiar types (tricksters, desirable women, jealous husbands or fathers)—rather than providential or natural forces. Kolve argues that the genre "admits no goals beyond self-gratification, revenge, or social laughter—the comedic celebration of any selfishness clever enough to succeed...If religious matters intrude, they are more likely to do so as a comic means of manipulation...than as an adumbration of the divine."[19] Laura Kendrick agrees: the fabliau "flagrantly satisfies erotic and aggressive desires," and deflates "repressive authority in general."[20] A common plot demonstrates how "A gylour shal hymself bigyled be," as Chaucer's Reeve pithily puts it (I.4321), and those who set out to beguile have, or think they have, authority. Glending Olson makes a convincing case for the sanctioned recreational uses of fiction. Aquinas recommended "justified" play for cultivated people as a remedy for anxiety or depression, and Petrarch praised the usefulness of "jesting words" in his sober defense of many kinds of literary profit and pleasure.[21] Humor is useful as well, in my view, in its power to focus "acutiy of regard" (Scarry) on facets of life and language not commonly granted that respect, and therefore addresses a "learning subject" (Singer) just as the "serious" tales do. I take all the tales to have this kind of aesthetic significance both in their individual craftedness and in relation to their pilgrimage and story contest frames.

A strategy characteristic of most fabliaux is the sudden release produced by playing on the ambiguity of signs (usually words, but sometimes the mental images they have elicited). Kendrick stresses this linguistic angle, positing that Chaucer's are the first fabliaux in English because the language itself had not achieved sufficient literary authority to make it a good target—there was earlier no "father tongue" to dethrone (*CP*, p. 76). Scott Vaszily argues that the willful *manipulation* of signs (since little humor is available through the *essential* ambiguity they allow) is the distinguishing characteristic of fabliau.[22] Although I agree that the sudden shift of a sign from one domain or register to another is very often present, it cannot be defining of fabliaux, or even of humor, since it is also the basis of tragic recognitions. Consider the granddaddy of tragic ironies (as Sophocles and Aristotle considered the matter): the warning to Oedipus that he would offend against father and mother. While Oedipus takes that warning to concern his adoptive parents, what eventually comes to light is that it concerns the birth parents he does not know. The shock of sudden intelligibility is aesthetic, but such cases elicit awe rather than laughter.

The Miller's Tale

The *Miller's Tale* is both a perfect instance of fabliau plotting and a tale that overflows the boundaries of the form, and not only because of the brilliantly evoked "naturalism" of Muscatine's account and of Kolve's. Or maybe I should say it involves three perfect fabliau-style jokes Nicholas's plot to cuckold John, Alison's simpler misdirection of Absolon's attentions, and Absolon's vengeful application of the glowing coulter also misdirected, since he was angry with Alison—all brought to crisis by the cry "Water!" This is a syntactic rather than a semantic ambiguity, since the single word "water" is not ambiguous, but its function in two different implied sentences is: Nicholas's yell means, "Bring me water to cool my burning behind!" and John hears, "The water of the second flood is rising!" Bergson claims that a "situation is invariably comic when it belongs simultaneously to two altogether independent series of events and is capable of being interpreted in two entirely different meanings at the same time" (p. 123). If the pleasure of the tale culminated in this alone, it would still be a magnificent comic plot—James H. Morey calls it "the most famous and well-crafted scene in all of Chaucer's poetry."[23]

But of course there is much more to attend to. Within the tale itself, the sensible details of everyday life in Oxford are presented in nuanced and pointed diction that makes them simultaneously (1) imaginatively vivid, (2) parodic of "serious" discourses, both courtly and religious, and (3) ultimately intelligible as contributions to the overall comic design of the tale. As the tale is addressed to the pilgrims, still other aspects of its signifying powers come into view, especially its quitting of the Knight and affront to the Reeve, and still others emerge as the whole pilgrimage is addressed to Chaucer's readers.

The thickness of this description of small-town life—hende Nicholas predicting weather and playing his sautrie in the upper chamber of a rich gnof's house, sprightly young Alison with her coquettishly plucked brows, self-regarding Absolon cavorting in his fancy shoes—is nonetheless economically rendered, all the details weighing in somehow before the end, and together weighing in to define the tone and register of the tale.[24] We know what Nicholas had in his room, right down to the color of the cloth on which his sautrie was laid. We know how the purse hanging from Alison's girdle was decorated and how Absolon parted his hair. Alison, John, Nicholas, and Absolon fill out their roles as desirable female, "sely" cuckholded husband, "hende" overreaching trickster, and golden haired narcissist of biblical fame. We seem to be in on *this* language game from the start, since the characters inhabit stock fabliau roles, but the ensuing fullness of their presentation distracts from any predictable implications. The plenitude and verisimilar detail of the Miller's telling, the sensible basis for its *enargeia,* produces surprise in spite of our knowing the genre.

The Miller's reference to music, for example, highlight both the specificity of the sensible and the intertextuality of the parodic. Nicholas keeps his sautrie in a place of honor on a red cloth on the top shelf. His private room rings with sweet renditions of "Angelus ad virginem" and "Kynges Noote" (I.3216–17), references to church and court. When he has won Alison's assent, he plays "fast" for her while he caresses her around the loins (hende indeed, and she has just told him to "do wey" his hands [3287]). His mode suggests privacy, slyness, and command of discursive realms above that of ordinary townspeople. Absolon, too, is musical; he plays the rubible and giterne, sings treble, and dances (3331–33). In his serenading of Alison while John is home, he positions her as the courtly lady, composing a couplet in his "gentil and smal" voice trilling like a "nightengale." His reference to the turtle dove in his second serenade echoes the *Song of Songs.* Befitting her description as an outdoor creature, Alison sings as loud and lively a song as a swallow on a barn (3257–58). The close attention paid to musical styles suggests music's traditional connection with joy and freedom from everyday necessity, but it also distinguishes the three musicians from one another, placing the clerics as two *different* representatives of culture and learning, the woman as natural in her own style. John the Carpenter did not sing; he merely groaned and snored (3646). All of this thickens the tale's sense of plausibility and at the same time provides an overplus of exuberant detail.

Plausibility is also served by the tale's "solidity of detail" in evoking spaces and objects.[25] Consider the cat hole in Nicholas's door: as John's knave looks into the room through it, it takes some time ("at the laste he hadde of hym a sight" [I. 3440–43]) for him to catch sight of the clerk gaping in an apparent trance. The poetry positions readers with the servant's maneuvers to get the right angle of vision. This is also the first, but not the last, use of the word "hole." The shot window is another detail with more than one function. Peter Brown has argued that Alison offers her bottom from the window of a privy: "The existence of a privy within John's bedchamber makes some of the narrative details more explicable; it enhances the scurrilous and scatological features of the tale; and it adds a further dimension to the theme of spatial transgression in which the boundaries of the private are breached and invaded."[26] Nicholas suggests that John take an axe into his tub to cut a hole (!) in the roof to let the tubs float out of the house (3569–71). All this amounts to extremely tight plotting designed to enmesh imagination and provide a counterweight against the outrageousness of the crisis to come.[27] The coherence of the tale also relies on its tight *verbal* weave.

The recurring use of the word "hole," which will play so large a part in the crisis of the tale, has its analogue in the four repetitions of the word "queynte" with its three potential meanings in Middle English. The couplet that uses queynte as identical rhyme contrasts two of those meanings: "As clerkes ben ful subtile and ful queynte; / And prively he caughte hireby the queynte" (I.3275–76). The cleverness of clerkes in general (3275), and Nicholas later in this tale, play a less important role in the first move he makes to seduce Alison than the hende-ness of his quick hands. This second instance of *queynte* cannot mean other than "cunt," which will throw light back toward the Knight's more genteel use of the word (genteel in that he tries to avoid its inevitable punning implications). The plot itself is called a *queynte cast* when John tells Alison about it (3605). In that case the term combines "clever" with "female sex"; this plot is about both. The doubleness of both *hole* and *queynte* is exploited in the fourth instance of the latter word. Mark Miller writes that the phrasing "hole"

> requires the Miller to gloss over the distinction between what, on his view, is desirable and what is disgusting—as again he must, and even more directly, in the triple pun of the punch-line that follows the scene, "his hoote love was coold and al yqueynte" (I.3754)—as though at this central moment in the Miller's gesture of comic exposure he could no longer tell the difference between what arouses desire and what quenches it, or could not make the difference stick.[28]

Miller's point here takes the direction of characterizing Absolon and the Miller; mine is that this repetition-with-difference results in a miniature joke, which is both self-contained and a working contribution to the larger comic effects of the *Miller's Tale*.[29]

Similarly telling is the verbal complexity of Nicholas's characterization as *hende*: "polite," "capable," "nearby" (he is the "nye sly" of I. 3392), and "good with his hands." If the tale is read from Alison's point of view, he is a useful tool in Heidegger's and Wittgenstein's deeper sense of "at hand." The *sely* carpenter is not merely foolish; he is *sely* in all the important medieval senses of the word. In the course of the tale, John is "unfortunate" and "foolish," even "pitiable," as he moves from the benefactor to the dupe, but he also embodies the otherworldly "innocent" of early medieval usage (in which the Virgin Mary is often addressed as *sely*) especially in his unself-regarding "Alas my wyf!" The helplessness suggested by some fourteenth-century instances of *sely* seems apt for his final appearance as injured and derided after his fall from the rafters.[30] Bergson makes a distinction between plotted comedic action expressed in words (and therefore translatable into other languages) and comedy that arises from the verbal texture itself (L, p. 127). The *Miller's Tale* fuses the kinds; this action would be funny if seen, but is funnier still when the equivocations of language itself contribute to the humor.

A considerable part of the overall comic effect of the tale depends on the *idea* of plotting. All the characters plot and comment on their plotting. (1) Nicholas and Alison are plotting a traditional fabliau trick on John, and Nicholas's glee in his ability to beguile a simple carpenter seems almost as delightful to him as bedding Alison. (2) Absolon is plotting a more traditional seduction, which he describes as "pley" (I.3686). After the kiss, he plans a cruel retributive trick, the physical violence of which gives the lie to his gentrified self-image. (3) Alison thinks up the ass kissing and invites Nicholas to laugh at it (3722), and her "Tehee" shows her own appreciation of her achievement. (4) John is plotting a *divina comedia* in which he and Alison (and Nicholas) escape the flood to a new Eden. All these plots depend on the playfulness and comic imagination that link laughter to the aesthetic. Within the tale, the characters are presented as free to hatch plots and laugh at them (for a while). The pilgrims are freed of their inhibitions against "churlishness," by their enjoyment of witty plotting, and so are (most) later audiences to the whole of the *Canterbury Tales*.

But the tale retains its edge by invoking more "serious" discourses as well. It is funnier to watch Absolon prepare for a courtly wooing scene, trying to seem "gracious," than it would be if he were aware of his uncultivated instincts only. Absolon's fastidiousness inheres in his mock-courtly techniques for wooing, but later also in his extreme anger at having been included in the coarse doings from which his personal habits should have protected him—after all he did put a love knot under his tongue, "therby wende he to ben gracious" (3693). His own long, well-tended hair contrasts with the rough "beard" that alerts him to his humiliation. The parodic force in this case works against both Absolon himself and the courtly love tradition that mystifies sexual feelings. Absolon is a man who (probably influenced by "coded texts") fooled himself but not the woman in question. That joke is compounded when Nicholas succeeds by being forthright about his similar aims. In terms of the Miller's intended quitting of the courteous Knight, Absolon's "refinements" of language and behavior parody the Knight's gentlemanly "port" and unwillingness to speak "vileynye." As so often is the case in well-crafted parody, the jury is still out on whether the Miller or the Knight loses more privilege in this elaborate game.

The weightier parody in the tale concerns the glimpses of religious discourse that flit through the tale. The Annunciation appears in Nicholas's musical repertoire and, perhaps in a more indirect way, in Alison's likeness to a weasel, a medieval symbol for the Virgin.[31] Reference to the flood is biblical, obviously. Kolve argues that the reference is so divergent from the biblical flood as to prevent its "bringing into the tale anything resembling the moral weight and doctrinal richness of its original."[32] Within the tale, of course, Nicholas and Alison must not be imagined as feeling that weight—there the joke is on John, who does. But some of the pilgrims will be aware of the way the scholar Nicholas is playing with fire (God's prerogative and privetee), and so are later audiences.[33] For Nicholas personally, it is fire, not flood that punishes (the fire next time). For all his cleverness, he is not able to see into "Goddes privetee" or even Absolon's immediate plans. Absolon's citation of the *Song of Songs* is congruent with the exalted and euphemized tone of his wooing. The prior texts here are orthodox and even scriptural, and the parodic undertow works against the tale's characters, especially Nicholas, whose clerical learning enables him to make these allusions. This strategy does not, I think, quite accord with Kendrick's assertion that fabliaux bring down, not just genres, but "repressive authority in general" (*CP*, pp. 98–99), but the *Miller's Tale* has united the pilgrims in a momentary freedom from authoritative strictures by irreverently reframing them.

So far, I have argued that the *Miller's Tale* marshals realistic detail in order to engage imagination in a fully realized world, that these details have provided small-scale jokes within the larger one, and that they have parodied "serious" discourses, expanding the genre to a "virtually philosophical" status through "an assertion of the binding, practical sequentiality of events."[34] The most obvious parody the tale provides is, of course, its point-by-point quittal of the *Knight's Tale,* demonstrating Bergson's dictum that wit makes ideas converse like people (L, p. 129). The quittal is so nearly a matter of consensus now that I will assume it and turn to the ensuing "philosophical" consequences. The tale contrasts with the Knight's "providentialism" by presenting a naturalistic account of the metaphysical and ethical world, not a world simply irrational and unjust (Bloomfield) or devoid of "metaphysical meanings" (Kolve).[35] The Miller's narrative efficiency invites his fellow pilgrims to share in the joke before the censor can block their participation in so licentious a point of view.[36] In other words, he invites them to exercise disinterested imaginative freedom severed from their real-life commitments. This densely configured story insists on a different cosmic order than the imagined providence of Catholic Christianity, an order in which inevitability resides in natural and human causal schemes. And as if that were not enough philosophical work for a fabliau, the tale also provides a self-reflexive commentary on reason and imagination.

I called providentialism an "imagined orderliness" in concert with Benedict Anderson and Paul Ricoeur's position that the cultural agreements defining communities are formed in imagination and sometimes challenged through imaginative forms. In *From Text to Action,* Ricoeur comments that if an image is confused with reality, the result is deceit, but with critical distance, imagination can lead to "a critique of the real."[37] "Men may dyen of ymaginacioun, / So depe may impressioun be take" (I.3612–13) is the Miller's own canny assessment of the carpenter's lack of critical distance. John was "taken in" by Nicholas's ruse so fully that the image of the future in his mind seemed a fact about the outside world. But then, so was Nicholas by his own self-aggrandizing vision of his control over Alison and John. And so was Absolon by his prescience that his itching mouth predicted his kissing Alison. And so are readers of the *Canterbury Tales* who regard the fiction as a documentary report on late fourteenth-century English folk, rather than as a "*locus amoenus* for interpretive play."[38] Such potentialities for imagination are just what medieval doctrine warned against when it rejected *phantasia.* The "resoun imaginatif" described in *Boece* is Ricoeur's higher kind, distanced by judgment. Such an oscillation between vivid immediacy and critical distance is essential to aesthetic response. The *Miller's Tale's* tight coherence (*integritas*) and proportionality of plot, setting, and characterization suggests sustained philosophical implications and problems; it both fulfills and overflows the fabliau shape.[39]

The Reeve's Tale

The *Reeve's Tale* is openly tendentious on several levels. The tale continues a quarrel with the Miller. Although the Miller tries to placate Osewold (who thinks Robyn's story discredits him rather than the Knight), the courtesy is not returned; the Reeve hopes that "God his [the Miller's] nekke mote to-breke," and concludes his prologue with an unjustified application of Luke 6.41–42. His story concerns a dishonest, overreaching miller (who plays the bagpipes and unhinges doors, like the pilgrim Osewold is quitting) to counter the Miller's hapless carpenter. It presents a rivalry between Oxford and Cambridge (perhaps the first in fiction) in terms of setting, and a confrontation between youth and age. It bears a formal parallel to the *Miller's Tale* as well. As Kolve observes, the "horse links the two plots, the stealing and the swyving, just as surely as the cry 'Water! Water!' brings together the Flood trick and the arse kiss."[40] In tone, though, the Reeve's performance contrasts with the "plenitude" and generalized good humor that characterized the Miller's; it is about scarcity and depletion from the prologue on, contributing to its sense of its narrator as an older, bitterer man. That tone invites an audience to relax its hold on everyday beliefs less heartily than the Miller's. The Miller and Reeve seem to be playing the same language game, but adopting different competitive styles in doing so. In stressing the "interests" his story serves, the Reeve risks sacrificing the playful appeal the *Miller's Tale* achieves so well. What the Reeve loses in comic effect, Chaucer gains for the *Canterbury Tales* by displaying his range of implication for the fabliau genre and the individuation of the pilgrims.

On a second level, the *Reeve's Tale* targets the "gentles" on behalf of the third estate, and, like the Miller's, offers yet another affront to the Knight's view of the world. It may even be argued that Chaucer (the author) is working out various responses to the class struggle imaged on the pilgrimage, producing a deeply coded tendentiousness, which may have been visible to some in Chaucer's early audience.[41] But it is striking to everyone that the Reeve registers the natural world "in harsher and more scholastic ways" than the Miller, as Kolve puts it.[42] I take his "scholastic" to mean that concepts, especially moral concepts, drive this plot and compromise its specifically aesthetic appeal to purposiveness without a final purpose. Its didacticism, which the Host foresees and chides in the prologue "The devel made a reeve for to preche" (I.3903) peeks through the details of the telling, absorbing as they are, more noticeably than with the Miller. The Reeve seems disillusioned (rather than cheerful, like the Miller) about the possibilities for *sentence* and *solas* in the human world. In Mark Miller's account, the Reeve's story exhibits a "clear commitment to a naturalistic view of human motive," as reflected in his figuring of human desire as a territory of animality that inevitably carries us away.[43] Such a "final purpose" is readable from the tale when contemplated, but energy and wit are foregrounded in the tale's breathlessly streamlined pace and delight in the jests of rebellious play on first reading.

For all its brevity, the details of *Reeve's Tale* provide a pleasurable "richness of specification," in tone and image, "that is rarely seen in French fabliaux," according to Muscatine. The telling is brisk; John and Aleyn are not clearly distinguished, Symkyn is monolithically the proud overreacher. Like the Miller's John the carpenter, who muses on the philosopher falling into a marl pit, the Reeve is ironic about learning—the scholars will be able "by argumentes" to make his little house a "myle brood" (I.4120–24). The story fits the Cambridge setting with unusual closeness, including its representation of dialect to characterize the students—the first attempt of its kind in English and unique to Chaucer.[44] Even this presentation of dialectal speech makes a point, highlighting the contrast between the clerks' bumpkin-like speech and Symkyn's more mainstream dialect and thereby feeding his arrogance toward the boys. The tale consists of macho one-upmanship and petty vengefulnesss, its harsh language consistent, except for the mock—aubade of Aleyn's parting from Malyne (4236–39). The varied music of the *Miller's Tale* is here reduced to the loud snoring of Symkyn's whole family, including Malyne. It keeps John and Aleyn awake, a harmonized, or perhaps antiphonal, "compline" (4170–71). Symkyn's snore resembles the snorting of a horse (5163), linking the miller with his trick to get the clerks out of his way, but also suggesting a drunken, coarser, more bestial snore than John's justified exhaustion after labor.

Symkyn's boast about his cleverness echoes Nicholas's: "Yet can a millere make a clerkes berd, / For al his art" (I.4096–97; he thinks that they think no one can bigyle them (4047), justifying the Reeve's later "gylour shal hymself bigyled be" (4321). Many of the major keywords of the *Miller's Tale* are picked up by the Reeve: thrift (4048), queynte (4051), pryvely (4057), hole (4298). Sely is particularly prominent: the sely tongue of dotage (3896), the sely clerks (4090, 4100, 4108), and two phrases in which nonadjectival forms stress the old meaning of health or good fortune, "Unhardy is unseely" (4210) and "swa have I seel!" (4239). These echoes suggest a full-scale taking up of the Miller's "issues," though in a quite different style and tone. As Robert Worth Frank observes, "For economy, swift forward motion, and sureness of effect the *Reeve's Tale* has no master."[45] This "explosive, vigorous" style, with its heavy reliance on verbs, simple or compound sentences, straightforward plot, and "low" diction requites the Miller's leisurely tale, richly detailed, allusive, complexly plotted, philosophically nuanced.

The Summoner's Tale

In the *Summoner's Tale*, Chaucer adopts yet another highly crafted shape for fabliau joking. Where the *Miller's Tale* unites a fullness of verisimilar detail with a tightly woven coherence and the *Reeve's Tale* answers it by reproducing its strategies in reduced form, the *Summoner's Tale* pays thematic attention to the "weight, number, and measure." The first part of the tale is focused on the appropriateness of Thomas's "gift" to Friar John's house. In this matter, as Harwood has succinctly put it, "the fart is a reward and a figure for the friar's sermon."[46] The friar produces mere "eir reverberacioun" instead of moral counsel or religious consolation, and is remunerated in kind. Later, when the lord actually uses that phrase for the gift fart, the question is how to divide it equitably, and this proportioning is also brought to an outrageous but suitable comic conclusion. There is a certain perfection in the alignment of the details of this narrative that makes it a kind of textbook case for Bergson's observations in "Laughter."

Among Bergson's overarching conclusions is that "mechanical inelasticity" in human behavior causes laughter (L, p. 67); we laugh "when a person seems a thing" or an automaton (p. 97). Like the question of proportion (which helps define the aesthetic effects of this joke), mechanical rigidity is a prominent feature of both parts of this two-part tale. Friar John's "mechanical behavior" is manifested in his automatic use of the "glosses" he brings together in his perfectly inadequate sermon, his lack of real *social* interaction with either Thomas or his wife, and his unflappable arrogance concerning the importance of his prayers. The easy way the *Summoner's Tale* settles itself in Bergson's spotlight may have something to do with the fact that the issue of mechanization came to Chaucer as an aspect of a cultural trend. Timothy O'Brien makes this assertion: "Chaucer's characterization of the Summoner reflects his age's excitement over the power of mechanics, e.g., the mechanical clock, heat and expanding gases," including a machine called a *sufflator* which heats to the point of explosion. This last emphasis exhibits an obvious relevance to the way Chaucer's tale conflates speaking, belching, and farting "as dynamics of expansion."[47] This is of course a comic conflation, which calls attention to the embarrassing claims of the body, the stupid monotony of its doing what it always does (p. 93), just when a more rarified tone is being attempted. Both the friar, who interrupts his claim to asceticism with a request for a sumptuous dinner, and Thomas, whose charitable donation is the deliberately insulting joke of a fart instead of soul-cleansing alms-gold, are funny in this way. In the case of the friar, this mechanical behavior is also funny by its perversion of his professional responsibilities, a professional callousness (p. 175) that Bergson also connects with laughable rigidity. Such callousness characterizes several of the pilgrims, of course, in many variations.

Bergson also stresses the comic way things return to their starting points (L, pp. 115–17) which is another facet of the shapeliness and *integritas* of these Chaucerian tales. The friar asks for a gift, which he duplicitously, but publicly, vows to divide with his order—that is what he ultimately gets. He asks for a large gift because "a ferthyng parted in twelve" has little efficacy (III.1968) and finds himself bound to a comic duty of division. This "getting what you asked for" can, of course, have noncomic consequences, as it does when Arcite asks Mars for victory, but the close timing and spatial precision in the fabliaux seems distinctively comic. (This is true as well of the cry "Water!" in the *Miller's Tale* and the placement of the cradle in the *Reeve's Tale.*) Contributing to the first climax in the Summoner's story is that great expectations come to nothing, or nothing but "eir reverberacioun."[48]

Bergson also stresses verbal sources of humor that push the word or expression until it turns against itself (L. p. 130), or make an expression flatly literal (p. 135). The friar tries to cajole Thomas into contributing to finishing ("parfourning") the "fundament" of his friary, and finds the contribution a performance of "fundament" of a different, more literal, kind. On a larger scale, this literalizing tactic accounts for the whole second phase of the tale, which turns Thomas's crude gesture into a logical, scientific problem to be disputed and a text to be *glossed* (suddenly suggesting a new *aspect* for regarding it). The friar is shocked at the pensive reaction of the lord:

How had this cherl ymaginacioun
To shew swich a probleme to the frere?
Nevere erst er now herde I of swich mateere.
I trowe the devel putte it in his mynde.
In ars-metrike shal ther no man fynde,
Biforn this day, of swich a question.
(II.2218–23)

The humor of this response lies in the lord's trancelike absorption in the problem of imagination. He wonders how a simple villager like Thomas could mentally represent an interesting *mateere*—the higher of Boethius's levels in the scholarly venue further suggested by *shew* ("set"), *probleme, ars-metrike, question, demonstracion,* and *inpossible*—to himself and then carry out the plot. How could he refigure his earthy joke as a challenge to the friar's vaunted intellectual superiority? Perhaps the devil sent Thomas a vision. Philip Pulsiano argues that in addition to images of Pentecost and Wheel of False Religion (Kolve), the spoked wheel may refer to the scientific problem "division of the winds," being discussed at Oxford in Chaucer's time.[49] This wealth of terms, specific to scholarly reasoning, fits nicely with Bergson's argument that the comic privileges "concrete terms, technical details, definite facts" (L, p. 143). In this latter phase of the tale, the close examination Friar John called "groping" in his inducement to confession and "glossing" in his sermon, is taken literally, and produces, as Linda Georgianna observes, an extended comic action instead of the abrupt conclusion typical of fabliaux.[50] The unusual proportionality of the tale is part of its comic effect; expecting a punch line, we get a further fabliau development. Again, the outline of the genre is both filled and overflowing.

In other ways, of course, the *Summoner's Tale* is, like the Miller's, a fine, though complicated, specimen of fabliau plotting. It bribes the censors that would object to the scatology and the abuse of friarly dignity by the extended mock-seriousness and "subtiltee" with which the vow to divide the gift is treated. Perhaps this humor is augmented by the recognition of a parody of the Eucharist or Wheel of False Religion as well.[51] Such parody would certainly "thicken" the hold on comic imagination, and the prologue suggests that it is not out of the Summoner's range, since the friars sheltered in the devil's ass parodically recalls their protection under the Virgin's cloak.[52] How parody works in the *Summoner's Tale* is part of the next section, since it depends on distinctions among the somewhat different language games involved in fabliau, satire, parody, and irony.

"Diverse Scoles Maken Parfyt Clerkes": Parody

M. M. Bakhtin makes laughter and polyglossia—the "interanimation of languages"—the central impulses of the Middle Ages in prefiguring modern novelistic fiction, and these impulses are decidedly pertinent to the *Canterbury Tales.* The fact that such fiction is always "double-voiced," demanding attention to both authority and transgression, resulted in its being "relativizing and deprivileging."[53] This attention to polyvocality is essential to the study of the *Canterbury Tales,* but in dealing with parody I want to take a position closer to Linda Hutcheon's, which allows for a wide range of effects from double-voicing from "respectful admiration to biting ridicule."[54] Parody always plays with prior "coded texts" (*TP*, p. 16), thereby "inscribing continuity while permitting critical distance" (p. 20), but it does not always "deprivilege" or even produce humor at the expense of either old or new text. It is, therefore, a large category, enabling a variety of effects, sometimes itself a genre, sometimes a contributor to other genres. Her distinction between parody, which alludes to coded texts and styles, and satire, which alludes to social life, is also useful to Chaucer studies. Irony is a trope rather than a genre; both parody and satire use it "as a rhetorical strategy...but not necessarily in the same way" (p. 52).

The satiric bent of the *Summoner's Tale* is overt and scathing, in the manner of a tendentious fabliau. It works unremittingly against the friar in the tale and thereby requites the pilgrim Friar. The "coded texts" behind the parodic aspect of the tale are images of the dispersal of the spirit at Pentecost (or its counterimage the Wheel of False Religion) that strongly resemble the final tableau of the tale. Identifying parody requires that we posit some knowledge of the previous text, and this is where Kolve's (strong) case for the familiarity of such images across a wide range of audiences comes in. I think of Chaucer's original audience as divided on points like these—for some the joke elements are more numerous and complicated than for others. But now that we know about them, we can use them to deepen our pleasure in the comic ingenuity of the squire's solution. Although an oblique depiction of Pentecost intensifies a scatological joke, the parody may be thought of as reinscribing a sacred image into a "habitable" social arena[55] rather than "deprivileging" it.[56] The allusion to the flood in the *Miller's Tale* may have worked in a similar way, calling to mind what "everyone knows"—that God promised not to flood the world again—and making John's gullibility patently obvious.

Although many of the tales incorporate parodic elements, the *Nun's Priest's Tale,* the *Wife of Bath's Prologue,* and *Sir Thopas* are among the most obvious candidates to be seen as belonging to the genre. Of these, *Sir Thopas* offers the clearest parody of form: versification, diction, plotting, and imagery. Hutcheon calls it "a parody of the form of metrical romances" and "a satire of the social institutions behind the chivalric system" (*TP*, p. 78). It seems to me more fully the first than the second. The two performances of the pilgrim "Chaucer"—*Thopas* and *Melibee*—may both be parodies, but they stand at opposite ends of Hutcheon's continuum between parodic critique, in which the earlier form is treated with humorous "difference" and small-scale difference that, except for its framing context, almost fades into translation.

Sir Thopas *and* Melibee

Sir Thopas mimes English metrical romance in its rhyme scheme, subject, and markers to oral address; one source of its humor is that the genre was itself "déclassé" as courtly entertainment by this late date.[57] *Sir Thopas* is, therefore, clearly established as what we now call parody.[58] Its internal humor arises from the anticlimax (a feature of humor discussed by Bergson and Kant) that characterizes almost every stanza. "He had a semely nose" (VII.729); "That coste many a jane" (735) are especially good examples. Many of these comedowns are located in word choices that would have been readily understood by Chaucer's earliest audiences, though nowadays scholarship has to uncover whether goshawks are appropriate for aristocratic hunters (and therefore part of the poem's pretended promotion of its hero) or a tip-off to the bourgeois pretension of the minstrel form (like the "jane"). These are matters of diction and imagery, and parodic reference in the story itself is even more self-revealing. The initial pointlessness of Thopas's "pryking" might simply melt into the style of the English romances if the repeated occurrence of the word didn't make it seem ludicrous and, perhaps, glancingly sexual. The otherworldliness of the elf queen is not in itself unprecedented, but she never appears to Thopas while he is awake; she is the mere dream of a sprite. Olifaunt is a good name for a giant, but he does not need to have three heads to signal his menace. Every plot element is carried too far. Some of these internally funny moments appear to mimic various English romances (in the manner of the "prefabricated henhouse," as George Orwell later called unoriginal writing) and, therefore, would seem to target the form itself.

The oscillation between direct and hyperbolic reference signals its belatedness and contributes to the joke, but not as a harsh dismissal of the value of the form. As Nancy Mason Bradbury points out, Chaucer uses many of the tags and phrasings so frequent in *Thopas* in *Troilus and Criseyde,* apparently finding them acceptable constituents of the multifaceted style he was crafting.[59] In *Thopas,* though, they are clustered so close as to attract attention to the narration instead of the plot. Frye comments on doggerel generally as making evident "how words are dragged in because they rhyme or scan, how ideas are dragged in because they are suggested by a rhyme-word," making deliberate poetry of this kind "a parody of poetic creation itself."[60] Seth Lerer finds this true in Chaucer, the pilgrim's image of himself in *Thopas* as "narrator errant," consciously working on his presentation without much success. The tag lines "redirect the audience's attention away from Sir Thopas's struggle with giants and toward the narrator's struggle with his own line."[61] The self-consciousness of the telling constitutes the overarching humor of the tale—Chaucer, the maker of all, presents his own persona as a worried and inept versifier in a dated genre—and rolls along incorporating smaller local jokes in its friendly parody of the minstrel style.

But Part Two of pilgrim Chaucer's storytelling performance is not locally funny. Some critics think it is "essentially without irony," and states the central theses of the *Canterbury Tales* directly. Others regard the performance as a whole to be parodic, though not, like *Thopas,* amusing line-by-line. It is generally agreed now that it is best approached as a *florilegium,* "a collection of sayings that can be retained in memory and produced on appropriate occasions," but not philosophical speculation or doctrine.[62] Nor can it be regarded as sustained allegory, insofar as the armored Christian of Pauline teaching could not urge peacemaking with "the flessh, the feend, and the world" (VII.1420). Prudence's practical advice about this world is no doubt serious, in the sense that much of it was believed useful and right, but the habit of allegorization (which

Prudence herself relies on) pulls sharply away from the pacifist lesson she tries to teach directly. (I say "tries" because the phrase "jumping up and down in the same place" comes to mind early in one's reading of her counsel.) The allegorical form here contrasts with deeply impressive and single-minded *exempla* like the parables of Jesus or the *Pardoner's Tale*. This particular amalgam of classical and biblical "flowers" cannot be made to converge on a particular source of right behavior, and, therefore, strikes me as parodic of an important medieval mode.[63]

Melibee consists of too many sentences and too little *sentence*. It lacks *integritas* (since more flowers could have been added at every juncture), proportionality (since it seems too long for its narrative point), and *claritas* (since nothing greets or surprises). The performance reminds me of Polonius's advice to Laertes: not untrue, exactly, but not the fountainhead of wisdom either, and subject to interpretive manipulation in new situations. I do not find the telling to be marked internally by ironic distance, nor do I think the idea of such collections of sayings is being mocked. The likeliest "target" of irony here is the characterization of the narrator Chaucer, who seems to turn from representing himself as an inept minstrel reciting *Thopas* to staging "himself as a writer of pedestrian orthodoxy and dutiful submissiveness" presenting *Melibee,* complete with the citations.[64] The pilgrim "Chaucer" is represented by two self-deprecating instances of the modesty topos. Although the *Melibee* is too slow moving to be funny or beautiful, it expands the range of the *Canterbury Tales* by sounding yet another note in the author Chaucer's repertoire.

The Nun's Priest's Tale

The *Nun's Priest's Tale* is also presented primarily as a parody of forms, although its plot is steadier and more engrossing than those of either *Thopas* or *Melibee*. Chapter 2 describes my reading of the parody of medieval rhetoric, perhaps specifically Geoffrey of Vinsauf's *Poetria Nova*.[65] The whole tale is parodic when its prior text is seen as Geoffrey's. As with other jokes, the massive playfulness of its unfolding has served as a bribe to listeners on the pilgrimage and ever since.[66]

But there is another and more delicate kind of humor involved in the tale as well. Larry Scanlon notes that the issue most central to a reading of the tale has to thread its way between its obvious stylistic parodies and its insistence (mock-insistence?) on its presentation of a serious doctrinal metanarrative. Kendrick calls this reading "up" for doctrine, "down" for *solas*. Both hermeneutics respond to the tale's irony, since irony involves saying more than and other than what you literally do say. The partisans of satiric reading argue that the tale reaches outside the discursive realm to target the pretensions of court and pulpit, which from time to time it certainly does. If the Summoner's friar exemplifies uncommitted preaching by calling up old stories without creating usable doctrine from them, so does Chantecleer. His succession of *exempla* recall the *Gesta Romanorum,* the *Summa praedicantium,* and other story collections for preachers. Further, the *Summa* compiled by John Bromyard actually contains one of the analogues Chaucer may actually have used as he wrote the overarching fable of the *Nun's Priest's Tale.* This is a moderately serious point and few would argue with it. The Parson's objections to including "fables and swich wrecchednesse" (X.34) in sermons underlines it. But there are actually two levels of pulpit parody here: the Priest presents a (mock) sermon that contrasts the simple virtues of the widow's style with the pride and ornament of Chantecleer's "realm," and the rooster offers sermon-like proofs for the predictive power of dreams. One aspect of tale's humor is that the Priest's frame is eclipsed by Chantecleer's.

An avowedly satiric reading the tone of the tale involves looking past its entertaining surface to anchor the rooster to his role as priest against the fox as friar; the tale then appears as a consistent "pattern of abstract principles which manifest themselves in common abuses of the time, abuses which Chaucer does not represent on the surface at all."[67] The "doctrine ywrite" in this allegory is the meaning of the tale, its kaleidoscopic surface a mere lure to encase the "pattern of abstract principles" that ought to guide faith and morals. In this reading, the tale is funny only until its rigorous essence is intuited. But it seems an odd strategy for purveying doctrine when the structure of the tale resembles, as Helen Cooper puts it, a series of nested Russian dolls, with the result that the doctrine in the tale "is subverted by the insistent fictionality of the text."[68]

Although I do not dispute that the priest-rooster and fox-friar are suggested by the tale, I cannot agree that such an interpretation discloses the "real meaning" or "fruit" of the tale. The formal craftsmanship of the tale suggests that the fruit is more likely to be found, as Muscatine argues, in the "free play" of its many elements, including not one but several allegories. In case this seems like merely taking sides in an old debate between Robertsonians and Muscatinites, let me be clear about the stakes. I agree with much current commentary that this tale has an especially important place in the Canterbury lineup. In aesthetic terms it is the very indeterminacy—the absence of hierarchy among its elements that causes it to overflow the boundaries of conceptual thinking—that characterizes aesthetic judgment. When it is regarded as entirely reducible to *any* of the "moralites" proposed for it, the tale is bereft of its "just out of reach" suggestiveness. If its crafted propensity to prohibit such a reduction is heeded (Scanlon's argument for this propensity is, I think, unanswerable), its aesthetic impressiveness is rooted in its laughter. Whether, as ideas, the "great capaciousness of Chaucer's humane vision" (Muscatine) trumps doctrinal principles presented obliquely (Robertson) is not my concern here. I am rather locating the humor of the *Nun's Priest's Tale* in the realm of the "free employment of imagination" which involves "such a multiplicity of partial representations...that no expression indicating a definite concept can be found for it," as Kant says about beauty in general.[69] Each of the elements of the tale is funny in itself and parodically calls up a range of genres and tropes, and the humor of the whole is that no one concept organizes the others.

The Wife of Bath

There are two other parodies of preaching among the tales: the *Wife of Bath's Prologue* and the *Pardoner's Prologue* and *Tale*. The mock-sermon the Pardoner offers as an example of what he tells the "lewed peple" lies, of course, in the realm of parody, but his portrait, introduction, prologue, and "epilogue" (the lines after VI.905) refer to the social and moral world, introducing an element of the satiric. This satire is radical and unrelenting in that it indicts both the pilgrim Pardoner and the sponsorship of pardons. Not all parody is funny, as Hutcheon has pointed out, and the Pardoner's does not elicit the pilgrim's laughter (except as a nervous, embarrassed response to raw anger in the epilogue). The Wife's sermon-parody, the *sermon joyeux* of her prologue, on the other hand, is thoroughly comic, both as satire of the social aspects of clerical teaching and as parody of familiar "coded texts." Lee Patterson argues that the "Wife of Bath's text, both here [in the Midas story] and elsewhere, solicits both body and mind," and in doing so defines a feminine rhetoric.[70] Many, if not most, accounts of the Wife's contributions to the Canterbury pilgrimage adhere to that logic. Although it is not wrong to attribute this broad "solicitation" to Alisoun's performance, it is my contention that it is neither hers alone nor distinctively "feminine," but a feature of all texts that justify aesthetic attention. Alisoun's *argument* is most certainly noteworthy for its "feminine" as well as "feminist" contentions, but her discourse is merely a heightened version of what all of the pilgrims are doing or trying to do: tell an aesthetically impressive story, one both sensible and intelligible. It is true, too, that one of the points she makes is that knowledges and principles are always embodied, both by their various authors and their audiences (individual bodies and social bodies), but in doing so she makes that claim for both men and women. In fact, she is pointing out how certain clerical interpretations of faith and morals follow from male somatic concerns (III.707–8) and one of her tactics for doing so is to show how she, as receiver of these doctrinal "truths" *feels them*. Carolyn Dinshaw makes this point about the Wife[71] and Antonio Damasio makes it about all knowledge—it is the overarching theme of *The Feeling of What Happens*.

The Wife's performance calls particular attention to sexual feelings. In connection with her *Prologue*, especially, Freud's description of erotic joking applies: it is that which makes its audience think about sex with arousal or embarrassment (*JRU*, p. 97). All the fabliaux do that, of course, but it is noteworthy when a woman is the teller—the other female pilgrims choose stories designed to block this response, as befits their cloistered vocations. The overarching comic effect is its parody of the arts of preaching. Patterson justifiably claims the first part of the Wife's account of herself a *sermon joyeux*, involving a biblical text, its interpretation, and its amplification by means of other scriptural references. Alisoun's form is readily recognizable; but her conclusions contradict common pulpit practice. This is itself a good joke (as well as a brilliant satire of clerical address),[72] but I want to expand the idea of sermon-parody beyond the *sermon joyeux* tradition and its association with women. The Wife's whole performance—*Prologue* and *Tale*—signals parody of the *ars predicantium*.

The initial sermon-like move is Alisoun's theme "wo that is in mariage" (III.3) tied to the interpretation of I Corinthians 7.28: "such [as marry] shall have trouble in the flesh." The troubles to which Alisoun subjects her husbands are unlikely to have been what St. Paul was referring to, but it is not self-evident that she is entirely wrong to insist on the slippage in his reasoning, as Lawrence Besserman has pointed out.[73] Her explications of that text and the biblical citations she brings in to support her claims (including the signifying absence of a biblical commandment to remain virgin) are funny precisely as they mimic pulpit exegesis without coming to its usual conclusions. Like other preachers, she turns to a second authority, the book of nature, which also encodes God's plan. There she reads the design of male and female bodies as his strategy for continuing the human race, and holds he did not and would not contradict himself by commanding that their use be forbidden (115–34).

Alisoun speaks for the text of both Bible and natural world and against the "spiritual" gloss,[74] just as the Wyclifittes (probably suspect, but not heretical when this was written) were doing. Like other public speakers, she must establish her distinctive ethos. Her pronouncement, "Divers scoles maken perfyt clerkes" (44b) insists on her authority in the domain of marriage and her contention with men who "devyne and glosen up and down" suggests familiarity with clerical interpretive strategies as well. Since her own experience is involved in her texts, she gives an unusually full account of it. It is a life lived in the shadow of these pulpit glosses, and she is like the "subject-who-remembers" in Mary Carruthers's account of Heloise taking the veil (above, chapter 3). Alisoun's oscillation between festivity and complaint brings to mind Kierkegaard's pronouncement that mature comedy includes pathos.[75] If hers is the "joly body" offering to tell a tale, it is this fullness of affect and thought that is suggested.

Alisoun's next move is to expand on her text through anecdote, in her case autobiographical anecdote, befitting the embodied nature of her knowledge. The three old husbands are handed out "trouble in the flesh" in several overlapping senses. They are tormented sexually by being "thral" to both her denials, until they have ceded her some "raunson" (III.410), and her excessive demands on their virility (202). Embedded in this larger sermon are two self-contained stories, the first a sermon allegedly *preached*—the word is used (366)—by her old husbands, the second a lucid dream-image that she herself allegorizes in a preacherly manner. The sermon is a parody of a pulpit adaptation based on Jerome and Theophrastus (described by G. R. Owst),[76] so the Wife's parody nests within it a fourteenth-century sermon, which refers to a fourth-century treatise, which refers to biblical doctrine. And then, as if that nesting were not deep enough, Alisoun admits that the husbands in question did not actually preach these sermons—she made them up. The Wife claims wit (426), and this is wit indeed, but apparently the old husbands could not disclaim such common medieval misogyny and could not be sure what they had said when drunk. Later she echoes this husband-preacher theme by turning their supposed preaching to her about Job's patience against them, arguing that if patience is good and men are the more reasonable sex, they ought to patiently let her win domestic quarrels (436–42). Her prologue-sermon parodies "real-world" sermons and simultaneously those she has produced herself by figuring her old husbands as preachers. This is a deep game, purposive without coming to rest in a concept.

The second embedded sermon ploy is her hermeneutic approach to her dream. Here the parodic target is even more clearly the gloss. The dream-image of Alisoun herself in a blood-drenched bed, killed by Jankyn, certainly needs a gloss to make it seductive, and the Wife, as always, has something ready. The blood is gold, and while there may be traditional precedents to call on, this tack also attracts attention to its outrageousness. Lollard attacks on glossing soberly referred to its denial of the plain meanings of scripture,[77] but here such denial is outright manipulation producing humor. Then the phrase "And al was fals" (III.582) is repeated verbatim from 382—once again she made everything up, dream and interpretation alike. This tactic figured in her seduction of her fifth husband.

Getting Jankyn, she got a preacher with some of her own gifts: storytelling ability, discursive stamina, and readiness to offer moral interpretation of unlikely materials. She has met her match, in both pulpit and domestic "wits." But her evenly matched struggle with her fifth is also the culmination of the long anecdote that forms the part of her sermon contained in her *Prologue*. Its major point is finally disclosed: when female mastery is acknowledged, it can be voluntarily relinquished to produce Edenic accord. Alisoun and Jankyn beat each other up, but neither is beaten into submission. Instead Alisoun's imagination threads its way through the tangle of patriarchal antifeminism and the personal responses to it she confronts in her *Prologue* to arrive at a parodic sermon conclusion based on a tempestuous rereading of both authority and experience by both husband and wife. Whether we believe that the pilgrim Wife experiences this Eden or not, the storyteller Wife yearns for and creates it verbally.[78]

Her sermon, as I am reading it, however, is not over. Like the Pardoner, she has a wonderful *exemplum* still to supply. Her *Tale* is that story, and, again like the Pardoner's, it is a perfect exemplification of her "moral." (Considered apart from the sermon shape of the *Prologue,* I discussed it in Chapter 2 as folkloric romance, but the reframing I want to do now enables seeing the Wittgensteinian duck as a rabbit.) As the finale of her sermon, the tale restates the long history of Wife's own psychic story, but in such a mode that it does not *seem* continuous until its entire shape is revealed as the final curtain is "cast up" (III.1249). There is a sermon within this part of the sermon too, but this time the hag's "pillow-lecture" is given authority within the tale, in contrast with the alleged sermons of the old husbands. Both the harshness and loopholes in patriarchal domination and cause-and-effect rationality are displaced and mirrored by the Arthurian setting and hints of magic, but in no literal way. The end is therefore truly surprising, both as the resolution of this fanciful tale and as the allegory of concord between contending wills. The sudden aesthetic thrill of finding that none of the portentous consequences predicted by these events actually occur bathes us readers in bliss, just as it does the knight. The further thrill is that of understanding, suddenly, that the "same" story has been told twice. The "realistic" mode of the *Prologue* and the allegorical mode of the *Tale* arrive at the same festive, utopian conclusion. This insight is not exactly funny, though it does produce comic release from dilemma and the sudden greeting of aesthetic satisfaction. It is parodic, but the overall sermon the Wife preaches does not denigrate scripture, biblical interpretation, or even preaching—it "refreshes" them.[79]

Turn the lens of attention once more and the Wife's performance can be seen as a festive enactment at which laughter is an expression of *joy*, in

Langer's sense, "the crest of a wave of felt vitality."[80] Seen as embodying this vitality, the Wife's performance contributes, like the Franklin's, to medieval structures of comic feeling that affirm both biological vitality and civilized respect for persons and promises. These tales seem forerunners to Shakespeare's festive comedies, "donative," as Ezra Pound calls texts that signal future understandings—in this case hopes for a fit between civilized human desire and the chaotic world. These are quite different from the comic rhythms of the fabliaux, where Bergson's claim that laughter cannot be just and should not be kindhearted generally applies (L, p. 188). But they return attention to the exuberance of the opening of the *General Prologue* and its stress on the promises of spring.

CHAPTER 7

IMAGINING COMMUNITY

epic is the story of the community.

Georg Lukács

The truth of our condition is that the analogical tie that makes every man my brother is accessible to us only through a certain number of imaginative practices.

Paul Ricoeur

Chaucer's handling of the formal elements of genre, characterization, and humor have been explored in previous chapters, frequently in terms of Wittgenstein's understanding of language as game, a game deeply embedded in social lifeworlds: "To imagine a language is to imagine a life-form."[1] This orientation toward language seems particularly relevant to Chaucer's work as it concerns community. In treating the various features of his aesthetics so far, I have argued for its generous inclusiveness (both realism and allegory, both personhood and typology, both fabliau and parody). Chaucer seems willing to play all the games going, as well as some he invents. This chapter attempts to address the broadest effects of that Chaucerian inclusiveness, the language game that surrounds those within it—the creation of an image of English community. As Wittgenstein asserts later in the *Philosophical Investigations*, "The game, one would like to say, has not only rules but also a point" (#564). This chapter is an inquiry into the narrative architecture of the *Canterbury Tales* that brings these *sondry folk* and their stories together—collectively as a pilgrimage and individually as competitors in the storytelling contest—into a coherent community without reducing their shared life to a thesis about Englishness. Chaucer is like the builder with a "hous to founde," sending out his "hertes line" in order to "caste his werk ful wisely."[2]

For centuries, the Canterbury pilgrims have been thought of as making up an imagined community. The textual panorama of these nine and twenty traveling together in a "myrie compaignye" with the common destination of the Becket shrine, their guide and their storytelling project freely chosen, calls up an image of community almost inevitably. Benedict Anderson's thesis in *Imagined Communities*—that the nation is an imagined, but bounded, political community—seems nicely suited to probing the Canterbury fiction.[3] By pointing out that an imagined entity like the nation can elicit the sacrifice of life on a large scale, Anderson acknowledges the importance of imagination and elevates its status in managing socially symbolic acts. His work has been used with good effect in discussions of literature with an eye to ideological analysis, but imagination is an even more important term in thinking about aesthetic matters. Although Chaucer's career lies well before the full establishment of the kind of nationhood Anderson describes, his is the authorial figure that later generations have associated with the beginnings of a specifically English sensibility. This association is all the more arresting when we consider how many of Chaucer's productions were in fact translations from Latin, Italian, or French "originals." This chapter investigates two related concerns: the extent to which the *Canterbury Tales* is justifiably credited with figuring a coherent (aesthetically graspable) emergent English community, and the extent to which that imagined community (since it is a crafted entity) can be judged beautiful.

In one sense, of course, the *Canterbury Tales* raises issues entirely different from those of Anderson's assertion, since the members of this community are themselves imagined, first by Chaucer himself and then by each of his interpreters, rather than by the apparently simultaneous recognition of communion living "in the minds of each" member of a nation even though they do not know one another (*IC*, p. 15). One might say that the community the pilgrims form is *only* an *imaginary* one—nobody will fight a war for it. But then again, people who do fight wars have to encounter images of those of their fellows, most of whom they have not met, and those images must resonate with their sense of those they have met in order for a community to form. Without erasing the difference between Chaucer's fiction of community and Anderson's posited political community, we might consider Richard Helgerson's comment: "We think more easily of people as agents and of the things they make or imagine as structures. But people themselves, whether individually or in groups, are made and imagined. Their identity—*our* identity—is a structure, a cultural construct."[4] Paul Ricoeur argues that the "social imaginary" is "the free play of possibilities in a state of noninvolvement with respect to the world of perception or of action," but yet available to be "put to cognitive use by a given community."[5] This formulation is strongly reminiscent of Kant's "purposiveness without purpose," because their conceptually unanchored state allows them an aesthetic force that binds loyalties and consolidates structures of feeling.

The role of art in the social imaginary has long been recognized as inspirational in forming new communities; shared art can characterize and unify a people. Aquinas regarded beauty as a cause of human community, and it is a persistent Kantian subtext, which receives its full elaboration in Matthew Arnold's *Culture and Anarchy*. It is, of course, this unity-producing feature of aesthetic power that ideology critique highlights in its suspicion of beauty. Discussion of this role for aesthetic force stretches from Plato to Terry Eagleton. Plato's attack on the poets (even Homer) acknowledges their power to produce a pervasive (or, alternatively, a confused) social imaginary; it is for that reason that poetry should not be allowed to arouse mental states unassimilable to the philosopher-king's fully conceptual plan for the republic. It would be particularly dangerous for different versions of ethical probity to be disseminated through art. Whatever is allowed to take hold of social imagination must be unrivalled and consonant with a morality useful to the state.[6] Eagleton fears that this very thing has already happened in bourgeois modernity: the unifying force of the aesthetic binds subjects by producing a hegemony that seems to come from within each of them, unobtrusively and without resorting to open coercion.[7] Both Plato and Eagleton give this matter too little nuance. Whether such a false consciousness issues from art or not will depend on how imagination and reality testing are put in touch with one another. I return now to Ricoeur's description of the poles from which imagination can operate: without critical consciousness, the image is "confused with the real, taken for the real," but with critical distance, imagination (and the art that arouses it) can lead to "a critique of the real."[8]

The variousness of the pilgrims and their stories in *Canterbury Tales* speaks to both Plato's suspicions and Eagleton's. Each tale is given an English slant, if only by being voiced by a teller firmly located in English society. The hearty, real-world tone of the frames, the broad range of social positioning for the pilgrims, and the alternation between highly serious *sentence* and playful *solas* exhibit its inclusiveness.[9] Attending to the *Canterbury Tales* as an epic, in Lukacs's sense, "the story of the community" brings into focus what an open-ended fiction it is, how stubbornly its purposiveness refuses reduction to a hegemonic, conceptualizable social purpose.[10] Everyone competes, and we suppose they all speculate about it, but no one knows who ought to win the storytelling contest. It is not even perfectly clear which of the pilgrims is on "the righte wey of Jerusalem celestial."

Anderson's definition of imagining involves bringing to mind something previously in existence, though differently experienced, recognizing society in a new aspect, rather than inventing the nation ex nihilo. This social imaginary is constructed from cultural memories shared by the group as well as from day-to-day experience. His formulation "imagined communities" is relevant here for two reasons. The first is that it seems to me particularly close to Chaucer's *resoun ymaginatyf*, in considering mental representations "nat present" together with beliefs and actions in the "real world."[11] This passage suggests that Chaucer's sense of imagination links memory and aspect recognition, and in terms of community, cultural memory and personal recollection are mutually implicated to disclose aspect.

The Knight describes Theseus's temple of Mars, presumably to enhance chivalry by locating it an honored antiquity, but the grisly personal memories of this veteran fighter cannot be edited out in favor of his conceptual project. The result is a problem of aspect recognition in which warfare may be seen as "pleyn bataille" or the babe in his cradle eaten by a sow. The *Wife of Bath's Prologue* tracks memory traces of a different kind. Within her account of her early marriages, three substantial interpolations from pulpit discourse appear: the sermon from Jerome's letter (III.248–302), the dream about Jankyn and its interpretation (575–84), and the stories from the book of wicked wives (669–787). These are "memories" from her specific experience of a common religious culture: "her" Jerome was preached from English pulpits, her dream was based on allegorical sermon styles, and the stories of wives were virtually everywhere in the preaching tradition (as well as in her third husband's book), and her discourse meshes them with her personal life history. The lord in the *Summoner's Tale* refuses to consign the division of the fart to the aspect of a coarse insult (as the Friar asks), taking it instead as an interesting mathematical problem. These are only three of the many instances in which matters of public import—chivalry, preaching, and scholarly dispute—are imagined in terms of memory and aspect. Although they are presented through particular (even idiosyncratic) characters, they are addressed to pilgrims and audiences of the *Tales* as matters of communal interest.

The second reason for Anderson's relevance is that Chaucer is always (and rightly) considered a poet of the social order. The hermeneutic/aesthetic circle, which posits that fore-conceptions are continually confirmed or modified as a text is interpreted and enjoyed, forms a bridge between Chaucer's social world and the world he created for his readers to imagine. I think that Chaucer depicted a specifically English community in the *Canterbury Tales*, that he was able to do so because such a community was, in some measure, already in existence, and that his image gestures toward a later, more obvious nationhood. In this matter, as in so many others, Chaucer appears as a "donative" author, in Ezra Pound's terms, or an enabler of emergent structures of feeling, in Raymond Williams's.

In both *Troilus and Criseyde* and the *Canterbury Tales,* Chaucer connects medieval notions of imagination with the public realm. Imagination stores sense impressions from life, receives them from cultural memory, art, or supernatural agents through dreams, and creates them from ideas through "resoun ymaginatyf." Such pictures have consequences—Arcite's return to Athens, John the carpenter's lashing himself to the ceiling in a kneading tub—that may prove either positive or negative. But before they influence the real world in social ways, "become real," one might say, as Anderson does,[12] they may be enjoyed as meditations on community. Their potentiality for creating new structures of feeling is derived in large measure from their aesthetic force. *Troilus and Criseyde* unfolds in a walled and besieged city, which provides a sharp contrast with the openness and movement of the temporary community of the *Canterbury Tales.* Since Troy is clearly marked for doom and its people are seriously at odds with one another, the focus of the poem on treasons—personal and political—are part of its tragic impact.[13] I will take up the imagined community of the *Canterbury Tales* in another key: in terms of the linguistic and religious affiliations which signal its Englishness, and in terms of citizenship (rather than subjecthood) underwritten by a shift from consciousness of time as cyclic and typological to time as linear and "empty," which enables national communities in Anderson's analysis.

Textual Communities: "The Kingdome of Oure Owne Language"

Chaucer's people form a motley and contentious crew, but seem consistently engaged with each other and with the group. They travel together as the result of a unanimous ("oon assent" [I.777]) decision ("conseil" [I.784]) indicated by the raising of hands, and they elect Harry Bailly as guide and governor of their journey, and as judge and reporter of the tales they will tell on the road (817). These are obvious references to a real-world (albeit festively presented) community. They are assembled on, and competitive over, the distinctive social and economic terrain of late medieval England. To contend this way, they use the varied registers available to Middle English and disclose their various takes on *English* controversies. To present them this way, Chaucer's text both creates images of what is not extant and interprets what is. What integrates the *Canterbury Tales* (what gives it its *integritas* in spite of its possibly remaining unfinished) is its foregrounding of an English community made of words. In order to produce the image of a bounded, coherent community, Chaucer's first resource was the English language, which was both near to hand and elastic enough to allow his remarkable expansions of its powers, both those based on "traditional" English usage and those he introduced from the continent.[14]

Chaucer was a not only a great translator, but a voice in contemporary debates about the competence of English, implicitly through his fictions and explicitly in his Prologue to the *Astrolabe*. Andrew Cole points out how closely Chaucer's vocabulary in this prologue resembles that of the General Prologue to the Wycliffite Bible, in common with others who argued for "vernacular translation."[15] In order to make its appeal available aesthetically, the images of English people traveling to an English shrine can best be told with the necessary *immediacy* in that "mother tongue." Chaucer addressed his audience in terms of the "language of a particular people that make meaning in a unique fashion," as Ruth Evans puts the matter.[16] Christopher Cannon's *The Making of Chaucer's English* interrogates the "myth of origin"—that Chaucer more or less single-handedly made English into a literary language—and finds it wanting; what he calls "revolutionary" is the movement within poetic passages from practices shared with earlier English writers to the inclusion of "Franco-Latin forms."[17] Seth Lerer concludes that Chaucer's poetry made use of a rich and varied international legacy in his "unique synthesis of styles."[18] What this suggests is that Chaucer saw his readers *as* in some distinctive ways English, but also as capable of responding to an augmented language, enriched by continental innovations in linguistic and generic patterns.

Anderson asserts that a condition of possibility for nationalism arises with the waning of the idea that "a particular script-language offered privileged access to ontological truth, precisely because it was an inseparable part of that truth" (*IC*, p. 40). As long as the linguistically adept of the Christian West were bound together in a transnational Latinate conversation, they were slow to form ties with their geographical neighbors across class lines. In this matter Chaucer's work registers a particularly strong element in the loosening of the prestige of Latin, but that prestige was "regularly contested by other languages of real or putative authority," as Christopher Baswell puts it.[19] The substitution of the international script-language Latin by English took centuries and was by no means complete when Edmund Spenser wrote to Gabriel Harvey in 1580, arguing for "the kingdome of oure owne Language." The authoritative presence of Latin in English culture long after Chaucer is exemplified by the trials of English Bible translators like Tyndale, the dearth of English books in the library at Oxford in 1600 (only 60 of the 60,000 titles), as well as the stipulation that even Queen Elizabeth could not address the faculty of Cambridge in English (she delivered a graceful and well-received address in Latin). The "kingdome of oure owne Language" is a resonant phrase, fusing the sense of entitlement to a national identity with the right to be heard in one's vernacular. Helgerson asserts that it "govern[s] the very linguistic system, and perhaps more generally the whole cultural system, by which people's identity and consciousness were constituted."[20] The capacity of the English vernacular to transmit sacred truths insisted on during the Reformation were already being championed within Chaucer's intellectual horizon, largely by Wycliffite positions that prefigured early modern debates over the authority of an English Bible.[21]

Anderson asserts that the transhistorical, transterritorial sodalities are communities of signs, not spoken language, signs which were regarded as "emanations of reality, not randomly fabricated representations of it," and notes that this view of language itself—"the non-arbitrariness of the sign"—is distinctly unmodern (*IC*, p. 21). But in the Christian West, this posited nonarbitrariness was a political rather than a philosophical or theological construct even in the early Middle Ages, since Latin was the original language of neither the Old nor the New Testament. Jerome's Latin Bible was no doubt a convenience for stabilizing the still unfixed canon and phrasing of sacred text for far-flung Christian congregations, but it could not be logically defended as the uniquely delivered Word.[22] It was, nonetheless, the institutionally sanctioned language, the language that made the sacraments efficacious, the one in which knowing his neck-verse could save a man from hanging.

Most English parish priests knew only enough Latin to announce their membership in that community, but not enough to participate in its controversies. Latin was not so much the actual currency of religious teaching[23] as the sign of connection with the long-standing community of believers, dead and living. Lollards were not the only proponents of vernacular presentations of devotional and doctrinal matters, although they are the best remembered, especially for their project for making Scripture "Common and open to laymen and women who are able to read," expressed in the preface to the "Lollard Bible." In 1362, Parliament ordained that all pleas "at the barre schulde be in Englisch tunge, and in no othir tunge," according to Capgrave's chronicle of 1464 (*MED*). More locally, there was the proliferation of vernacular *escrowez* or broadsides posted for public consumption which, as Steven Justice asserts in *Writing and Rebellion*, "embodied a claim as well as a message: merely by existing, it asserted, tendentiously or not, that those who read only English—or even could have only English read to them—had a stake in the intellectual and political life of church and realm."[24] Richard Firth Green's detailed account of the obligations of contracts, promises, and oaths suggests a densely figured cultural and legal system of traditional, local linguistic understandings.[25] Caroline Barron has discovered many varieties of reading experience available in the late medieval London—"tables" and bills in churches, guildhalls, and outdoors—which indicate "textual communities" usually thought to have developed much later.[26] Recent estimates of lay literacy in English suggest that as many as 50 percent of adult males may have been able to read the mother tongue and there must have been literate females as well, since they are mentioned as readers of an English Bible.

Along with his knowledge of a public literate in the vernacular, Chaucer was aware as well of the unstandardized state of English dialectal speech: "for ther is so gret diversite / In Englissh and in writyng of oure tonge, / So prey I God that non myswrite the [the 'litel book'], / Ne the mysmetre for defaute of tonge" (*Troilus and Criseyde* [V.1792–96]). Varied as its pronunciation and written forms might be, it is "oure tonge." In spite of this felt limitation, Chaucer gambles on the expressive potentialities of English in many registers, often explicitly foregrounding the pilgrims' linguistic modes and habits. In the *Reeve's Tale,* a northern dialect is represented, and not as a sign of *lewedness,* by the better educated (and in the end, cannier) *clerkes,* Aleyn and John. The narrator fears the "gentles" may object to the Miller's coarse language (I.3169), Harry Bailly is concerned that the Clerk should speak intelligibly, without the terms, colors, and figures of the high style (IV.15–20), and the Franklin apologizes for his "rude" speech (V.718), a disarming use of the modesty topos, since so much of what he says *is* learned and even eloquent. Paul Strohm has concluded that Chaucer's poetry presupposes readers capable of grasping his varied narrative effects, "an audience of some literary sophistication."[27]

Anderson nicely catches the paradox of the hold on imagination exerted by the transterritorial sodalities: "Christendom assumed its universal form through a myriad of specificities and particularities: this relief, that window, this sermon, that tale, this morality play, that relic" (*IC*, p. 29). Yet those very specificities, since they incorporate an element of the local, might under the right conditions mobilize imaginative loyalties *to* the local as well as to the transcontinental communion of the faithful, like Chaucer's Parson. In other words, I find Anderson's sharp distinction between an identity imagined as commitment to Christianity (thought of as Latin Christianity) and an early form of nationality too stark. I am positing a Chaucerian text that calls on both simultaneously.

Certain textual gestures look like appeals to national identity. For example, the unscrupulous Pardoner is said to be "of" Rounceval, near Charing Cross, which is a daughter house of Roncesvalles in Navarre; his chicanery over the papal bulls is directly associated with Rome. The archdeacon's courts, which come off so badly in the Summoner's portrait and the *Friar's Tale*, are opposed in part because they were managed by non-English appointees.

Some textual details support inferences about Chaucer's attitudes toward the competing claims of Latin and English for authoritative teaching, an issue closely entwined with religious controversy in Chaucer's immediate circle. The *General Prologue's* description of the Parson, for instance, calls him "lerned" (I.480), doubtless in the technical sense of "literate in Latin." This places him as part of the "bi-lingual intelligentsia mediated between heaven and earth," in Anderson's phrase (*IC*, pp. 22–23), typical of the prenational social formation. But he appears to make use of the plainest English possible in both the *General Prologue* (I.499–504) and his tale, and he refuses to supplement his income by reciting Latin prayers at Saint Paul's in London. He does have the power of excommunication, but uses it sparingly, relying instead on setting an ethical example and "snybbing" his parishioners sharply in English. This generally idealized figure is presented as both a performer of efficacious sacraments and an instructor in the ethics of daily life, and his aura is notably English.

His vernacularity is in contrast to the Friar's Latinity. The Friar also exercises the power of confession and is slyly accused of misusing it, as well as his pleasant *In principio*, to bilk poor widows out of their farthings. Chantecleer's Latin is also false dealing, this time a mistranslation that achieves the double effect of impressing Pertelote with his command of a tongue reserved for men and flattering her female vanity by attributing "joye" and "blis" to her influence instead of *confusio*. The Summoner knows a bit of Latin too—he speaks nothing but Latin in his cups—using it occupationally for extortion, like the summoner depicted in the *Friar's Tale*.[28] The Pardoner's bulls are not likely to be authentically papal (since some are credited to the patriarchs!), but how will the *lewed* people recognize this, if the proofs are in Latin? These instances suggest that what Chaucer saw when he looked at his cultural world was clerical familiarity with Latin, but not necessarily as the sole repository of "emanations of reality."

The Prioress tells a tale about a boy just beginning his studies, who praises the Virgin by singing a song he has learned by heart and understands only as homage to Mary, "Noght wiste he what this Latyn was to seye" (VII.523). His failure to understand the text he sings is, of course, immediately attributable to his being such a young scholar, but, as Eamon Duffy has written,

> In a culture where the whole liturgy was celebrated in Latin most lay people would pick up a wide range of phrases and tags, with a depth of understanding perhaps not more profound than Chaucer's Summoner's grasp of legal Latin.[29]

The boy's fascination with Mary arises in the first place from his seeing her image as a statue. Once again, there is an immediate *English* controversy stirred up by Wycliffites over the efficacy of images and the value of lay literacy and an English Bible. The boy's piety and claim to martyrdom when the Jews, offended by his song, cut his throat, is both aroused and expressed by works of art, imagination touched by sculpture and song, rather than by ethical or intellectual appeals. It is true that dominant discourse in the Middle Ages accorded "learning by heart" a higher status than moderns do, stressing the emotional tagging of the memory-image, as well as its rational content, often associating it with "desire and fear, pleasure or discomfort." Such personal storing away of learning was regarded as "morally virtuous in itself," as Carruthers puts it,[30] certainly by the Prioress, who expresses herself in her prologue in a similar rehearsal of poetry learned by heart. She places herself in the medieval mainstream by joining those who held that the power of scripture, the liturgy, and even the primers were, as Duffy puts it, "full of 'vertue' which 'availed' by God's grace, independently of the reader's or hearer's comprehension." As late as the motto on Henry VIII's coins, Mary was imagined as preferring certain phrasings of praise, "this prayer shewed our lady to a devoute persone, sayenge that this golden prayer is the most swetest and accepablest to me."[31] This sort of appeal to religious imagination is replicated in the fact that the boy's memorized Latin is almost completely opaque to him beyond its association with the image of Mary.

Both the Prioress's self-presentation and her presentation of the boy suggest the world of the unquestioning faithful, those who grasp spiritual themes through precisely worded prayers and songs and affecting statues—Anderson's "myriad of specificities and particularities" (*IC*, p. 29). This is the world of most lay piety, as Duffy sees the matter, and would have continued to be had it not been for the divisiveness of the Lollards and later the rapaciousness of the Reformers. The *General Prologue* suggests, however, the shortcomings of a markedly nonintellectual Prioress whose ethical sense conflates manners with morality and squeamishness with compassion. Her inert piety contrasts with the vigorous struggles to understand spiritual and ethical ideas in characterizations and performances like those of the Clerk, Parson, Knight, Franklin, and even the Pardoner and the Wife. These gestures can be read as undermining a straightforward sponsorship of the tale and its teller's "take" on her story. They suggest that the Prioress represents a well populated circle of nuns whose appeal to pathos is still widely felt by lay listeners (on the pilgrimage, "Whan seyd was al this miracle, every man / As sober was that wonder was to se" [691–92]), but not immune from a subtle, immanent critique offered through aesthetic strategies that do not come to rest in concepts.

Chaucer's imagined *hous* is intricately various, with wings and gables in many styles strongly marked by its investment in English language and discourse. The community I am positing among the pilgrims is not one of unanimous agreement, but one that shares distinctive controversies over belief as well as distinctive beliefs. If it can be granted that Chaucer evokes the image of an English community, the first claim on aesthetic attention has been met, that is, the pilgrim's community is seen as foregrounded, a coherent entity. The *General Prologue* introduces that fore-conception, the links reinforce it, and some of the tales specify it. But there is, in addition, an element of surprise in Chaucer's presentation of his imagined community, one that is best considered in terms of *claritas*. Luminous details in several of the pilgrim's stories light up an aspect of this journey that suggests a potential for citizenship for his characters.

Time and the Citizen: The "Shock of the Possible"

I have argued that Chaucer's commitment to the English language leads him to depict the pilgrims' linguistic modes and habits explicitly, to give them very specific locations in the discursive systems of the late fourteenth century. Although estates satire is called upon in the *General Prologue*, it does not interfere with the creation of characters who in the course of the fiction grow larger, more complex, than their social roles require and demand attention in a variety of intricate ways. They are presented as speaking as they are inclined to by a complicated network of affiliations like constitution (Martian and Venusian for the Wife, sanguine for the Franklin), gender, estate, age, religious profession, and the like. I speculate that Chaucer presented them this way because he imagined—both in the sense of creating mental pictures and in the sense of reading the world he saw—an emergent community of citizens. The idea of citizenship had a certain currency in the fourteenth century; the *OED* connects it with living in a city and with being "an enfranchised inhabitant of a country." The legal designation "free of the city," which gave city dwellers certain mercantile rights and governmental participation, dates from the early part of the century.[32] *Citizen* was also used more broadly to indicate enfranchisement in an existing or imagined polity like the community of the godly. The rising rates of vernacular literacy, the use by villagers themselves of charters and documents, the fact that communication and record keeping were increasingly set down in English, the quick response to the Wycliffite Bible and the teaching of the "poor priests," and of course the Revolt itself may have been among the signs Chaucer was interpreting. These signs are not to be taken as indications that fourteenth-century society generally understood itself as a nation of citizens; it is likely that Chaucer's fiction produced, in its milieu, "the shock of the possible," in Paul Ricoeur's striking phrase.[33]

Important as the characterization of Chaucer's pilgrims is, another, subtler feature of Anderson's preconditions for the emergence of the nation is also relevant: the modern apprehension of time. Where typology apprehends events in the shape of a recurring motif in salvation history, modernity sees a causal chain, sequential and temporally continuous. It must be acknowledged that much in the English Middle Ages conforms to Anderson's description of prenational typology; markers of a premodern apprehension of time, resembling Erich Auerbach's "omnitemporal" occurrence "which has always been, and will be fulfilled in the future" abounds in the medieval record.[34] Saints and visionaries saw the Holy Family in their own houses; Margery Kempe was offered soup by the Virgin. Even Wyclif, modern in many ways, writes as if the biblical term anti-Christ specifically referred literally to the fourteenth-century popes, and Wycliffite sermons refer to the friars of his own day as "oure pharisees" or "modern pharisees." The continued usefulness of *exempla* in the pulpit suggests an appetite for the form "in spite of the contradiction between its mode as fiction and its role as purveyor of eternal truths," as Peter Haidu puts it.[35] In this mode, no Frederic Jameson was saying, "Always historicize"—instead Berthold Brecht, "It always happens that way."

Anderson contrasts typological logic with the modern conception of the "homogeneous, empty" time that finds "a precise analogue of the idea of a nation," in which a citizen does not know what his countrymen are up to at any given time, yet "has complete confidence in their steady, anonymous, simultaneous activity" (*IC*, p. 31). The nation takes for granted the logic of "a complex gloss on the word 'meanwhile'" (p. 31). Anderson links this secular conception of time with print culture as a contributing cause for the establishment of the modern state and likens imagining the nation to following the plot of a realistic novel. Perhaps I am reversing the force of his simile in thinking of the *Canterbury Tales* as in this matter a precursor of the realistic novel, which suggests the emergence of a precursor to the English nation.

Long before print, other predisposing causes were in motion. Two of those causes bear particularly on the design of the *Canterbury Tales*. The first is embedded in Western Christianity. From the earliest meditations on it, theological time is described both as an island in the vast sea of eternity—consider Bede's beautiful image of the sparrow who flies into the meeting hall, as into time, from the undelineated reaches outside[36]—and as the mundane arena in which a person's faith and conduct must be tested. Jacques Le Goff puts it thus: "the Christian must simultaneously renounce the world, which is only his transitory resting place, and opt for the world, accept it, and transform it, since it is the workplace of the present history of salvation."[37] In Le Goff's analysis, the secularization of time, indicated by clocks that measured and rang out hours, was motivated by mercantile and urban concerns and marked the transition from the agrarian "natural" day to the closely measured time of the urban working day. And it began earlier than Anderson's shift toward the modern nation, its pressures being felt from the end of the thirteenth century. From this point of view, fourteenth-century Christians were taught by their faith *and* by their economic lives, especially in cities, to think of time as both cosmic recurrence and linear sequence.

The second pressure comes from the structures of narrative itself. As Ricoeur says, emplotment draws "a configuration out of simple succession,"[38] which must presume succession and "meanwhile" understandings of time in the first place. The strongest version of the typological attitude needs no precise succession: Wyclif's rendering of John 8.58 is, "Before Abraham was, I am." Incidents are isolated and repeated in an undifferentiated history: Moses' vision of the unburnt burning bush is restated in the unviolated virginity of Mary. But narrative as Aristotle describes it, draws events toward "the linear representation of time," both because it causes readers to wonder what is coming next and because, in retrospect, it allows its episodes to be seen as leading toward this particular ending, suggesting that time can be read either forward or backward toward its "thought."[39] This narrative feature serves a text's *integritas*, and yet allows for historical awareness.

Even more directly relevant to the *Canterbury Tales* is Ricoeur's comment that "[p]eregrination and narration are grounded in time's approximations of eternity, which, far from abolishing their difference, never stops contributing to it."[40] A pilgrimage is a traditional typological figure, but each separate pilgrimage and each stage in it is an episode enacted sequentially. Chaucer's pilgrims are wandering through time, some perhaps toward "Jerusalem celestial," but the "wey" they must take is measured in incidents, hours, and days that unfold in familiar places in England and occupy mundane, measurable time—the Friar remarks about the "long preamble" of the Wife's performance (III.831) and the Knight expresses impatience with the temporal extension of the Monk's store of tragedies (VII.2767–68).

For the pilgrimage frame story and many of the tales, Anderson's modern "complex gloss upon the word 'meanwhile' " is directly apposite. The trip to Canterbury is charted against clock time, Anderson's "empty time," indicated every now and again by the position of the sun (which may be read both as a realistic detail and a nod to the still-agrarian habits of the era). The last tale, though, returns to the "timeless" truths of contrition and penitence. Paul Strohm argues that as Chaucer's career moves from the providential early poems to the *Canterbury Tales,* "his treatment of time and narrative becomes, in a word, progressively more social," marked by more modern time schemes.[41] I think that the individual *Canterbury Tales* are varied in their handling of the temporal, the strongly "exemplary" *Monk's Tale,* for example, at one end of a spectrum, and the strongly "modern," like the *Miller's Tale,* at the other. Other tales exhibit a mixed sense of narrative time within themselves. This internal oscillation of the text and the contrast between one tale and another gestures toward the problem of apprehending narrative time. As with other features of the sign systems at his disposal, Chaucer fashions a storytelling instrument that registers both old and new understandings of the world; in this case the mix tilts toward the "modern," the "meanwhile."

The privilege given to the modern system is fully evident in the frame tale.[42] There, both sequence and the "empty time" of each day's passing are insisted on. The narrator-Chaucer acquaints himself with the other pilgrims at the tavern, describes them, and relates their conversation on the road. The Miller responds to the Knight, the Reeve to the Miller, the Friar to the Wife, in what we would now classify as a "real-time" representation of people's interactions. Many of the tellers make a point of locating their narratives, old or contemporary, in time, as with the Knight's "Whilom, as olde stories tellen us," the Wife's "In th' olde dayes of the Kyng Arthour," the Clerk's elaborate footnotes on the source of his tale, and the Physician's "as telleth Titus Livius." Even the fable setting of the *Nun's Priest's Tale* is located temporally: "For thilke tyme, as I have understonde, / Beestes and briddes koude speke and synge" (VII.2880–81). The Reeve, on the other hand, begins "At Trumpyngtoun, nat fer fro Cantebrigge, / Ther gooth a brook" (I.3921–22), suggesting both a recent time setting and a place that corresponds to the Oxenford of the *Miller's Tale,* further locating his telling of his tale as a response to the pilgrimage conversation. Within the tales, some gestures are writ even larger. The *Clerk's Tale* depends on twelve years worth of meanwhile; the children were being raised as aristocrats by Walter's sister, Countess of Panik, while Griselda was imagining their decomposing bodies back in Lumbardye. That large-scale "meanwhile" is reinforced by a narration that quite self-consciously marks the shifts from one focus to another, in phrases like "But to this markys now retourne we" (IV.597) and "But to Griselde agayne wol I me dresse" (IV.1007).[43] Examples like these suggest that Chaucer's narrative investment in "empty time."

The Franklin's Tale

The Franklin introduces his story in terms of its venerable age and generic type, but his telling assumes a largely modern sense of meanwhile, turning from an account of Arveragus's joyful return with "of the sike Aurelius wol I tell" (V.1100). As events unfold according to a relatively realistic sense of causality, he seems to reach an impasse: his story arrives at a nearly intolerable existential situation for the characters (and perhaps the audience) when Arveragus tells Dorigen to go to the garden to keep her promise. This *gentil* teller is constrained to let on that he knows the ending:

> Paraventure an heep of yow, ywis,
> Wol holden hym a lewed man in this
> That he wol putte his wyf in jupartie.
> Herkneth the tale er ye upon hire crie.
> She may have bettre fortune than yow semeth;
> And whan that ye han herd the tale, deemeth.
> (V.1493–98)

I find this aside by the Franklin-narrator luminous in its revelation of the two aspects of time the narration is simultaneously aware of. Without explicitly claiming providential intervention, the Franklin undermines the open-ended, "real-time" sense of his tale by suddenly invoking expectations for a shapely fable as well. One effect of this passage is that the idealistic, gregarious, bourgeois Franklin, who wants to avoid offending his listeners, is subtly characterized in addition as able to differentiate between competing narrative time schemes. Differing levels of awareness about the modes of presenting time, then, seems to be part of the characterization with which the poet-Chaucer endows the tellers of the *Canterbury Tales*.

The Monk's Tale

Some tales, of course, are not nuanced with the Franklin's attention to time and sequence—the Man of Law's, the Prioress's, the Second Nun's, Chaucer's *Melibee*—seem in one way or another fitted to the allegorical mode with its link to typology.[44] In each of these tales, narrative seems designed as "an historical anecdote employed in a rhetoric of persuasion," an instrument of edification, which is the way Le Goff defines *exempla* in *Medieval Imagination*.[45] The *Monk's Tale* is perhaps the most striking example of unhistoricized storytelling; the Monk resembles the friar in the *Summoner's Tale,* who lines up historical tales at odd angles to his avowed didactic purpose. His scriptural, historical, and modern examples are all attached to the same "moral," seemingly without regard for the telling differences in their patterns of detail. The Monk has no sooner introduced his series of object lessons against trusting Fortune than he has to veer away from it to account for Lucifer, "nat a man" and, therefore, not able to be harmed by Fortune. He credits Cenobia and Julius Caesar, for example, with uncommon moral strengths and nowhere indicates their failing to resist Fortune. He gets sidetracked by Dalida into drawing an entirely different moral from Sampson's story (the *Nun's Priest's Tale* revisits the misapplied *exemplum* in general and this mistrust of women's council in particular). When "omnitemporality" is treated most seriously, no sampling from the whole range of history is needed or proper; the very fact that the Monk is impelled to tell so many stories weighs against him; his failure to please might be stated as a recognition that no two anecdotes will match perfectly with each other or with the timeless lesson they are intended to illustrate, and may involve direct contradiction.

The Pardoner's Tale

The *Pardoner's Tale* would seem the most exemplary tale (perhaps in both the generic and the hortatory modern sense) in the Canterbury collection. The misguided youths who seek Death as if he were a person might have played out their story with only minimally altered details any time, any place (and indeed its *sentence* has been dramatized many times, for example, in films like *The Treasure of Sierra Madre* and, recently, *A Simple Plan*). Two details, though, stress the idea of "meanwhile" and they deeply inflect the plot. First is the precipitating death of the rioters' friend *while* they were drinking and, second, the poisoner's purchase of ratsbane *while* the two conspirators plan his murder. Of all the exempla related in the *Canterbury Tales,* the Pardoner's is the one which most clearly participates in the various time frames Le Goff discusses: the "segment of narrative time—historical, linear, and divisible" within the fiction, the shape of the whole plot which "drew upon and nourished the time of private memory," and the ultimate, timeless lesson that "pointed toward eternity."[46] Le Goff links this complication in the history of moral teaching to the practice of auricular confession mandated by the Fourth Lateran Council (1215) requiring "introspective self-examination" and memory of a personal sort. A long logic would connect such capacities with citizenship.

Like most successful *exempla,* the Pardoner's offering makes a surprising turn with considerable emotional impact. Unlike Custance's or Cecilia's story or that of the "litel clergeon" of the *Prioress's Tale,* though, pathos is not its mode; the shock of the tale works on an intellectual level. No emphasis is given to any suffering the young men might have experienced as they died, and there are no wicked mothers-in-law or Jews to execrate. What the story enacts is exactly what biblical and Augustinan tenets about the intrinsic connection between the lust for gold and the death of body and soul. Linear time unfolds for the characters in the tale and for the pilgrims as they listen and respond, but the point of the *exemplum* resides in a timeless present. This tale, therefore, seems both deeply medieval and subversively modern. Looking to eternity but also to citizenly responsibility and intellectual acumen, it produces and satisfies a drive toward intelligibility.

The Miller's Tale

In other tales, "meanwhile" is a linchpin in the storyline. The *Miller's Tale* is the most obvious example. Anderson's chart and discussion of a hypothetical novel is precisely relevant to the *Miller's Tale* in concluding that (in novels) "all these acts are performed at the same clocked, calendrical time, but by actors who may be largely unaware of one another" (*IC*, p. 31). Moreover, Chaucer's tale *only works because* Alison, Nicholas, John, and Absolon act in the same time frame largely unaware of each other's plots. That John is generally ignorant of Nicholas's wooing is a stock feature of fabliau plotting, but that he waits for the second flood in his own kneading tub lashed to the ceiling of his own house while Nicholas enjoys his bed raises the ante. Absolon's first serenade crowds the meantime still further. It is, however, the finale that allows the tale to be read as an attempt to push the idea of meantime as far as it will go. Nicholas's cry "Water!" signals the culmination of Absolon's successful plot against him, the disclosure of his adultery with Alison, and the crumbling of John's delusion about the flood. On the grounds of narrative timing, the *Miller's Tale* may be the most modern of the Canterbury tales.

The Knight's Tale

Although in many ways the *Knight's Tale* presents a direct contrast to the *Miller's Tale,* in its management of time the contrast is more nuanced. It is true, of course, that time passes more slowly for Palamon and Arcite and that an epic sense of range over both time and space is enacted in the tale. And it is true that the Knight/teller seems bent on invoking Boethian patience in the face of long time spans, justified by frequent references to *destiny* and *purveiaunce.* The Knight may strive to make an allegory or parable out of his narrative through his commentary, but the deeper logic of the story depends almost as much on "meanwhile" as the Miller's. For example, the *Knight's Tale* turns from the adventures of Arcite in exile to Palamon in prison, basing the *debat* that concludes Part I on the simultaneity of Arcite's freedom and distance from Emily and Palamon's incarceration and nearness to her. The Knight stresses *destiny* and *purveiaunce* in Theseus' turning up during the battle between the cousins, digressing rather heavy-footedly about both external occurrences and internal inclinations as "reuled by the sighte above" (I.1673), but the plot need not explain why "Duc" Theseus might have gone hunting in his own domain. What accounts for this development in the plot is that the cousins have arranged to fight and *simultaneously* the Duc has decided to go hunting. The fateful appeals to deities made by Palamon, Emelye, and Arcite are carefully timed (Palamon's two hours before daybreak, Emelye's at daybreak, and Arcite's shortly after that at Mars' hour). Each of these nearly simultaneous appeals is made in ignorance of the others, laying the groundwork for the outcome of the plot. Even though the teller's every ploy in the *Miller's Tale* suggests his insistence on the intricate play of human agency and those of the *Knight's Tale* teller consistently stress destiny, both of these plots manifest Anderson's "complex gloss on the word 'meanwhile'" (*IC*, p. 31). In the *Knight's Tale* it just takes longer.

The Canon's Yeoman's *Story*

If the *Miller's Tale* presents the most modern handling of time, the Canon's Yeoman is more like a modern citizen than the other pilgrims, especially a citizen under the capitalism just beginning to appear on Chaucer's horizon.[47] Joining the *compaignye* after the pilgrims have traveled together for some time, he provides his own introduction through an autobiographical *Introduction* and *Prologue* as specific as those of the Wife and Pardoner. The Yeoman frees himself of feudal encumbrances through his offense to the Canon, who would not stay to hear *his* mystery disclosed. The freedom gained in this way is both exhilarating, as his telling shows, and tragic, since now he has only his labor to sell, but he has seized the kingdom of his own language:

> Syn that my lord is goon, I wol nat spare;
> Swich thyng as that I knowe, I wol declare.
> (VIII.718–19)

This gesture and stories he tells to declare "swich thyng" constitute a luminous detail revealing Chaucer's sense of time and the citizen. As the Yeoman tells his tale, he is between a medieval and a modern world, masterless and unemployed, but hopeful of joining the pilgrims' community. Although Chaucer's pilgrims are seen in terms of their work—as social role or estate—the Yeoman wields the word *work* differently from the others. The word *work*, in most other cases, belongs to a religious rather than an economic discourse.[48] Particularly striking is its frequent use in the *Second Nun's Tale,* where all ten instances refer to piety, mental and rhetorical labor, not salable, while the fourteen instances in the *Canon's Yeoman's Tale* are nearly all about such physical exertions as are called work under modern conditions. On the grounds of their differing inflection for *work* alone, it would seem evident that the *Second Nun's Tale* speaks to an (idealized) image of social responsibility characteristic of Christian feudalism while *The Canon's Yeoman's Tale* introduces a (non-idealized) vision of modern, proto-capitalist society through the practices of the marginal (literally: "in hernes and in lanes blynde" [VIII.658]) alchemical lab.

Both his account of the lab he worked in (*Prologue*) and his tale of the swindle unfold in "real time." The Yeoman has been working for the Canon for seven years. He explains his usual job in detail: he blows on the fires, measures the ingredients, seals the vessels, conducts the calcinations. Then he offers a brilliant description of the explosion that shows why the desired results never came to pass. The walls of the lab can scarcely contain the violence of the explosion in which everything is lost, and the devil himself seems to be there. The men begin to blame each other for the failure of the experiment: "Somme seyde it was long on the fir makyng; / Somme seyde nay, it was on the blowing—/ Thanne was I fered, for that was myn office" (922–24).[49] The fact that the cause of the explosion cannot be determined adds to the "greet strif" among the workers (931). Afterward the master appears, encouraging them to clean up the mess and prepare for the next try. Hope is once again kindled, but it remains uncertain whether the canon himself believes that the goal will be reached or whether he is merely using up the "thrift" of these men, like the "fend" and tempter the Yeoman sometimes calls him (705–9 and 916–17). This account formally resembles an industrial novel—first the general conditions of work, then a particularly disastrous event, and finally a comment about the workings of the "system." It seems to me a luminous detail that matches the barnyard chase after Chantecleer and the fox: loud and bright, it illuminates the Yeoman's lifeworld thriftily and at the same time suggests an emerging form of life for the larger social order.

The tale itself conforms even more obviously to Anderson's sense of meantime. Like the *Miller's Tale,* the scam depends on independent actors, the alchemist/canon and the priest, carrying on their activities in empty time, the priest, like the carpenter, unaware of what his "benefactor" is up to. Like the Miller's contribution, as well, it ends without a providential or morally conventional turn of phrase. The con-man simply skips town with his ill-gotten gain, which suggests that there is mobility between towns (John the Carpenter has to go on living in Oxenford after his humiliation) and other dupes just as suitable for his enterprise. Such mobility also fits with the on-the-move way the Canon and Yeoman have joined the pilgrims.

Handling time and causality so differently in the different tales, Chaucer creates yet another way in which his community is imagined as consisting of *sondry folk*, differentiated in their relation to the historical scene they inhabit. The language game that situates them in a coherent community "has not only rules but also a point," in Wittgenstein's phrase. In imagining and presenting his *compaignye* as proto-citizens, but framing their presentation with pilgrimage, estates satire, and in some cases typology, Chaucer blunts the "shock of the possible," sneakily allowing his fiction to be seen in traditional terms, and often making good on those terms. In accord with a medieval aesthetic, the variety of the persons may signal verisimilitude, the focus on their connectedness *integritas* and proportionality, many moments in this long poem luminousness, and the logic of the pilgrimage frame an incitement to moral good. For us, Chaucer's sly equivocation in producing a medieval community so seemingly traditional, yet so poised to accept emergent cultural tendencies, produces admiration for the way it overflows constraining concepts. Looking back, we can see that familiar *sensible* details, the "scraps, patches, and rags of daily life," as Homi Bhabha calls them,[50] are being pressed into service as subtly *intelligible* sources of new knowledge and attitudes about a shared community. The pilgrims have told stories about various kinds of subjectivity and exhibited them as they traveled together. They have laughed and wept, raged and made peace without violence or banishment of any of their number. There is a characteristic parsimony in Chaucer's pulling off this trick; his community of pilgrims functions as a religious trope and at the same time a record of the heterogeneity, contention, and good will, citizens in more modern communities ideally exhibit. Beauty, says Kant, is "attended by a feeling of the furtherance of life" (*CJ*, p. 91), including, in this case, the life of the community.

Further aesthetic appeals the *Canterbury Tales* exerts concern its generosity, its inclusiveness, and respect for various "forms of life," even when harshly satiric. Such "capaciousness of regard" is part of Elaine Scarry's definition of aesthetic effects and it belongs to medieval thought as well. Aquinas wrote that whenever creatures find common cause (*unionem*) it is because of beauty (*habent ex virtute pulchri*).[51] Some pilgrims reveal a combination of vividness and ugliness that Bonaventure would have equated with well-modeled gargoyles; we are better positioned to see them in terms of motivated subject-positions within the larger social frame that signals genuine drama. Contentious as the pilgrims sometimes are, the company seems to want to keep itself together in spite of its fissures; the Knight's efforts to reconcile the Host and Pardoner are especially notable in this regard. And sometimes all the pilgrims like the same things, forming a cohesive interpretive community in their laughter over folly or pity for distress. The Yeoman sees this camaraderie, and it impels him to join the compaignye, knowing that to do so will lose him his place with his master. While national projects are often defined in terms of an ancestral enemy or an excluded other, another aspect of Chaucerian generosity is its sense of an English community in the *Canterbury Tales* that minimizes such "othering" (although it is present in the Prioress's telling and in some episodes of the Man of Laws'). Chaucer's narrative architecture produces a *hous* not a fortress. The stress is on shared cultural memories and social landscapes, locations ample enough to accommodate a *sondry folk* each deeply imagined and all imagined as together on the pilgrimage: the Middle Earth of the social with a specifically English slant. We would be justified, I think, in calling such an image of community beautiful.

NOTES

1 Introduction: Why Aesthetics?

1. Werner Heisenberg is quoted by S. Chandrasekhar, *Truth and Beauty: Aesthetics and Motivations in Science* (Chicago, IL: University of Chicago Press, 1987), p. 65.
2. Both Roberts and Wilczek are quoted in "The Tiniest of Particles Poke Big Holes in Physics Theory," *New York Times*, February 9, 2001.
3. Philip Fisher, *Wonder, the Rainbow, and the Aesthetics of Rare Experiences* (Cambridge, MA: Harvard University Press, 1998), p. 138; the phrasing of Plato's position is from Hans-Georg Gadamer's discussion of "Phaedrus," in *Truth and Method*, trans. Joel Weinsheimer and Donald G. Marshall (New York: Continuum Books, 2003), p. 481. Hereafter cited in the text as *TM*.
4. *Itinerarium Mentis in Deum*, ed. Philotheus Boehner, *Works of Saint Bonaventure*, Vol. 11 (New York: Franciscan Institute, 1956), 52. George Boaz's translation, *The Mind's Road to God* (New York: Bobbs-Merrill, 1953), p. 16.
5. Although they are not precise synonyms ("beauty" usually refers to objects, texts in our case, and "aesthetics" to the study of the effects these objects exert), I will discuss "beauty" and "aesthetics" without insisting on a sharp distinction between them.
6. Only two of the many recent handbooks and anthologies of literary study, now widely current, so much as mention aesthetics, art, or beauty (and those two without explaining or integrating the notion into the rest of what it has to say). For example, in Frank Lentricchia and Thomas McLaughlin's *Critical Terms for Literary Study*, 2nd edn. (Chicago, IL: University of Chicago Press, 1995), five of the twenty-eight authors of the chapters use the term, three of those levering their positions against it. The most recent position to take account of aesthetics in Charles Kaplan's *Criticism: The Major Statements*, 2nd edn. (New York: St. Martin's Press, 1986) is an essay by John Crowe Ransom from 1941.
7. Fisher writes that "beauty for the Greeks was mathematical, and the geometrical and the proportional were the meeting point of aesthetics and science." *Wonder, the Rainbow, and the Aesthetics of Rare Experiences*, p. 36. The quotations about intelligibility are on pp. 138 and 123.

8. Jacques Rancière, *The Politics of Aesthetics*, trans. Gabriel Rockhill (London and New York: Continuum Books, 2004), p. 35 and *passim*.
9. Charles Altieri has argued that "it seems both narrow and historically inaccurate to assume that we participate fully only in those works that either directly mirror our lives or are appropriable within that sphere." Charles Altieri, *Canons and Consequences: Reflections on the Ethical Force of Imaginative Ideals* (Evanston, IL: Northwestern University Press, 1990), p. 64. I am of course in sympathy with his position—in fact I would put it even more strongly: such narrowness blocks a conscientious attempt to understand human endeavors in both past and present.
10. *Troilus and Criseyde*, V. 1793–96. All citation from Chaucer's work is from *The Riverside Chaucer*, ed. Larry D. Benson, 3rd edn. (Boston, MA: Houghton Mifflin, 1987).
11. In Fredric Jameson, *The Cultural Turn: Selected Writings on the Postmodern* (London: Verso, 1998), Fredric Jameson traces the ascendancy of the "Sublime" to the influence of Hegel (p. 84). I will say more about this in chapter 3.
12. Lee Patterson, "'What Man Artow?': Authorial Self-Definition," in *The Tale of sir Thopas* and *The Tale of Melibee*," *SAC* 11 (1989): 173. Patterson then connects this autonomy with the literary and the aesthetic, which "has played a central role in the articulation of Western civilization, and with Chaucer we witness its entrance into English culture." These remarks suggest that an aesthetic mode of intelligibility was understood and influential before the formal aesthetics of the eighteenth century.
13. Elaine Scarry, *On Beauty and Being Just* (Princeton, NJ: Princeton University Press, 1999), p. 7.
14. As the argument I am about to launch contends, aesthetic experience is subjective; others may be called upon to share it, but they cannot be argued into sharing it. Therefore, when I say "we" in describing contemporary responses, it is a shorthand for my own experiences informed by those of many students and colleagues. They are claimed "for everyone," in the manner argued for by Kant.
15. An example, but a very nuanced and well argued one, is Terry Eagelton's *Ideology of the Aesthetic* (Oxford: Balckwell, 1990), in which the chapter on Adorno is called "Art after Auschwitz."
16. Oscar Kenshur, "The Rhetoric of Demystification," in *Aesthetics and Ideology*, ed. George Levine (New Brunswick, NJ: Rutgers University Press, 1994), p. 74. Hans Robert Jauss takes up the issue from another angle by insisting on the inappropriateness of the "categories of affirmation and negation" as exclusive leys to understanding medieval texts ("The Alterity and Modernity of Medieval Literature, *NLH* 10: 194).
17. J. W. T. Mitchell has aptly described the "mutual embarrassment" with which aesthetics and Marxist commentary have faced one another. See *Iconology: Image, Text, Ideology* (Chicago, IL: University of Chicago Press, 1986), p. 202.

18. Theodor Adorno, *Aesthetic Theory*, ed. Gretel Adorno and Rolf Tiedemann, trans Robert Hullot Kentor (Minneapolis: University of Minnesota Press, 1997), p. 347.
19. Adorno, *Aesthetic Theory*, p. 17.
20. Denis Donoghue, *Speaking of Beauty* (New Haven, CT: Yale University Press, 2003), pp. 121 and 122.
21. I cite James Creed Meredith's translation of the *Critique of Judgement* (Oxford: Clarendon Press, 1952) throughout (as *CJ*), except in the phrase "purposiveness without a final purpose," which I prefer because of its familiarity. The quotation is found on p. 42. I will use Kant's formulations because of their attempt at philosophical precision and because they have so often been the target of attacks on aesthetic claims.
22. Raymond Williams, *Marxism and Literature* (Oxford: Oxford University Press, 1977), p. 151. Hereafter cited in the text as *ML*.
23. "Polyvalent" is Adorno's term in "Commitment," *New Left Review* (1974): 87–88.
24. The phrase is Denis Donoghue's in *Speaking of Beauty*, p. 128.
25. Kenshur, "Rhetoric of Demystification," p. 74.
26. The term is usually used negatively to impart the notion that beauty is *merely* a class-associated asset one spends to achieve other goals, but Cornel West sees it as an asset that should be sought by marginalized groups who might use it to shape new consensuses. West argues that critics need "the self-confidence, discipline, and perseverance necessary for success without an undue reliance on the mainstream for approval and acceptance," and that this becomes especially hard for those of color. See "The New Cultural Politics of Difference," quoted in Arnold Rampersad, "Values Old and New," in *Aesthetics and Ideology*, ed. George Levine (New Brunswick, NJ: Rutgers University Press, 1994), p. 37.
27. Pierre Bourdieu, *Distinction: A Social Critique of the Judgement of Taste*, trans. Richard Nice (Cambridge, MA: Harvard University Press, 1984), p. 241. Reading *Distinction* as an American, I cannot translate Bourdieu's categories, either those of class distinctions or culturally elite art. Bardology, for example, has had such an off-again-on-again history in my country. Shakespeare's plays were sometimes performed in minstrel shows for broad public, sometimes reserved by high prices for the well heeled, and now proffered to the millions on film and television.
28. Elaine Scarry speaks of beauty as carrying a greeting, and Alan Singer of the "new," the surprise addressed to a "learning subject" (Singer, "Beautiful Errors," 32). This is not to deny that some elements of subjectivity itself are not "structured" (as Williams claims) in social terms, but to insist that the structuring is not all there is.
29. Music and painting are less likely to be reduced to concept, but this is only comparatively the case. Sometimes a certain style of perspective or

musical chord is associated with a conceptual system (Renaissance figure placement with patronage or a Wagnerian chord with fascism).

30. As Wendy Steiner puts it, art is "neither identical to reality nor isolated from it, but a virtual realm tied to the world by acts of interpretation." *The Scandal of Pleasure: Art in an Age of Fundamentalism* (Chicago, IL: University of Chicago Press, 1995), p. 8.
31. "One must assume that all persons are constituted like the judge" (*CJ*, p. 147, n. 1).
32. Scarry begins *On Beauty and Being Just* by stressing the impulse to share and replicate the experience of encountering beauty. The impulse to share is a widely acknowledged effect of aesthetic pleasure: "Come to the window, sweet is the night air."
33. Hans-Georg Gadamer, *Philosophical Hermeneutics*, trans. and ed. David E. Linge (Berkeley: University of California Press, 1976), pp. 95–104; quotation from pp. 95–96. (The essay was published in German in 1964.) It is cited in the text as *PH*.
34. Hans Robert Jauss writes "It is no atemporal, basic element which is always already given" but "the never-completed result of a process of progressive and enriching interpretation," although he takes issue with the use of the term; see Hans Robert Jauss, "The Alterity and Modernity," 183 n. 3. Warren Ginsberg calls Jauss's assertions "metaphysical inventions" by which history "darkens knowledge." *Chaucer's Italian Tradition* (Ann Arbor: University of Wisconsin Press, 2002), pp. 7–8. I would argue that the opposite is the case: asking old texts new questions continually extends our knowledge of their energies.
35. Jauss, *Toward an Aesthetic of Reception*, trans. Timothy Bahti (Minneapolis: University of Minnesota Press, 1982), p. xii.
36. Rancière, *The Politics of Aesthetics*, p. 50.
37. *TM*, p. 267. Rita Copeland sees a close relation between Gadamer's hermeneutics and medieval rhetorical theory in that both can be associated with Aristotle's discussion of practical wisdom; *Rhetoric, Hermeneutics, and Translation in the Middle Ages* (Cambridge: Cambridge University Press, 1991), pp. 18–19. She finds in Gadamer's openness to new interpretation a vantage point for our understanding of the medieval exegesis of *its* textual inheritance (pp. 83–84).
38. Laura Kendrick quotes Byron in *Chaucerian Play: Comedy and Control in the* Canterbury Tales (Berkeley and Los Angeles: University of California Press, 1988), p. 21; Skeat and Gwynn are discussed by T. L. Burton and Rosemary Greentree in *Chaucer's Miller's, Reeve's, and Cook's Tales: The Chaucer Bibliographies* (Toronto, Canada: University of Toronto Press, 1995), p. xxi.
39. For Althusser's version of ideology in which people are led to see "their specific place in a historically peculiar social formation as inevitable, natural, a necessary function of the real itself," see James Kavanagh's essay "Ideology," in *Critical Terms for Literary Study*, ed. Frank Lentricchia

and Thomas McLaughlin, 2nd edn. (Chicago, IL: University of Chicago Press, 1995), p. 310. Both "lived relations to the real" and "structures of feeling" are in common usage in many critical venues now, and I will use them without quotation marks.

40. George Levine, "Introduction: Reclaiming Aesthetics," in *Aesthetics and Ideology*, p. 15.
41. Kenshur, "Rhetoric of Demystification," p. 74.
42. This effect of art is especially important for those who study the Middle Ages. Andrew Taylor defends the desire to fully know the objects of the past against the charge that medievalists, especially those who study manuscripts, are guilty of fetishizing them. His account of the scholar's involvement in medieval objects of study stresses a particular hold on imagination that produces desire, which in turn is "a necessary element in cultural exchange that gives the object meaning"; Andrew Taylor, *Textual Situations* (Philadelphia: University of Pennsylvania Press, 2002), pp. 197–208, the quotation is on 205.
43. For "utopia," see Levine, *Aesthetics and Ideology*, pp. 15–16 and for "National Park," Claude Levi-Strauss, *The Savage Mind* (Chicago, IL: University of Chicago Press, 1966), p. 219.
44. Williams, "Dominant, Residual, and Emergent," pp. 121–27. Williams describes new structures of feeling as often manifesting themselves first in literature (p. 133).
45. Ricoeur *From Text to Action*, trans. Kathleen Blamey and John B. Thompson (Evanston, IL: Northwestern University Press, 1991), p. 174.
46. Wendy Steiner' s account, although addressed to a current confrontation between aesthetic and legal issues, is apt for the Middle Ages as well: "Because art acts both as a sign of reality and as a self-contained entity, it creates a confusion between meaning and being and has a necessarily ambiguous relation to the extra-artistic world. It appears to provide a particularly intense experience of reality while not belonging to that reality in a straightforward manner" (*Scandal of Pleasure*, p. 76).

2 Chaucerian Resoun Ymaginatyf

1. The earliest occurrences of the term in English were in 1798, 1821, and 1832, according to the *Oxford English Dictionary*.
2. Mary Carruthers, "Sweetness," *Speculum* 81 (2006): 999. Sweetness does not map onto a Kantian sense of aesthetic taste precisely, but it similarly registers the immediacy and pleasure of the effects of beauty, and their distinction from moral judgments. "Carruthers's" account complicates the notion of sweetness by linking it to knowing and showing its involvement with its contrast terms bitter and salty (1000).
3. "The Study of Classical Authors from the Twelfth Century to c. 1450," *Cambridge History of Literary Criticism*, ed. Alastair Minnis and Ian Johnson (Cambridge: Cambridge University Press, 2005), p. 235.

4. Robertson "Some Observations on Method in Literary Study," NLH 1 (1970): 21–33 and more fully worked out in *A Preface to Chaucer* (Princeton, NJ: Princeton University Press, 1962).
5. Allen, *The Ethical Poetic of the Later Middle Ages: A Decorum of Convenient Distinction* (Toronto, Canada: University of Toronto Press, 1982). Allen writes that his medieval research "flatly contradicts purely aesthetic approaches to literature" except as they work to "demonstrate ethical values" (p. 38), denies that "art" meant "something aesthetic" (p. 79), and throughout the book refers to aesthetic understanding as solipsistic—sinful in theological terms (p. 181). I share his position that poetry is not wholly divorced from philosophy (p. 72), but find his sense of what philosophy is too inattentive to its variousness in the Middle Ages.
6. Edwards, *Ratio and Invention: A Study of Medieval Lyric and Narrative* (Nashville: University of Tennessee Press, 1989), pp. xvi, xviii, and 148.
7. In the *Confessions* Augustine refers to it in terms of the sensible and the intelligible, for example 12.5, 13.18. Page numbers are to John K. Ryan's translation (Garden City, NY: Doubleday, 1960).
8. *De Doctrina Christiana*, 2.6.8; Augustine Corpvs Christianorum; *On Christian Doctrine*, trans. D. W. Robertson Jr. (Indianapolis, IL: Bobbs-Merrill, 1958), p. 38.
9. *De Musica*, VI.xiii.38 in *Philosophies of Art and Beauty*, ed. Albert Hofstadter and Richard Kuhns (New York: Random House, 1964), p. 191; *De Ordine*, 11.34, in Hofstadter, p. 175.
10. *De Ordine*, 16.44, in Hofstadter, p. 181. In the previous chapter, Augustine speculates that there is a "very number by which all things are numbered," a key to the mysteries of the universe. In his first three chapters, Edwards glosses and complicates Augustine's position on *ratio* in music and its relation to aesthetic order generally. Two recent fictions come to mind as echoes of this remarkable wish: the film *Pi* and the novel *Riddley Walker*, in both of which the protagonists seek after and suffer for such a number and the various interests that it might end up serving.
11. Robertson, *On Christian Doctrine*, 1.5.5, pp. 9–10.
12. *Itinerarium Mentis in Deum*, ed. Philotheus Boehner, *Works of Saint Bonaventure*, Vol. 11 (New York: Franciscan Institute, 1956), 1.3. I have used George Boaz's translation, *The Mind's Road to God* (Indianapolis, IL: Bobbs-Merrill, 1953) for the English citations.
13. This tenet closely resembles S. Chandrasekhar's argument for the aesthetic impulse as a signpost to truth in physics: "It is, indeed, an incredible fact that what the human mind, at its deepest and most profound, perceives as beautiful finds its realization in external nature." See Chandrasekhar, *Truth and Beauty*, p. 66, discussed above p. 1, n1.
14. O'Brien ("'Ars-Metrik': Science, Satire, and Chaucer's Summoner," *Mosaic* 23 [1990]: 16) discusses this debate in explaining the "ars-metrik" of the *Summoner's Tale*. Proofs using the *via rationis* were called *secundum imaginationem*.

15. This discussion takes place in the *Sentences*, and is quoted by Umberto Eco in *Art and Beauty in the Middle Ages* (New Haven, CT: Yale University Press, 1986), p. 102.
16. Pasnau, *Thomas Aquinas on Human Nature* (Cambridge: Cambridge University Press, 2002), p. 293. His commentary on the discussion of mind in *Summa Theologiae* 1a 75–89 brings a consideration of Aquinas's other writings to that text and compares them to some contemporary thinking on the subject. I have also used the Blackfriars edition of the *Summa*, Vol. 12 (New York and London: McGraw-Hill, 1968).
17. Pasnau, *Human Nature*, p. 285.
18. Pasnau's translation, *Summa Theologiae*, 1a.85,3, p. 281.
19. Pasnau discusses Aquinas's rather inconclusive treatment of the content and mechanism for storing mental images; Pasnau, *Human Nature*, p. 292. The fact that Aquinas stresses both pictures and words enables Stephen David Ross to write that he is concerned to show the "rational order of a universe intelligible to understanding...an infinite play of metaphors, symbols, and figures in the mind, filling it with exhilaration" (Ross, *The Encyclopedia of Aesthetics*, p. 240).
20. Pasnau, *Human Nature*, pp. 270–78. I will be discussing Wittgenstein's position in the next chapter.
21. Pasnau, *Human Nature*, p. 275.
22. Eco, *The Aesthetics of Thomas Aquinas* (Cambridge, MA: Harvard University Press, 1988), pp. 58–59. He quotes and translates the *Summa* 1–2, 27, 1 and 3 here and notes the way sight and hearing are privileged.
23. Eco, *Thomas Aquinas*, pp. 80–81.
24. Eco, *Thomas Aquinas*, pp. 252–53, n. 130, is particularly interesting on the scholarly debates over *claritas*; on p. 143 Eco discusses the "pleasure in bringing a beautiful metaphor to light."
25. Quoted in Eco, *Thomas Aquinas*, p. 125.
26. *Summa Theologiae*, 1a.86,4. See Pasnau's discussion in *Human Nature*, p. 283 and Murray Wright Bundy, *The Theory of Imagination in Classical and Medieval Thought* (Urbana: University of Illinois Press, 1927), pp. 403–06.
27. Boethius's ubiquitous *ubi sunt* theme betrays what Eco calls "aesthetic yearning" (Eco, *Thomas Aquinas*, p. 10) signaled by its frequent association with *shynyng*, "radiance, splendor."
28. Eco describes Boethius's "bias toward theory" in *De Institutione Musica*, in *Thomas Aquinas*, pp. 244–45, n. 32.
29. *The Sources of the* Boece, ed. Tim William Machan with the assistance of Alastair Minnis (Athens, GA: University of Georgia Press, 2005), prints facing pages of the French and Latin texts Chaucer probably used. This passage is on pp. 208–9; see also the account of Chaucer's decisions in Ralph Hanna, Tony Hunt, Nigel Palmer, and Ronald Keightley, in "Latin commentary and vernacular literature," *Cambridge History*, pp. 365–66. "Resoun ymaginatyf" seems to have been a conscious choice from Jean de Meun's "*raison ymaginative*" rather than the Latin "*ymaginaria racione*."

30. Such widely shared medieval notions, though not altogether reconcilable, had a long history of currency: from Hugh of St. Victor's position "when [sense impression is] brought within the domain of man's understanding, it becomes the subject matter of imagination—the imagination not of the brute, but of the man of reason" (quoted in Bundy, *Theory of Imagination*, p. 383).
31. Bacon is discussed by Vincent Gillespie in the *Cambridge History*, pp. 160–71, cited p. 171.
32. Quoted in Eco, *Thomas Aquinas*, p. 15.
33. James J. Murphy has argued that Chaucer probably knew Geoffrey's treatise from Trivet, and that his other reflections on the "colors of rhetoric" were gathered from his eclectic reading rather than academic study of classical sources. The sense of the "hous to founde" passage is in Luke 14. Chaucer used this idea in *Boece* (4. Prosa 6, 90–96); it may have been useful to him here as the kind of traditional saying Pandarus is fond of.
34. *De Musica* in Hofstadter, pp. 185–202; cited p. 187.
35. Haidu, "Repetition: Modern Reflections on Medieval Aesthetics," *MLN* 92 (1977): 884–85.
36. See Alastair Minnis's recent account of this much-discussed controversy ("Medieval Imagination and Memory," in *Cambridge History*, p. 273), in which Lollard's objections to actor's images eliciting pity echo Augustine's self-reproach for weeping over Dido (*Confessions*, I.13.20–22).
37. Minnis, "Medieval Imagination and Memory," in *Cambridge History*, p. 273.
38. Le Goff, *The Medieval Imagination*, trans. Arthur Goldhammer (Chicago and London: University of Chicago Press, 1985), p. 6.
39. Carruthers, *The Book of Memory* (Cambridge: Cambridge University Press, 1990), p. 1.
40. The drive toward intelligibility in the realm of nature has sometimes split off into scientific investigation, which is why physicists sometimes use the word beauty to describe a theory that matches the phenomenon it renders intelligible. In that somewhat specialized use of the term, the medieval sense that beauty is knowledge-bearing is reflected directly. Carl Sagan's delight in describing the night sky, for just one example, fused his immediate visual pleasure with his delight in scientific explanation.
41. Marjorie Hope Nicholson, *Mountain Gloom, Mountain Glory* (New York: W. W. Norton, 1959).
42. Carruthers, *Book of Memory*, p. 197.
43. Carruthers, *Book of Memory*, pp. 18 and 22 on the first point, p. 23 on the second; both points may be related to Aquinas's theories of mind in the *Summa* 1a. 75–89.
44. Damasio, *The Feeling of What Happens: Body and Emotion in the Making of Consciousness* (New York: Harcourt Brace, 1999) *FWH* in the text, and Daniel Dennett, *Consciousness Explained* (Boston, MA: Little, Brown, 1991). *CE* in the text.

45. "Movies are the closest external representations of the prevailing storytelling that goes on in our minds," Damasio, *What Happens*, p. 188. Damasio goes on with another arresting formulation: "You exist as a mental being when primordial stories are being told, and only then.... You *are* the music while the music lasts" (p. 190).
46. I was myself a highly resistant reader for this argument and am not offering it here as the latest solution to the mind/body problem or as a consensus view of contemporary science. It serves instead as a persuasive (I finally agreed reluctantly) statement of current concerns that may be balanced against (and correlated with) medieval mysticism's assumption of spirituality. Robert Pasnau likens the multiple drafts formulation to Aquinas's resistance to the assumption that consciousness all happens "in some one place" (*Human Nature*, p. 198).
47. Dennett, *Consciousness Explained*, pp. 399–400. See also, Daniel Dennett, *Elbow Room: The Varieties of Free Will Worth Wanting* (Cambridge, MA: MIT Press, 1985), p. 12.
48. Eco, *Thomas Aquinas*, pp. 112–14. Poetic fictions in particular were permitted and respected for their simultaneous presentation of "the ideal reality belonging to eternal archetypes" (luminosity), and their moral claim to verisimilitude, according to Hans Robert Jauss. See *Question and Answer: Forms of Dialogic Understanding*, ed. and trans. Michael Hays (Minneapolis: University of Minnesota Press, 1989), p. 9.
49. Mitchell, "Representation," in *Critical Terms for Literary Study*, ed. Frank Lentricchia and Thomas McLaughlin (Chicago and London: University of Chicago Press, 1995), p. 14. Mitchell's discussion of the whole issue is wide-ranging and incisive.
50. Quoted by Mary Warnock, *Imagination* (Berkeley: University of California Press, 1976), pp. 200–201.
51. Ludwig Wittgenstein, *Philosophical Investigations*, trans. G. E. M. Anscombe, 3rd edn. (Oxford: Basil Blackwell, 2001), I.19, p. 7e; hereafter *PI* in the text.
52. John Gibson, "Reading for Life," *The Literary Wittgenstein*, ed. John Gibson and Wolfgang Huemer (New York and London: Routledge, 2004), p. 117. See also Bernard Harrison's "Imagined Worlds and the Real One," pp. 92–108 in the same volume.
53. Seneca uses *ingenium* for the creative redeployment of images in memory, an active faculty, but Chaucer's instances go farther toward modern "engine," driving force. Seneca is quoted in Mary Carruthers, *The Book of Memory*, p. 192. Edwards discusses the role of *ingenium* in classical and medieval accounts of invention (*Ratio and Invention*, pp. 82–83).
54. The Parson also uses the "engyn" as an aspect of mind, which can figure as a benign gift of nature or as a deadly sin when "malice ymagined" arises from pride (X.445–50). He lists "subtil engyn" among the gifts of soul bestowed by nature, along with "vertu natural" and good memory. A similar implication may be seen in the *House of Fame* when the narrator invokes Thought to unlock the dream images in his mind and present

them (to "every maner man / That English understonde kan") aright, displaying his "engyn and myght" to do so (II.509–10, 28).

55. Even more fully contrivances, although not employed stealthily, are the astrolabe, which the modest Chaucer does not want Lewis to think as his own invention ("myn engyn," Prologue 61), and the catapult whose stone makes such a noise in the *House of Fame* (III.844).
56. He does use "imagination," however, to achieve a pointed satiric effect in the *Nun's Priest's Tale*. The col-fox bursts through the hedge to plot against Chauntecleer by "heigh ymaginacioun forncast" (VII.3217). This dignified phrasing suggests foreknowledge, perhaps even a reference to Dante (see Riverside's note), but it forwards the plot by indicating that the fox had imaged a long-range plan to dine on the rooster. This mental picturing was less sealed off from reality testing than January's, and it almost succeeded.
57. Mary Warnock, writing on Wittgenstein concludes: "images themselves are not separate from our interpretations of the world; they are our way of thinking of the objects in the world.... The two are joined because forms have a certain meaning, always significant beyond themselves. We recognize a form as a form *of* something, as Wittgenstein said, by its relation with other things," (pp. 194–95; Gadamer agrees: "Perception always includes meaning." Gadamer, *Truth and Method*, p. 92).
58. Ray Monk considers Wittgenstein's emphasis on aspect worthy of a long chapter (pp. 489–519) in his biography, *Ludwig Wittgenstein: The Duty of Genius* (Harmondsworth, UK: Penguin Books, 1990).
59. The narrator concludes that, although Funes had learned five languages, "I suspect, nevertheless, that he was not very capable of thought.... In the overly replete world of Funes there were nothing but details, almost contiguous details" (pp. 114–15); Jorge Luis Borges, "Funes," in *Ficciones* (New York: Grove Press, 1962), pp. 114–15.
60. Dillard, "Sight into Insight," in *Popular Writing in America*, ed. Donald McQuade and Robert Atwan (New York: Oxford University Press, 1977), pp. 247–51. Denis Donoghue discusses *seeing as* in terms of both ways a work of art is itself framed, the way it shapes what "being beautiful" entails, and the way a particular cultural setting enables an angle of vision in *Speaking of Beauty* (New Haven, CT: Yale University Press, 2003), pp. 89–106.
61. It would account for Anderson's response to Gellner's contrast between awakening to self-consciousness and inventing nationhood that does not exist. Anderson replies by insisting that invention be linked to imagining and creativity rather than fabrication and falsity (Benedict Anderson, *Imagined Communities* [London: Verso, 1986], p. 15).
62. A glancingly presented example of the "seeing as" use appears in the *Clerk's Tale*: The sergeant leaves Griselda after taking away her baby boy, ostensibly to be killed, to report to Walter, "ful faste ymaginyng / If by his wyves cheer he myght se / Or by her word aperceyve, that she / Were changed" (598–601). Riverside glosses "ymaginyng" as "considering" and

Donaldson as "pondering," but neither Fisher's edition nor Robinson's gives it a gloss and there is little reason not to take it to mean "interpreting through imagination." The sergeant is bringing reason and experience to the image of Griselda's behavior he has seen, trying to interpret it *as* either obedience to Walter's will or veiled rebellion. He concludes that it is obedience.

63. Quoted in Eco's *Thomas Aquinas*, p. 84. This seems congruent with Donoghue's resonant phrasing: "form is the distinguishing characteristic of art." *Speaking of Beauty*, p. 121.
64. Scarry, *On Beauty and Being Just*, pp. 47–48.
65. Burke, *Counter-Statement* (Berkeley and Los Angeles: University of California Press, 1931), p. 31.
66. This is Eco's summary of Aquinas's thinking (*Thomas Aquinas*, p. 119).
67. Helen Cooper, "Responding to the Monk," *SAC* 22 (2000): 432.
68. Jauss, *Aesthetic of Reception*, p. 23.
69. Scarry, *On Beauty and Being Just*, pp. 3 and 26, n. 7.
70. Fisher, *Wonder*, p. 49.
71. Scarry, *On Beauty and Being Just*, p. 19.
72. Scarry, *On Beauty and Being Just*, pp. 67–68.
73. Ezra Pound, *Selected Prose, 1909–1965*, ed. William Crookson (New York: New Directions, 1973), p. 22; hereafter cited in the text as *SP*.
74. Raymond Williams's claim that some literature predicts and impels new structures of feeling (*ML*, p. 133) is relevant here, as is Gadamer's principle of *Wirkungsgeschichte* or "effective history" (*TM*, p. 300, above p. 11).
75. I discuss *virtù* in Chapter 12 of my *Time-Bound Words* (New York: St. Martin's Press, 2000). In English the term, spelled "virtue" retained its sense "power" in some early modern instances, but had already begun its shift toward "goodness," its chief modern meaning. Pound is making use of his term to hint at the attractiveness of verbal efficacy.
76. *Practicing New Historicism* (Chicago, IL: University of Chicago Press, 2000), p. 16.
77. Kant calls that thing good, "which by means of reason commends itself by its mere concept" while "the beautiful must depend on the reflection on an object precursory to some (not definitely defined) concept, freeing it from interest" (*CJ*, p. 46). Albertus Magnus distinguished beauty and goodness in much the same way: "the beautiful and the good are the same in subject...but differ logically." Beauty must be apprehended by the senses and weighed by reason to appreciate the "due proportion of its members and splendid colors, while the good may be discovered by cognition alone," quoted in Eco, *Thomas Aquinas*, p. 25. The underlying assumption, however, remains that the two logics will find beauty and goodness together.
78. Eden, *Hermeneutics and the Rhetorical Tradition* (New Haven, CT: Yale University Press, 1997), p. 58. She goes on to argue that the inclusiveness of his reading practice avoids the extremes of both "Jewish legalism and Greek allegorism" (p. 62).

79. Augustine, *On Christian Doctrine*, II.XL.60, p. 75.
80. Petrarch's letter to Boccaccio is quoted in Mark Musa and Peter Bondanella's Norton Critical Edition of *The Decameron* (New York: W. W. Norton, 1977), pp. 184–87.
81. Haidu, "Repetition," p. 884. Haidu goes on: "We may even guess that the belief in free variation was one of those magnificent inventions of self-deception which enable historical change to take place without the awareness that it is taking place, and awareness that if present, might have impeded that historical development."
82. Oscar Kenshur, "Rhetoric of Demystification," in *Aesthetics and Ideology*, ed. George Levine (New Brunswick, NJ: Rutgers University Press, 1994), p. 74.
83. I owe this phrasing to James Franklin Knapp.

3 Playing with Language Games

1. Philip Fisher argues that aesthetic pleasure is not passive but intellectual, "active thinking closely related to discovery in science" (Fisher, *Wonder*, pp. 40 and 138).
2. There are of course many others including Joel Fineman's key to the positioning of the tales by "allegory" of the *General Prologue*, which he identifies as "the hierarchized sexuality already built into the piercing of March by the potent, engendering liquidity of April." See "The Structures of Allegorical Desire," in *Allegory and Representation*, ed. Stephen Greenblatt, English Institute Essays, 1979–80 (Baltimore, MD: Johns Hopkins University Press, 1981), p. 39.
3. Helen Cooper, *The Structure of the Canterbury Tales* (Athens: University of Georgia Press, 1984), pp. 8–55, emphasizes Chaucer's departures from the known genres of his sources. Jill Mann, *Chaucer and Medieval Estates Satire* (Cambridge, MA: Cambridge University Press, 1973), concentrates on the portraits of *General Prologue*. Frederick Tupper ("Chaucer and the Seven Deadly Sins," *PMLA* 29 [1914]: 93–128) proposes that the pilgrims are going to Jerusalem celestial by confessing their sins and sinful outlooks through their tales. Glending Olson, *Recreation in the Later Middle Ages* (Ithaca and London: Cornell University Press, 1982), stresses medieval justifications for textual enjoyment; see also his "The Profits of Pleasure" in *Cambridge History of Literary Criticism*, Vol. 2: *The Middle Ages*, ed. Alastair Minnis and Ian Johnson (Cambridge: Cambridge University Press, 2005), pp. 275–87. There are, of course, many more recent variations of these general propositions.
4. *Philosophical Investigations*, trans. G. E. M. Anscombe (Oxford: Blackwell, 1963), p. 19. Language games in general may be distinguished from one another by the functions they fulfill, rather than regarding all language as asserting propositions whose truth claims may be investigated. See also Ray Monk's discussion of the matter in *Ludwig Wittgenstein: The Duty of*

Genius (Harmondsworth, UK: Penguin Books 1990), esp. pp. 330–31 and 364–65.

5. Wallace, *Chaucerian Polity: Absolutist Lineages and Associational Forms in England and Italy* (Stanford, CA: Stanford University Press, 1997), p. 64.
6. Late in the term, I arrange a modest "soper" for my Chaucer seminar, at which I ask them to vote on the best tale, first from the standpoint of a particular pilgrim, then from their own.
7. Wallace, *Chaucerian Polity*, p. 97.
8. Cooper, "Responding to the Monk," *SAC* 22 (2000): 432. Cooper goes on to write that defining a genre and then fulfilling its expectations is "not enough," since some tales are found wanting or interrupted for reasons other than their generic deficiencies. Paul Strohm finds a lack of "truly neutral [generic] terminology" for Middle English writers, except in the case of tragedy ("Storie, Spelle, Geste, Romaunce, Tragedie: Generic Distinctions in the Middle English Troy Narratives," *Speculum* 46 [1971]: 348–59); the broadest aspect of generic marking distinguishes between "tale" as new creation and "story" as closer to the historical record (Strohm, "Some Generic Distinctions in the *Canterbury Tales*," *Modern Philology* 68 [1971]: 321–28).
9. Kant, *CJ*, p. 70 and *passim*. Alan Singer also argues that the judgment of beauty is distinct from that of the logical perfection of a genre in "Beautiful Errors," 7–34.
10. Williams, *Marxism and Literature*, pp. 182–83. Adena Rosmarin thinks of genre primarily in terms of critics rather than general readers: "A genre is a kind of schema, a way of discussing a literary text in ways that link it with other texts and, finally, phrase it in terms of those texts." Its value lies in its usefulness as a hypothesis that leads us to perceive similarities among instances of a genre "in the midst of and in spite of differences"; see *The Power of Genre* (Minneapolis: University of Minnesota Press, 1985), pp. 21 and 46.
11. Croce also wrote that all books dealing with genre "could be burned with out any loss whatsoever." *Aesthetic as Science of Expression and General Linguistic*, trans. Douglas Ainslie (London: Macmillan, 1922), p. 188. See also Susanne Langer's discussion of Croce in *Feeling and Form* (New York: Scribners, 1953), pp. 375–78 and *passim*.
12. Rosmarin regards the "horizon" as something out of sight that defers a ground for genre in the text itself (*Power of Genre*, p. 35), but I picture the horizon as the farthest distance that *can be seen*.
13. Hans-Georg Gadamer, *Truth and Method*, trans. Joel Weinsheimer and Donald Marshall, 2nd rev. edn. (New York and London: Continuum Books, 2003), p. 304.
14. See Gadamer, *The Relevance of the Beautiful and Other Essays*, trans. Nicholas Walker, ed. and intro. Robert Bernasconi (Cambridge: Cambridge University Press, 1986), pp. 19–20.

15. Haidu, "Repetition: Modern Reflections on Medieval Aesthetics," *MLN* 92 (December 1977): 875.
16. Cooper, *Structure*, p. 55. I will return to Cooper's metaphor of windows repeatedly, because seeing is always motivated in Chaucer's time and in ours: "the innocent eye is blind," as W. J. T. Mitchell writes in discussing Ernst Gombrich. Mitchell earlier used the metaphor of looking out the window himself (*Iconlogy*. pp. 38 and 30). As attractive as I find this metaphor, it must be admitted that the entry of sin and death through windows was a persistent medieval trope, sometimes based on Jeremiah 9. 21. Suzannah Biernhoff discusses the eye as metaphoric window in *Sight and Embodiment in the Middle Ages* (Basingstoke, UK, and New York: Palgrave Macmillan, 2002).
17. Admittedly, "realism" is an awkward term, since it evokes the Platonic world of ideas in medieval parlance, but I will use it within imaginary quotation marks because alternatives like "representational" carry with them other equally heavy baggage.
18. Quoted in V. A. Kolve, *Chaucer and the Imagery of Narrative: The First Five Canterbury Tales* (Stanford, CA: Stanford University Press, 1984), p. 19.
19. Bloomfield, "Chaucerian Realism," in *The Cambridge Chaucer Companion*, ed. Piero Boitani and Jill Mann (Cambridge: Cambridge University Press, 1986), p. 179.
20. Owst, *Literature and the Pulpit in Medieval England* (Cambridge: Cambridge University Press, 1933), pp. 23, 55, and 46. The cultural trend Owst describes "find its obverse in Fredric Jameson's contention that in the current collapse of the overarching narratives, aesthetic attention finds itself transferred to the life of perception as such, abandoning the former object that organized it." See Jameson, *The Cultural Turn: Selected Writings on the Postmodern* (London: Verso, 1998), p. 112.
21. William Courtenay, "Nominalism and Late Medieval Religion," in *The Pursuit of Holiness in Late Medieval and Renaissance Religion*, ed. Charles Trinkaus and Heiko Oberman, Studies in Medieval and Renaissance Thought (Leiden, The Netherlands: Brill, 1974), p. 57. Nor is Ockham unusual in this emphasis (although his positions were much discussed in Chaucer's time); see Gillespie, *Cambridge History of Literary Criticism*, pp. 145–235.
22. The term is Elaine Scarry's (*On Beauty and Being Just*, p. 84), but the Chaucerian aura has sometimes been similarly described (cheerful and accepting) obscuring his wide variations in subject matter and tone. Scarry's commentary on the bifurcation of aesthetics is based on Kant's *Observation on the Feeling of the Beautiful and Sublime*, an earlier work than the *Critique of Judgement*. Wendy Steiner's *Venus in Exile: The Rejection of Beauty in 20th-Century Art* (New York: Free Press, 2001) recognizes that Kant himself did not privilege the sublime over the beautiful, but argues that modernists could not resist the "uncompromising, " 'masculine' distance of the sublime" (p. 16).
23. Jameson, *The Cultural Turn*, p. 84.

24. Singer, "Beautiful Errors," 11.
25. Howard Felperin aptly describes this position: "the world of [literary] reference has no objective reality or ontological stability, but recedes into an infinite play of signs and deferral of affirmed or authoritative meaning." He is writing about drama, but he generalizes his point to all fictional forms; "'Tongue-Tied Our Queen?': The Deconstruction of Presence in *The Winter's Tale*," in *Shakespeare and the Question of Theory*, ed. Patricia Parker and Geoffrey Hartman (New York: Methuen, 1985), p. 14.
26. Gibson calls this "the wonder of agreement"; see "Reading for Life," in *The Literary Wittgenstein*, ed. John Gibson and Wolfgang Huemer (New York: Routledge, 2004), p. 117. Gibson's observation is not unlike many of the medieval positions discussed by Vincent Gillespie in the *Cambridge History*, especially pp. 171–235.
27. Stewart, *On Longing* (Durham, NC: Duke University Press, 1993). We Pittsburghers, even those who usually avoid cinema, have avidly watched recent films made in our city.
28. Thomas Hahn and Richard Kaeuper, "Text and Context in Chaucer's *Friar's Tale*," *SAC* 5 (1983): 67–101.
29. Jauss makes a similar point: in the Middle Ages, fictions were permitted and privileged (in such measure as they were allowed), for two quite different reasons: as a "Platonic residue" in which the sense world imagined is the vehicle for presenting "the ideal reality belonging to eternal archetypes," and as a moral claim for presenting the sense world under the imperative of verisimilitude. See Hans Robert Jauss, *Question and Answer: Forms of Dialogic Understanding*, ed. and trans. Michael Hays (Minneapolis: University of Minnesota Press, 1989), p. 9.
30. Angus Fletcher, *Allegory: The Theory of a Symbolic Mode* (Ithaca, NY: Cornell University Press, 1964), pp. 1–3 and 339. Fletcher is arguing against the use of allegory as a measure of value.
31. White, *Figural Realism* (Baltimore, MD: Johns Hopkins University Press), Chap. 6 and specifically: Freud's "conception of the relation between dream-thoughts and the dream-contents is precisely analogous to that form of poetic discourse...[called] allegorization" (p. 103).
32. *Select English Works of John Wyclif*, ed. Thomas Arnold (Oxford: Clarendon Press, 1869–1871), I.30 and II.277–78.
33. The full account of the medieval theories of signification is A. J. Minnis's *Medieval Theory of Authorship* (Philadelphia: University of Pennsylvania Press, 1988), pp. 73–159.
34. Frye, *Anatomy of Criticism* (Princeton, NJ: Princeton University Press, 1957), p. 72.
35. Quilligan, *The Language of Allegory* (Ithaca, NY: Cornell University Press, 1979), pp. 26 and 31.
36. Tuve, *Allegorical Imagery: Some Medieval Books and Their Posterity* (Princeton, NY: Princeton University Press, 1966), p. 221. Tuve's case for *Solomon* is made in detail by Ann W. Astell in *The Song of Songs in the Middle Ages* (Ithaca, NY: Cornell University Press, 1990).

37. Reynolds, *Medieval Reading: Grammar, Rhetoric, and the Classical Text* (Cambridge: Cambridge University Press, 1996), p. 139. The book describes how medieval Christian culture made use of its inheritance from the pagan classical past, using the glosses on the satires of Horace as principle examples.
38. Tuve, *Allegorical Imagery*, p. 331.
39. Kolve, *Imagery of Narrative*, p. 60.
40. Scarry, *On Beauty and Being Just*, pp. 14 and 48. From a different starting point Michael Witmore sees "regarding" as seeking out wider implications for value than a detail might otherwise claim. *Culture of Accidents: Unexpected Knowledges in Early Modern England* (Stanford, CA: Stanford University Press, 2001), p. 83. The next chapter has more to say about regard.
41. *De Doctrina*, II.vi.7: *Sed quare suauius uideam, quam si nulla de diuinis libris talis similitude promeretur, cum res eadem sit eademque cognito, difficile est dicere et alia quaetio est.* Augustine, *On Christian Doctrine*, trans. D. W. Robertson Jr. (Indianapolis, IN: Bobbs-Merrill, 1958), p. 38.
42. *De Doctrina Christiana*, I.ii.2; *On Christian Doctrine*, p. 8.
43. Fletcher, *Allegory*, pp. 305 and 339.
44. Christine de Pizan objected to this laundering; see Gillespie's discussion of this "outlandish and contradictory" allegoresis in the *Cambridge History*, p. 181.
45. Frye, *Anatomy of Criticism*, p. 90.
46. Paul de Man calls this a "pagan pleasure" and insists that the "'realism' that appeals to us in the details of medieval art is calligraphy rather than mimesis, a technical device to insure that the emblems will be correctly identified." I disagree. It seems to me that the precise figuration of much medieval art, and certainly of Chaucer's, was intended to please precisely *as something in the world*, which is to say, as mimesis. Mitchell argues that even the hermeneutic most suspicious of images must get to its critique by "working its way through the surface" of representation (*Iconology*, p. 174).
47. Larry Scanlon, *Narrative, Authority, and Power* (Cambridge: Cambridge University Press, 1994).
48. Carruthers, *Book of Memory*, p. 197, see above, chap. 2, pp. 27–28.
49. Armstrong, *The Radical Aesthetic* (Oxford: Blackwell, 2000), p. 87. Later in the book, Armstrong works out an elaborate defense of the link between rationality and feeling, including Paul Ricoeur's insight that emotion both acknowledges and assuages the gap between knower and known "by making the relation mobile and dynamic" (p. 137).
50. "Compulsory" is Fletcher's term (*Allegory*, p. 341); "dogmatic" Gadamer's (*Truth and Method*, p. 79).
51. Michael Stugrin, "Richardian Poetics and Late Medieval Cultural Pluriformity: The Significance of Pathos in the *Canterbury Tales*," *Chaucer Review* 15 (1980): 165. I will have more to say about pathos in chapter 5.
52. We now know, if we read the newspapers, about domestic abuse; we know that some women *can* obey their husbands even when it costs their

children's lives. We can try to read the Clerk's story as an exemplum, but we resist its moral in the strongest terms, unlike Harry Bailey.

53. I always wonder if the elaborate allegorizations of the *Song of Solomon* erased or eclipsed for medieval people the erotic responses the poem invites at first reading.
54. *Philosophical Investigations*, II, p. 181; cf. Monk's discussion of aspect-seeing and its relation to gestalt psychology, *Wittgenstein*, pp. 508–17.
55. Robertson, *A Preface to Chaucer* (Princeton, NJ: Princeton University Press, 1962), pp. 47, 82, and 269. A vast record of scholarly commentary on whether the tale is allegorical or exemplary has followed Robertson's *Preface*. John Finlayson sees the importance of Boccaccio's influence as well as Petrarch's and concludes that Chaucer offers both a tale of suffering and a severe allegory; "Petrarch, Boccaccio, and Chaucer's *Clerk's Tale*," *Studies in Philology* 97 (2000): 255–75. Warren Ginsberg stresses the subtle ways Chaucer takes control of his Petrarchan source; *Chaucer's Italian Tradition*, pp. 264–65. Anne Middleton ("The Clerk and His Tale: Some Literary Contexts," *SAC* 2 [1980]: 121–50) and Charlotte Morse ("The Exemplary Griselda," *SAC* 7 [1985]: 51–86) take opposite sides of the debate on where Chaucer and his Clerk imply. None of these accounts, or those I refer to in my *Chaucer and the Social Contest*, consider the ethical weight of Griselda's duties to her children. To emphasize the mental agility the Griselda tale requires, I ask my students to read Marga Cottino-Jones's "Fabula vs. Figura" in the Norton Critical *Decameron*, pp. 295–305 (first published in *Italica* 50 [1973]: 38–52).
56. Augustine's indictment of curiosity is found in *Confessions*, 10.35.57: *Veram tamen in quam multis minutissimus at contemptibilibus rebus curiositas cotidie nostra temptetur et quam saepe labamur, quis enumerate?* See also, *City of God*, III.13. To Angus Fletcher, it looks like the daemon-haunted man described by: "some characters are so possessed by an influence that excludes all other influences...that he has no life outside an exclusive sphere of action" (Fletcher, *Allegory*, pp. 41–59).
57. David Wallace, writing from a somewhat different angle opposes the reading as *exemplum* for five reasons (Wallace, *Chaucerian Polity*, pp. 286–93).
58. Haidu's fuller claim is that "even where intentionally established to function in subordination to an ideological superstructure (a Neoplatonic Form or Idea), is inherently subversive of such vehiculation, and betrays that externally imposed purpose by its very nature" (Haidu, "Repetition," 886).
59. Some elements in the story seem familiar to us as well. Marshall Leicester says his students thought of the taverners as fraternity boys "'Synne Horrible': The Pardoner's Exegesis of His Tale and Chaucer's," in *Acts of Interpretation*, ed. Mary Carruthers and Elizabeth Kirk (New York: Pilgrim Books, 1982), p. 37.
60. Pearsall, "Chaucer's Pardoner: The Death of a Salesman," *Chaucer Review* 17 (1983): 362.

61. Dinshaw, "Eunuch Hermeneutics," in *Chaucer's Sexual Poetics* (Madison: University of Wisconsin Press, 1989), p. 180.
62. This is, of course Kittredge's famous "paroxysm of anguished sincerity," in "Chaucer's Pardoner" (1893), rept. *Chaucer: Modern Essays in Criticism*, ed. Edward Wagenknecht (New York: Galaxy, 1959). Tuve describes the Pardoner's odd return to bilking as his disappearance into his allegory of avarice: "As we watch, the Pardoner becomes the very thing" (*Allegorical Imagery*, p. 177).
63. At the end of her book, Quilligan links the whole allegorical tradition with communion (*Language of Allegory*, p. 290). If she is right, the Pardoner's attempts to sell pardons at the end of his tale has an especially disruptive effect—not only does he shatter what might have been a shared moment of awakened moral awareness for the pilgrims, he has referred to the sacramental bread and wine in concluding his tale. This moment takes us close to the Kantian sublime and away from "good-heartedness."
64. Donatism arose in the year AD 311 as a jurisdictional dispute in the African Christian Church. Donatists took the position that unbelieving or openly sinful clerics could not administer the sacraments efficaciously. Defeated by Augustine himself, who provided "the first reasoned defense of the persecution of Christians by Christians," Donatism was nonetheless numerically preponderant in Africa in the fifth century and apparently survived until at least the seventh. It was not a heresy, but an attempt to return church offices to an Apostolic purity and resist their secularization. See *Encyclopedia of Religion and Ethics*, ed. James Hastings (New York: Scribners, 1955). Several parallels to fourteenth-century Lollardy suggest themselves in the scathing denunciations of anointed priests who are too vicious, neglectful, or undereducated to preach true doctrine.
65. See H. Marshall Leicester's challenging argument about the Pardoner's inner life in *Disenchanted Self* (Berkeley and Los Angeles: University of California Press, 1990), Part Two. I think the Pardoner may be credited with this complicated angst, but I wouldn't want to blunt the clear disapprobation the text invites us to feel about him. The counterfigure to the benevolent Parson, the Pardoner is a despoiler of the common people who cannot read his authorizing "bulls" from Rome. Fred Hoerner, in "Church Office, Routine, and Self-Exile in Chaucer's Pardoner," *SAC* 16 (1994): 69–98 describes the Pardoner's powerful performance as "a demonic version of charisma" and links him with his creation, the Old Man, in terms of the futility of their quests (75).
66. See Dinshaw's "Eunuch Hermeneutics," in *Sexual Poetics*, pp. 156–84.
67. Jon Whitman, *Allegory: The Dynamics of an Ancient and Medieval Technique* (Cambridge, MA: Harvard University Press, 1987), p. 77.
68. Sherry Reames ("The Cecilia Legend as Chaucer Inherited It and Retold It," *Speculum* 55 [1980]: 38–57) and others have pointed out subtle variations from the *Golden Legend* and the *Passio* that was Chaucer's second major source, but although the changes make Cecilia stronger, they do not detract from her moral reasoning.

69. Johnson, "Chaucer's Tale of the Second Nun and the Strategies of Dissent," *SP* 89 (1992): p. 324.
70. Wallace, *Chaucerian Polity*, p. 370. Interpretation, as the generations pass, will also *respond* to literary constructs in terms of its historical conditions of understanding.
71. Fletcher, *Allegory*, p. 8. Since the audiences for the *Canterbury Tales* inhabit different historical venues over the decades (and centuries), these effects would be differently felt.
72. Haidu, "Repetition," 884. John Foxe regards Chaucer as a Lollard author, although not on the grounds of tales like the Nun's; he thought of Chaucer as covering his tracks by masking his sympathies with humor; see John Foxe, *Acts and Monuments* (1583), rept. (London: AMS Press, 1965).
73. I will refer to the translation of Margaret Nims (Toronto, Canada: Pontifical Institute of Medieval Studies, 1967), p. 84.
74. Frye, *Anatomy of Criticism*, p. 186.
75. Fletcher argues that "allegory does not *need* to be read exegetically; it often has a literal surface that makes good enough sense all by itself. But somehow this literal surface suggests a certain doubleness of intention" becoming "richer and more interesting if given interpretation" (p. 7). I want to be more explicit about that "somehow" in the case of Chaucerian texts.
76. Many critics have commented on this echo from the Prologue. See, for example, my "Alisoun of Bath and the Reappropriation of Tradition," *Chaucer Review* 24 (1989): 45–52.
77. Mitchell, *Iconology*, p. 31 and Felperin, "Tongue-Tied Our Queen," p. 14 (see n. 25).
78. Among others, see the work of Georges Duby, *Medieval Marriage* (Baltimore, MD: Johns Hopkins University Press, 1978).
79. For example, Robertson argues that the Franklin's wrongheadedness is demonstrated in that none of the promises in the tale (except that which is included in the sacrament of marriage) deserve to have any binding force *Preface*, p. 276). From an entirely different vantage point. Susan Crane thinks taking the promise so seriously shows the Franklin's lack of courtly gentility by misvaluing breezy aristocratic love-talking. "Franklin as Dorigen," *Chaucer Review* 24 (1990): 243.
80. Muscatine, "The Emergence of Psychological Allegory in Old French Romance," *PMLA* 68 (1953): 1180 and 1161. Muscatine's point is that "in the psychology of the romances we are always in sight of the fictional situation, always aware of the forces surrounding the psychic event," which distinguishes them from Prudentius's style of moral allegory. They therefore present inner life in a manner "broadly characteristic of what has been called the period of subjectivity, of self-reliance and independent activity," following the crusades.
81. Although he does not admire her ethics, Robertson does take her to be a "realistically" conceived character, and faults her both for thinking her

case similar to those she cites in her rehearsal of noble suicides, and for abandoning the conclusion she had come to on account of them (*Preface*, p. 274).

82. Carruthers, "The *Gentilesse* of Chaucer's Franklin," *Criticism* 23 (1981): 295.
83. Crane, "The Franklin as Dorigen," 243.
84. Carruthers argues that Arveragus's generosity was not unrecorded or unpraised, even among aristocrats, but Crane is right that as a generic crux, the Franklin is departing from convention.
85. Whether there was a substantial "fabliau" tradition in English before Chaucer is discussed by Melissa Furow in "Middle English Fabliaux and Modern Myth," *ELH* 56 (1989): 1–18. She concludes that the generic category is best used for French instances and Chaucer's, Miller's, Reeve's, Summoner's, and Shipman's tales. For the *Wife's Prologue, Thopas, Nun's Priest's Tale, Merchant's Tale, and Manciple's Tale* she finds the term "bourd" more appropriate (p. 16).
86. Patterson, "Perpetual Motion," *SAC* 15 (1993): 25, n. 1.
87. The term "journalistic "is based on Cooper's account (*Oxford Guide*, p. 370). Charles Muscatine observes that nowhere else in Chaucer "is there such a solid, unspiritual mass of realism." See *Chaucer and the French Tradition* (Berkeley, CA: University of California Press, 1964), p. 220.
88. Strohm, "Some Generic Distinctions," 323.
89. Molinet, using Livy's version of the story, comes to another awkward moralization: "Virginia is daughter of God in that she is *anima*, yet must be beheaded by her helpless father if he is to keep her from the World," reported by Tuve, *Allegorical Imagery*, p. 308.
90. Not only does *Troilus and Criseyde* announce its genre early and late, from "double sorrow" (I.1) to "Go litel bok, litel myn tragedye" (V.1786), it plays out a tragic irony in the careers of both lovers. Each seeks to know and belong to the other, and the decisive steps taken toward that end lead to its destruction. Although it is somewhat unusual in the Middle Ages for lost love to be figured tragically, it is not out of keeping with either a fall from bliss or an Aristotelian sense of a protagonist's inadvertent self-defeat, since loving Criseyde was Troilus's "project." In this long poem, Chaucer demonstrates that a tragic conception can be freighted with temptations to see it allegorically without losing its tragic edge. On a smaller scale, the *Franklin's Tale*, while its plot does not go all the way to tragedy, also invokes tragic irony in that Dorigen makes her rash promise in an attempt to return her husband safely to her side and almost loses him thereby.

4 Beautiful Persons

1. Lee Patterson, "On the Margin: Postmodernism, Ironic History, and Medieval Studies," *Speculum* 65 (January 1990): 92. See also Susan Crane's incisive note on this essay and other positions that deny a simple progress narrative from early modernity toward our current sense of autonomous individuality; *The Performance of Self: Ritual, Clothing, and Identity During*

the Hundred Years War (Philadelphia: University of Pennsylvania Press, 2002), p. 179, n. 1.

2. Burckhardt, *Civilization of the Renaissance in Italy* (London: Phaidon, 1965), p. 81. But David Wallace argues that this passage might be taken to mean that medieval people were acutely conscious of themselves politically. *Chaucerian Polity: Absolutist Lineages and Associational Forms in England and Italy* (Stanford, CA: Stanford University Press, 1997), p. xiv.
3. Partner goes on: if the deep structure "could change so rapidly and profoundly, altered by the comings and goings of institutions and beliefs, then there could be no discipline of history at all, and our human endowment of memory would be a cruel deception"; "Reading *The Book of Margery Kempe*," *Exemplaria* 3 (Spring 1991): 61–62, I choose Partner's comment to face Burckhardt's because both are historians and the examples of Margery Kempe and Heloise that I will be using in the next few pages concern historical personages, although available to us only in textual form. Of course this choice also testifies to the interdependence of historical and literary analysis.
4. Gadamer, *Truth and Method*, pp. xxxiii–xxxiv and 340.
5. Carruthers, "Introduction," *Book of Memory*.
6. Crane, *Performance of Self*, p. 176.
7. Gadamer, *Truth and Method*, p. 474.
8. Even Harold Bloom, whose title *Shakespeare: The Invention of the Human* (New York: Penguin, 1998) and main contention would seem to point to the absence of full subjectivity in the Middle Ages, comes around to writing primarily about modes of representation (pp. 714 and 747). He often cites Chaucer as the prime influence on Shakespeare's inventive mode of characterization (e.g., pp. 278, 284, 288, 312, 401, 725, 727, and 732).
9. Peter Abelard, *The Story of Abelard's Adversities*, trans. J. T. Muckle (Toronto, Canada: Pontifical Institute of Medieval Studies, 1992), p. 40.
10. Carruthers, *Book of Memory*, pp. 179 and 182. See also, Barbara Newman, "Authority, Authenticity, and the Repression of Heloise," *JMRS* 22 (1992): 121–57, and Peggy Kamuf, *Fictions of Female Desires: Disclosures of Heloise* (Lincoln, NE: University of Nebraska Press, 1982), pp. 1–43.
11. Carruthers is working out a contrast between medieval mindsets and our emphasis on originality, but Bob Dylan was recently quoted as saying, "I seem to draw into myself whatever comes my way, and it comes out of me. Maybe I'm nothing but all these things I soak up" (*New York Times*, May 11, 2001): B 26. Dylan is a good writer (although not as good as Heloise) and often praised for originality.
12. Partner, "No Sex, No Gender," *Speculum* 68 (1993): 419–43.
13. Robertson *Preface to Chaucer* (Princeton, NJ: Princeton University Press, 1962), pp. 330–31.
14. Dollimore, *Radical Tragedy* (Chicago, IL: University of Chicago Press, 1986), p. 271.
15. As Patterson puts it, "It is of course true that human self-consciousness has been reified into the concept of a wholly autonomous individual,

a concept that has in turn been transformed into a fully fledged ideology of individualism. But this impeaches neither the fact of subjectivity itself nor its capacity to act within the world." See *Chaucer and the Subject of History* (Madison: University of Wisconsin Press, 1991), p. 12.

16. Hans Moravec, *Robot: Mere Machine to Transcendent Mind* (New York: Oxford University Press, 1999), pp. 194–95. A third-generation robot will be able to carry on a perfectly civilized conversation, and it will "believe itself to be conscious, just like other people!" (p. 113). Later on: "The next chapter suggests how we parents can gracefully retire as our mind children grow beyond our imagining" (p. 126).
17. In *The Feeling of What Happens*, Damasio's research is based on the observation of human behaviors and the impairment of normal functioning, often involving neuroimaging techniques.
18. Damasio, *What Happens*, p. 150.
19. Pasnau, *Aquinas on Human Nature*, p. 293.
20. Daniel Dennett, whose philosophical positions often pay close attention to AI and robotics, rejects the movie-in-the-brain image for that of consciousness as a nonmysterious "center of narrative gravity," which calls on various neural subroutines to control our adaptations to the world. This center is the self. See Dennett, *Consciousness Explained*, p. 418. In *Elbow Room: The Varieties of Free Will Worth Wanting* Dennett makes an extended argument for free will in a rationally understood universe.
21. Witmore, *Culture of Accidents*, pp. 93–94.
22. Scarry, *On Beauty and Being Just*, pp. 14 and 48.
23. Kolve, *Imagery of Narrative*, p. 60.
24. Cooper, *Structure*, p. 80.
25. Norman Holland said he wanted to write a book using psychoanalytic notions to interpret poetry without retelling the Oedipus story; the result was *5 Readers Reading* (New Haven, CT: Yale University Press, 1975), an engaging exercise in analyzing five of his students interpreting a poem, which nicely illustrates the "ego theme" as a touchstone for what is most loved.
26. Pound, *Selected Prose, 1909–1965*, ed. William Crookson (New York: New Directions, 1973), p. 25.
27. Pound, *Selected Prose*, p. 30.
28. Pound, *Selected Prose*, p. 22.
29. Foucault, *The Order of Things* (New York: Vintage Books, 1973).
30. Foucault, *The History of Sexuality I* (New York: Random House, 1980), p. 59.
31. Lochrie, *Covert Operations: The Medieval Uses of Secrecy* (Philadelphia: University of Pennsylvania Press, 1999), p. 14.
32. Lochrie, *Covert Operations*, p. 4.
33. Raskolnikov, "Confessional Literature, Vernacular Psychology, and the History of the Self in Middle English," *Literature Compass* 2 (2005). Online. http://www.blackwell-compass.com/subject/literature.
34. Patterson, *Chaucer and the Subject of History*, p. 385.

35. Lochrie, *Covert Operations*, Chap. 1, especially pp. 32–42. The priest has to extract every secret wish he can, but he might fall into sin himself, either by informing the confessant of new sins or by taking pleasure in hearing sins described.
36. His description accords closely with received doctrine, for which see Morton Bloomfield's *The Seven Deadly Sins: An Introduction to the History of a Religious Concept* (East Lansing: Michigan State University Press, 1952).
37. Foucault, *History of Sexuality*, p. 59.
38. Leicester, *The Disenchanted Self: Representing the Subject in the* Canterbury Tales (Berkeley and Los Angeles: University of California Press, 1990) p. 108.
39. Patterson calls his chapter on her "The Wife of Bath and the Triumph of the Subject," in *Subject of History*, quotation on page 282.
40. Dinshaw, *Chaucer's Sexual Poetics*, p. 124.
41. For example, although it is important for Dinshaw's argument that Alisoun seem like a real person in order to show that other scriptural exegetes are real persons, she also sees her as a figure of "the body of the text" in a general discussion within the *Tales* (*Sexual Poetics*, pp. 120–28).
42. Medieval audiences would have credited a well-stocked memory with a certain moral value, as Carruthers concludes (*Book of Memory*, p. 9).
43. Both Patterson (*Subject of History*, p. 309) and Cooper (*Structure*, p. 76) refer to her as a nightmare of the misogynist.
44. In disputing directly with the Fathers, Alisoun seems like Heloise, who learned disputation from Abelard, but whose letters "the formidable rhetorician, must have read…as an implicit challenge to his powers of argument," Kamuf, *Female Desire*, p. 26.
45. This interlace of sensible image with cognitive discernment is a feature of Aquinas's understanding of mind; see Pasnau on this subject, especially pp. 285–93.
46. Leicester, *The Disenchanted Self*, p. 42.
47. G. L. Kittredge, *Chaucer and His Poetry* (Cambridge, MA: Harvard University Press, 1915), p. 117.
48. Pound, *Selected Prose*, p. 25.
49. Harwood, "Chaucer and the Silence of History: Situating *The Canon's Yeoman's Tale*," *PMLA* 102 (1987): 343.
50. For example Catherine Belsey, *The Subject of Tragedy* (London: Metheun, 1985); Francis Barker, *Tremulous Private Body* (London: Methuen, 1984); Jonathan Dollimore, *Radical Tragedy*;and Terry Eagleton, *The Ideology of Aesthetics*.
51. See Karl Marx, *Capital: A Critique of Political Economy*, trans. Ben Fowkes, intro. Ernest Mandel (New York: Random House, 1977), pp. 272–73.
52. The Yeoman's description of the craft is so good that a few critics think Chaucer was in on the alchemical secret, others that he was cheated by a real-life alchemist and wrote his tale in revenge, adding it belatedly to

the in-progress plan of the *Canterbury Tales*. See John Reidy's notes in *Riverside Chaucer.*

53. Spearing, "'Introduction' to *Reading Dreams*, ed. Peter Brown (Oxford: Oxford University Press, 1999), pp. 2–3.
54. Spearing, *Medieval Dream Poetry* (Cambridge: Cambridge University Press, 1976), p. 49.
55. Medieval dreaming has attracted impressive array of commentary, notably Kathryn Lynch's *The High Medieval Dream Vision* (Stanford: Stanford University Press, 1988) and Steven Kruger's *Dreaming in the Middle Ages* (Cambridge: Cambridge University Press, 1992) in addition to Spearing's, but my point here is not to elaborate or adjudicate these findings, but to show how the dreams reported in the *Canterbury Tales* and *Troilus and Criseyde* imply inner life for his various dreamers.
56. English poetry in the second half of the fourteenth century relied heavily on the trope of the dream vision (one-third of the poems made use of it), in Peter Brown's count (without including Gower and Chaucer); see "On the Borders of Medieval Dream Visions" in *Reading Dreams*, p. 22. This particular dream territory acquired a certain weight through its connection to antiquity (appropriately invoked by the Knight's setting for his tale), and yet refuses a philosophically sound connection with "the transcendental world" (p. 23), perhaps to signal the trickery of the pre-Christian pantheon. Bonaventure begins *Mind's Way* with a Christian dream vision of St. Francis, presumably a trustworthy breaking through of transcendence.
57. Freud, *Interpretation of Dreams*, standard edn., Vol. 5 (1900–1901), trans. James Strachey (London: Hogarth Press, 1953): "significant secretions, such as semen, are replaced by indifferent ones" (II.359); for this case, I would say "more readily interpretable ones."
58. *Interpretation of Dreams*, I.97.
59. Leicester, *Disenchanted Self*, p. 102.
60. *Interpretation of Dreams*: what is fulfilled in some unpleasurable dreams is both the transgressive wish and an "equally an unconscious wish, namely that the dreamer may be punished for a repressed and forbidden wishful impulse" (II.557). I am not arguing that Alisoun's desire for Jankyn is repressed and punished in the dream, but that the dream is constructed as if it were.
61. Spearing *Medieval Dream Poetry*, p. 10.
62. *Interpretation of Dreams*, II.460.
63. *Livre de Seintz Medicines*, ed. J. Arnould, Anglo-Norman Text Society (Oxford: Blackwell, 1940; rept. New York: Barnes & Noble, 1966), pp. 16–17.
64. Pound in *Gaudier Brzeska: A Memior* (New York: New Directions, 1970), p. 89.
65. Green. "Chaucer's Victimized Women," *Studies in the Age of Chaucer* 10 (1988): 18.
66. Burrow, *Gestures and Looks in Medieval Narrative* (Cambridge: Cambridge University Press, 2002), p. 87. The distinction between deliberate and

symptomatic looks goes back to Augustine's discussion of signs in Book II of *On Christian Doctrine.*

67. For another view of Griselda's swoon in the final scene, see Elaine Tuttle Hansen, *Chaucer and the Fictions of Gender* (Berkeley: University of California Press, 1992), pp. 193–94: "She knows that any power she has lies in continuing to excel at suffering...and that the promise of a happy ending precludes her potential for martyred apotheosis, and forces her to awaken into the reality of her material, gendered powerlessness."
68. Crane, *Performance of Self*, p. 11.
69. Crane, *Performance of Self*, p. 37. Throughout her analysis, Crane takes material signs and gestures as reliable signs of inner constitutions (more than I do), attributing real negotiating powers to women like Griselda. But some critics who attend to the gestural, take the term as entirely negative and empty. For example, Francis Barker dismisses *Hamlet*'s vaunted subjectivity as an illusion, a "nothing," disclaiming that no reading of it from his words and actions is valid; *Tremulous Body*, p. 36. But refusing to interpret Hamlet's gestures is ultimately dismissing all conjecture about human innards, consigning them to Moravec's enigmatic "salty squirts" though even Moravec (in *Robot*) quotes Hamlet. I am more positive about gestures than Barker, but less than Crane.
70. For a similar conclusion from a different perspective, see David Wallace, *Chaucerian Polity* (Stanford, CA: Stanford University Press, 1997), pp. 261–93.
71. Witmore, *Culture of Accidents*, p. 17.
72. Erwin Panofsky, some time ago, connected vanishing point perspective and the particularization of portraiture in painting with Ockhamite nominalism and a shift in the mental habits that govern interpretation in all the arts. Images then came to be perceived as arresting in themselves, rather than offered "in a prefabricated projection"; *Gothic Architecture and Scholasticism* (London: Meridian Books, 1957), p. 17 and *passim.*
73. Finding this direction in fourteenth-century Italian art is, of course, entirely in keeping with Burckhardt's chronology for "Renaissance" individualized attention; Dante is one of his primary exemplars (*Civilization*, pp. 84–85).
74. *Gestures and Looks*, pp. 125–26.
75. Robertson, *Preface*, p. 34; Singer, "Beautiful Errors."
76. Robert Payne, for example, argues in *The Key to Remembrance* (New Haven, CT: Yale University Press, 1963), that Criseyde is a type, "a way of saying something about the lovely vanity of human wishes" (p. 226), but also acknowledges the nuanced style of her portrait. Sheila Delany, "Techniques of Alienation in *Troilus and Criseyde*," in *Chaucer's Troilus and Criseyde "Subgit to alle Poesye" Essays in Criticism*, ed. R. A. Shoaf (Binghamton, NY: Center for Medieval and Early Renaissance Studies, 1992), similarly contrasts the passages through which she demonstrates the alienation effect with "the psychological depth and realism to which the poem has accustomed us" (p. 36).

77. Dennett, *Consciousness Explained*, p. 306. Here Dennett is making a distinction very much like Augustine's treatment of signs.
78. I agree with Dieter Mehl in referring to Chaucer's technique in Book II in this way. He writes about another passage in Book II as, "interior monologue or reported thought which hardly appears in English fiction before Jane Austen," and goes on to discuss several of Chaucer's strategies in terms of eighteenth- and nineteenth-century novels. See "The Audience of *Troilus and Criseyde*," in Chaucer's *Troilus: Essays in Criticism*, ed. Stephen Barney (Hamden, CT: Archon Books, 1980), p. 221.
79. Benson, *Chaucer's Troilus and Criseyde* (London: Unwin Hyman, 1990), p. 110.
80. Delany, *Troilus and Criseyde*, p. 37. Reading these gestures depends partly on whether one sees them as "expressing" inner states intentionally or not, rather than "reporting" them, which certainly involves intention and may involve lying or posing, as Delany argues. Christopher Conner, a student of mine from the drama department told me that actors can be taught to blush on cue.
81. Chrétien de Troyes, "Erec and Enid" and "The Story of the Grail," in *Arthurian Romances*, trans. William Kibler (Harmondsworth, UK: Penguin Books, 1991), pp. 48 and 432.

5 The Beauty of Women

1. *The English Text of the Ancrene Riwle*, ed. A. C. Baugh, EETS 232 (London: Oxford University Press, 1956), p. 4. The pit in Exodus is a hazard to cattle, and the question at issue is about restitution for a trapped ox. See also *Ancrene Wisse*, EETS 325 (London: Oxford University Press, 2005).
2. Ferrante, *Woman as Image in Medieval Literature from the Twelfth Century to Dante* (New York: Columbia University Press, 1975), p. 80.
3. Both Jerome (*Selected Letters*, ed. F. A. Wright [London: Loeb Classical Library, 1954], p. 161) and Hortensius (quoted by Constance Jordan, "Boccaccio's In-Famous Women" in Carole Levin and Jeanie Watson's *Ambiguous Realities* [Detroit, MI: Wayne State University Press, 1997], p. 30) put the matter that way. See Carolyn Bynum's *Holy Feast and Holy Fast* (Berkeley and Los Angeles: University of California Press, 1987), p. 28 and n. 68 for other examples.
4. Ferrante, *Woman as Image*, p. 63.
5. Eagleton, *The Ideology of the Aesthetic* (Oxford: Blackwell, 1990), p. 16.
6. Armstrong, *The Radical Aesthetic* (Oxford: Blackwell, 2000), p. 31. The first thing wrong with the aesthetic is that it combines with other domains and confounds discrimination; it is "runny."
7. Wollstonecraft is quoted by Mary Poovey in "Aesthetics and Political Economy in the Eighteenth Century: The Place of Gender in the Social Construction of Knowledge," in *Aesthetics and Ideology*, ed. George Levine (New Brunswick, NY: Rutgers University Press, 1994), p. 92.

8. Eagelton (*Ideology of the Aesthetic*, p. 28) is alluding here, with approval, to Max Horkheimer's position.
9. Williams, *Marxism and Literature*, p. 156. I find this formulation awkward and evasive, but even so it acknowledges the importance of aesthetic effects.
10. Marcuse, *The Aesthetic Dimension* (Boston, MA: Beacon Press, 1977), p. 62.
11. Ferrante, *Woman as Image*, p. 74. Elaine Scarry's comment suggests the same emphasis: the beautiful thing is a wake-up call to perception. See *On Beauty and Being Just*, p. 81.
12. This paradox in medieval thought is aptly characterized by Suzannah Biernhoff in *Sight and Embodiment in the Middle Ages*,. Spiritual vision may appear as "both the *opposite* and the *analogue*of bodily sight" (p. 112, italics in the original).
13. Bonaventure, *The Mind's Road to God*, p. 17. This position is very much like Scarry's throughout her book.
14. Singer, "Beautiful Errors," 8.
15. Marcuse, *Aesthetic Dimension*, p. 62.
16. *Psychomachia. In Prudentius*, trans. H. J. Thomson (Cambridge, MA: Harvard University Press, 1949), I.301–03.
17. That suggestion is, of course, in the word *queynte*. See my *Time Bound Words: Semantic and Social Economies from Chaucer's England to Shakespeare's* (London: Palgrave Macmillan, 2000), pp. 130–42.
18. Sugrin, "Richardian Poetics and Late Medieval Cultural Pluriformity: The Significance of Pathos in the *Canterbury Tales*," *Chaucer Review* 15 (1980): 165.
19. Augustine, *Confessions*, 3.2.2–3.
20. Frye, *Anatomy of Criticism*, p. 38.
21. Thomas Bestul, "The Man of Law's Tale and the Rhetorical Foundations of Chaucer's Pathos," *Chaucer Review* 9 (1975): 223.
22. Augustine, *Confessions*, 3.2.2–4.
23. Frye, *Anatomy of Criticism*, p. 39.
24. Bloch, "Chaucer's Maiden's Head: *The Physician's Tale* and the Poetics of Virginity," *Representations* 28 (Fall 1989): 128 and *Medieval Misogyny and the Invention of Western Romantic Love* (Cambridge : Cambridge University Press, 1991).
25. Scarry, *On Beauty and Being Just*, p. 47.
26. Evans, "Virginities," in *The Cambridge Companion to Medieval Women's Writing*, ed. Carolyn Dinshaw and David Wallace (Cambridge: Cambridge University Press, 2003), pp. 33–35.
27. From a different angle, Evans concludes that the tensions over virginity in the tale serve as a "displacement of anxiety about social mobility" ("Virginities," p. 35).
28. Guerin, "Chaucer's Pathos: Three Variations," *Chaucer Review* 20 (1985): 101.
29. Helen Cooper notes that the " most distinctive stylistic feature of the tale is its generous proportion of comment to narrative (*Oxford Guide*, p. 135).

30. See David Wallace, *Chaucerian Polity* (Stanford, CA: Stanford University Press, 1997), p. 202.
31. Frye, *Anatomy of Criticism*, p. 39. The *Tales* are in general wary of appeals to pity by the sufferer. The Merchant, goaded by the Host to speak of his own suffering in marriage, declines: "but of mine owene soor, / For soory herte, I telle may namoore" (IV.1243–44), only to present a displaced, and not self-regarding, image of male suffering in his tale.
32. Hill, *Chaucerian Belief: The Poetics of Reverence and Delight* (New Haven, CT: Yale University Press, 1991), p. 148.
33. Lynch, "Despoiling Griselda," *SAC* 10 (1988): 60.
34. Wallace, *Chaucerian Polity*, p. 82.
35. Hofstadter, *Gödel, Escher, Bach* (New York: Vintage Books, 1980), p. 564.
36. Hill, *Chaucerian Belief*, p. 115.
37. Beverly Kennedy finds certain passages in early manuscripts of the *Wife's Prologue* interpolations by a scribe who moves Alisoun's characterization to a closer fit with clerical versions of women's frailties. See "Cambridge MS Dd.4.24: A Misogynous Scribal Revision of the *Wife of Bath's Prologue*?" *Chaucer Review* 30 (1996): 343–58 and "The Rewriting of the *Wife of Bath's Prologue* in Cambridge MS Dd.4.24," in *Rewriting Chaucer: Culture, Authority and the Idea of the Authentic Text, 1400–1602*, ed. Thomas Prendergast and Barbara Kline (Columbus: Ohio University Press, 1999), pp. 203–33. Suzanne Reynolds discusses the attempts of medieval glossators to guide reading practices toward the assimilation of pagan texts into Christian culture (*Medieval Reading* [Cambridge: Cambridge University Press, 1996]).
38. Umberto Eco is here translating Chalcidius's commentary on the *Timaeus* and claiming this stance toward the beauty of the natural world to be "fundamental in the formation of medieval thought." *Art and Beauty in the Middle Ages*, trans. Hugh Bredin (New Haven, CT: Yale University Press, 1986), p. 17.
39. Aspect is discussed in *Philosophical Investigations*, II.166–82. The idea of the dawning of aspect (*aufleuchten*), which links Wittgenstein's thinking with *claritas* as well as *integritas*, is discussed on II.166.
40. Near the end of the poem, the narrator excuses himself from condemning Criseyde "Forther than the storye wol devyse" (V.1094), which clearly points to a meaning combining elements of "exemplify" and "explicate." The usage that stresses fashioning or construction is in use as late as Samuel Harsnett's *Declarations*, where he calls Catholic exorcists "devisers of new devils"; quoted in Stephen Greenblatt, *Shakespearean Negotiations* (Berkeley and Los Angeles: University of California Press, 1988), p. 104.
41. Biernoff, *Sight and Embodiment*, p. 163.
42. *Kynde* here is likely to have both its primary meaning, in Middle English, "nature," but also its emerging one "genre."
43. Her lack of steadfastness in love counts against her with the greatest force if the poem is seen in terms of romantic love-loyalty; in epic tales love must take second place to civic duties, as it does when Aeneas deserts Dido.

44. The coherence of the image of Criseyde is the result of its designer's *idea*, which Aquinas likens to God's conception "according to whose pattern the world was made" and the architect's mental design for a house (quoted in Erwin Panofsky, *Idea: A Concept in Art Theory*, trans. Joseph J. S. Peake [New York: Harper and Row, 1968], p. 41). Chaucer (after Vinsauf) uses the same metaphor as Aquinas in *Troilus and Criseyde*, I.1065–71: "For everi wight that hath an hous to founde" (see above p. 24).
45. Strohm, *Social Chaucer* (Cambridge, MA: Harvard University Press, 1989), p. 63.
46. Evans notes that "medieval people read the virgin-martyr lives symbolically as well as literally" in identifying Margaret as the patron saint of childbirth because she had emerged unscathed from the belly of the dragon ("Virginitas," p. 23).
47. Quoted in Peter Haidu, "Repetition: Modern Reflections on Medieval Aesthetics," *MLN* 92 (1977): 881 and 883.
48. Robertson, *A Preface to Chaucer*, pp. 472–73; further citations appear in the text parenthetically.
49. Denomy, "The Two Moralities of Chaucer's *Troilus and Criseyde*," in *Chaucer Criticism:* Troilus and Criseyde *and the Minor Poems*, ed. Richard J. Shoeck and Jerome Taylor (Notre Dame, IN: Notre Dame University Press, 1961), pp. 147–159.
50. "Techniques of Alienation," in *Chaucer's Troilus and Criseyde "Subgit to alle Poesye," Essays in Criticism*, ed. R. A. Shoaf (Binghamton, NY: Center for Medieval and Early Renaissance Studies, 1992), p. 30.
51. A softer version of the allegorical reading takes Criseyde to be a figure for Nature. The error of misplaced trust invites reader sympathies for characters who must love without the revelation offered by Christ. The beauties of the early books will seem in this reading genuine, but limited, rather than ironic, when salvation history is known, as it is in the epilogue. See my "The Nature of Nature: Criseyde's 'Slydyng Corage,'" *Chaucer Review* 13 (1978): 133–40.
52. Robertson, *Preface*, p. 473. For a detailed argument that *The Consolation of Philosophy* does not underwrite the "tragedy of Fortune," see Monica McAlpine, *The Genre of* Troilus and Criseyde (Ithaca, NY: Cornell University Press, 1978), Chap. 2. Moreover, Boethius does not assert the worthlessness of the world's gifts and his treatise does not end with a "coda" that banishes the "hydra" of the world's confusion, but retains "the openness of life itself" (p. 84).
53. Eco, *Art and Beauty*, p. 56.
54. E. Dinshaw, "Reading Like a Man: The Critics, Troilus, the Narrator and Pandarus," in *Chaucer's Sexual Poetics*, p. 51.
55. That this "necessity" is transhistorical is a point first made most forcefully by Gayle Rubin in her indispensable essay "The Traffic in Women: Notes on the 'Political Economy' of Sex," in *Toward an Anthropology of Women*, ed. R. R. Reiter (New York: Monthly Review Press, 1975).
56. Dinshaw, *Sexual Poetics*, p. 62.

57. Elaine Tuttle Hansen, *Chaucer and the Fictions of Gender* (Berkeley: University of California Press, 1991), p. 156.
58. In this reading, it is doubtful that Criseyde's physical beauty causes anything, and her qualities of mind and heart (including her agency, which the men assume, but is actually lacking) are thoroughly problematized (Hansen, *Fictions of Gender*, p. 178).
59. It is not clear to me how any author could stand in any other relation to his or her created character, but for Hansen this state of affairs arises from the social power of men.
60. Hansen, *Fictions of Gender*, p. 162.
61. McAlpine, "Criseyde's Prudence," *SAC* 25 (2003): 199–224.
62. Aers, *Chaucer, Langland and the Creative Imagination* (London: Routledge, 1980), p. 129.
63. Williams, *Marxism and Literature*, p. 133.
64. Singer, "Beautiful Errors," p. 16.
65. Aers, *Creative Imagination*, p. 123.
66. Ian Watt's influential thesis in *Rise of the Novel* is that interest in the psychology of its characters is the hallmark of the novel, especially from the 1840s on, is just one of many loci for this premise.
67. Greenblatt, *Renaissance Self-Fashioning* (Chicago, IL: University of Chicago Press, 1980), Chap. 1.
68. Ricoeur, quoted in Cathleen Bauschatz's "Montaigne's Conception of Reading," in *The Reader in the Text*, ed. Susan Suleiman and Inge Crosman (Princeton, NJ: Princeton University Press, 1980), p. 284. For Augustine, I am of course invoking the famous *tole et lege* passage in the *Confessions* (8.12.29).
69. Mehl, "The Audience of *Troilus and Criseyde*," in *Chaucer's Troilus: Essays in Criticism*, ed. Stephen Barney (Hamden, CT: Archon Books, 1980), p. 221. I agree with Mehl about prose fiction, although on the stage such internal rumination was represented in Shakespeare and several of his contemporaries. The likeness to Austen is very apt: Book II closely resembles *Emma*, Vol. 1, Chap. 16, in which Emma's internal musings are reported by a narrator with just enough distance to allow for both empathy and critique.
70. Aers, *Creative Imagination*, p. 119.

6 The Aesthetics of Laughter

1. Dennett, *Consciousness Explained* (Boston, MA: Little, Brown, 1991), pp. 62–65.
2. *Summa Theologiae*, 1–2.1.6 ad 1; discussed by Umberto Eco, *The Aesthetics of Thomas Aquinas* (Cambridge, MA: Harvard University Press, 1988), pp. 17 and 50.
3. Freud, *Jokes and Their Relation to the Unconscious*, Standard edn., Vol. 8 (1905), trans. James Strachey (London: Hogarth Press, 1960), pp. 10–11; hereafter cited in the text as *JRU*.

4. Bergson, *Laughter: An Essay on the Meaning of the Comic*, trans. Cloudesley Brerston and Fred Rothwell (New York: Macmillan, 1912), p. 61; hereafter cited in the text as L.
5. *Understanding Brecht*, quoted in Terry Eagleton, *The Ideology of the Aesthetic* (Oxford: Blackwell, 1990), pp. 337–38. Kant is also attentive to the somatic effects of laughter (*CJ*, p. 201), coming to conclusions similar to Benjamin's.
6. Kant also respected the "rare talent" involved in creating humor (*CJ*, p. 201).
7. De Bolla, *Art Matters* (Cambridge, MA: Harvard University Press, 2001), pp. 95–96.
8. Muscatine, *Chaucer and the French Tradition* (Berkeley and Los Angeles: University of California Press, 1957), p. 224.
9. The principle of thrift had been available in the rhetorical tradition since the ancients; see Kathy Eden, *Hermeneutics and the Rhetorical Tradition* (New Haven, CT: Yale University Press, 1997). I have also described thrift in terms of Daniel Dennett's "epistemic hunger" and its satisfaction (above, chapter 2).
10. Robertson, *A Preface to Chaucer*, pp. 20–22. Robertson's reasoning is explicit, but Dryden's edition purged "undecent" words and Byron (not exactly a prude himself) found some of the tales "obscene and contemptible." Dryden and Byron are discussed in Laura Kendrick's *Chaucerian Play: Comedy and Control in the* Canterbury Tales (Berkeley and Los Angeles: University of California Press, 1988), pp. 23–24. Hereafter cited as *CP*.
11. Michael Camille makes an argument similar to mine in connection with humorously carnal images drawn in the margins of liturgical texts: "it is not always clear that the margins depict the deadly distractions of the flesh that are meant to be transcended through the spirit of the letter, as has been strongly argued [note to Robertson]; *Image on the Edge: The Margins of Medieval Art* (Cambridge, MA: Harvard University Press, 1992), p. 28.
12. Although Bergson (pp. 148 and 170) and Kant find humor less intrinsically worthy of attention than "fine art," it is nonetheless the product of an "enlivening...originality of mind" (Kant, *CJ*, p. 203)
13. Kendrick, *Chaucerian Play*, p. 158.
14. Ideology critique, though, has encouraged critics to make an "interested" investment in contending pilgrim's positions. Some favor the theologically "correct" and some are on the side of those who represent a disenfranchized class status in the medieval hierarchy. A tendentious investment in a joke cannot yield specifically aesthetic pleasure because it pleases through interest, both in justifying one's own position and in enjoying the fun the joker deliberately "intended." De Bolla's "Toward the Materiality," in *Art Matters*, p. 26 is relevant here.
15. *Chaucer and the Imagery of Narrative: The First Five Canterbury Tales* (Stanford, CA: Stanford University Press, 1984), pp. 5 and 20. "Imaginative

vividness" is Kolve's rendering of *enargeia* (p. 59); I would link some instances of it with *claritas*.

16. Two terms from ancient rhetoric seem to have been used as near synonyms later. Energeia suggests movement, even wildness; *enargeia* vividness and stylistic energy. Madeleine Doran, *Endeavors of Art: A Study of Form in Elizabethan Drama* (Madison: University of Wisconsin Press, 1954), p. 242.
17. Hutcheon, *A Theory of Parody: The Teachings of Twentieth-Century Art Forms* (New York: Methuen, 1985), p. 16; hereafter cited in the text as *TP.*
18. Kolve, *Imagery of Narrative*, p. 60.
19. Kolve, *Imagery of Narrative*, pp. 160–61.
20. Kendrick, *Chaucerian Play*, pp. 57 and 98–99. Kendrick points to two ways of responding to irreverent humor: "If the function of serious exegesis was—and is—to cooperate with the censoring artifices of fiction, to mask and prolong the forbidden pleasures of the text by further sublimating and authorizing them," unserious interpretation (then and now) wallowed in them (p. 32).
21. Olson, *Literature as Recreation in the Later Middle Ages* (Ithaca, NY, and London: Cornell University Press, 1982), on Aquinas (pp. 49 and 98) and on Petrarch (pp. 128–29). I cannot agree with Olson, though, that Chaucer did not regard his "cherles tales" with the same seriousness as those in other genres, in part because they can always be seen as taking on another layer of complication by being told within the "inner frame" of the storytelling contest and the "outer frame" of the pilgrimage; pp. 156–57.
22. Vaszily, "Fabliau Plotting Against Romance in Chaucer's *Knight's Tale*," *Style* 31 (1997): 531.
23. Morey, "The 'Cultour' in the *Miller's Tale*: Alison as Iseult," *Chaucer Review* 29 (1995): 373.
24. As Muscatine puts it, "It is the solidity of detail, along with the characterization interlaced intimately with it, that gives the ingenious plotting its overpowering substantiality." This economy in the use of narrative detail is another contrast with the *Knight's Tale*, which contains "a richness of detail far in excess of the demands of the story" (*French Tradition*, pp. 226 and 177).
25. The phrase is from Muscatine, *French Tradition*, p. 226.
26. Brown, "'Shot Window' (*Miller's Tale* I.3358 and 3695): An Open and Shut Case," *Medium AEvum* 69 (2000): 106. Commenting on another material object in the tale, James Morey concludes that hot coulters were still understood as involved in ordeals that tested for sexual fidelity, though they were forbidden in Chaucer's day; see "The Cultour in the *Miller's Tale:* Alison as Iseult," *Chaucer Review* 29 (1995): 373–75.
27. I am not as convinced as I used to be of the outrageousness of John's believing Nicholas's prophecy, now that I read about the far bigger sacrifices some of my contemporaries are making in connection with a predicted apocalypse. Nonetheless, the outrageousness of the tale is still striking in its alignment and timing of motives and accidents.

28. Mark Miller, "Naturalism and Its Discontents in the *Miller's Tale*," in *Philosophical Chaucer: Love, Sex, and Agency in the Canterbury Tales*. Cambridge Studies in Medieval Literatu no returnre. Ser. 55 (Cambridge: Cambridge University Press, 2004), p. 63.
29. A similar repetition is that of sweetness. Nicholas is "as sweete as is the roote / Of licorys or any cetewale" and his room was full of sweet herbs (3206–7); Alison's mouth was "as sweete as bragot or the meeth" or drying apples (3261–62). Absolon chewed cardamom and *lycorys* to smell sweet (3690–91) before his wooing expedition, and calls Alison "sweet" under her window. Note that, in this matter, the characters distinguish themselves in terms of nature and culture just as they did in their musical talents.
30. See my *Time-Bound Words* (New York: St. Martin's, 2000), Chap. 10 for the early history of the term *sely*. The fact that the term can carry pathos as well as mockery recalls Kierkegaard's dictum: "The pathos which is not secured by the presence of the comic is illusion; the comic spirit that is not made secure by the presence of pathos is immature"; *Concluding Unscientific Postscript*, trans. David F. Swenson and Walter Lowrie (Princeton, NJ: Princeton University Press, 1941), p. 81.
31. The weasel in some medieval bestiaries conceived through the ear and was therefore associated with Mary's virginity. See Joseph D. Parry, "Female Agency in the *Miller's Tale* and the *Merchant's Tale*," *PQ* 80 (2001): 147.
32. *Imagery of Narrative*, p. 206.
33. Fredrick M. Briggs and Laura L. Howes argue that Nicholas's claim to knowledge of a second flood may complicate this part of the religious parody by suggesting a reference to the "back parts" (Incarnation) God allowed Moses to see and its medieval commentaries on the limits of human knowledge; see "Theophany," *MAE* 65 (1996): 270–73.
34. Muscatine, *French Tradition*, p. 224.
35. Morton Bloomfield, "The *Miller's Tale*—An UnBoethian Interpretation," in *Medieval Literature and Folklore Studies: Essays in Honor of Francis Lee Utley*, ed. Jerome Mandel and Bruce A. Rosenberg (New Brunswick, NJ: Rutgers University Press, 1970), pp. 205–12. Kolve, *Imagery of Narrative*, p. 160.
36. Mark Miller stresses, as I do, but with somewhat different emphases, "the philosophical seriousness of the tale, the depth to which it engages the normative problems raised in the Knight's Tale rather than merely evading the with a joke: Chaucer means the tale as more than an occasion for laughs, and as more than the expression of a churlish man who simply fails to see what the Knight's concerns are" (Miller, "Naturalism and Its Discontents," p. 45). I agree that the tale is not *merely* a joke, but it *is* a joke on the Miller's part and an occasion for laughter among the pilgrims. After reflection, it seems a comic challenge on Chaucer's part to the Miller as well as his satiric targets who, as Mark Miller argues, assumes that the normative questions the Knight asks need to be answered (p. 49).

37. Ricoeur, *From Text to Action*, p. 171.
38. The phrase is from Kendrick's *Chaucerian Play*, p. 148.
39. The shape of the genre probably took on definition through its French, rather than its Middle English instances, as Melissa Furrow has argued in "Middle English Fabliaux and Modern Myth," *ELH* 56 (1989): 1–18.
40. Kolve, *Imagery of Narrative*, p. 252.
41. This tendentious joke, as both Lee Patterson and Britton Harwood see it, is aimed at both the character Symkyn and the Reeve himself. Patterson (*Chaucer and the Subject of History* [Madison: University of Wisconsin Press, 1991]) takes the view that the Reeve's requittal of the Miller disrupts any sense of unified interests among the third estate and "reinvokes" religious perspectives (pp. 274–75). Harwood ("Psychoanalysis as Politics," *ELH* [2001]: 1–27) deduces from place names and other features a detailed account of the substructure of historical concerns that can be read out of this tale, and particularly its instances of incoherence. "In the text surrounding the Reeve, the relationship is antagonistic because Chaucer identified himself with two potentially antagonistic points of view" (16–17).
42. Kolve, *Imagery of Narrative*, p. 253.
43. Mark Miller sees the requiting among Knight, Miller, and Reeve as pointedly concerned with the role of human reason and control—Knight and Miller worried, Reeve cynical (*Philosophical Chaucer*, p. 56). He is complicating Muscatine's estimate of the *Reeve's Tale* as the prime example of naturalism "unequalled in medieval times" *French Tradition*, p. 197).
44. Muscatine, *French Tradition*, p. 199.
45. "The *Reeve's Tale* and the Comedy of Limitation," in *Directions in Literary Criticism: Contemporary Approaches to Literature*, ed. Stanley Weintraub and Philip Young (University Park: Pennsylvania State University Press, 1973), p. 61.
46. Harwood, "Chaucer on Speche: *House of Fame, The Friar's Tale*, and the *Summoner's Tale*," *Chaucer Review* 26 (1992): 344.
47. O'Brien, "'Ars-Metrik': Science, Satire, and Chaucer's Summoner," *Mosaic* 23 (1990): 2, 4, and 8.
48. Kant identifies this sort of anticlimax as an aesthetic pattern (*CJ*, p. 199).
49. Pulsiano, "The Twelve-spoked Wheele of the *Summoner's Tale*," *Chaucer Review* 29 (1995): 383.
50. Georgianna, "Lords, Churls, and Friars: The Return to Order in the *Summoner's Tale*," in *Rebels and Rivals: The Contestive Spirit in* The Canterbury Tales, ed. Susanna Greer Fein, David Raybin, and Peter Braeger (Kalamazoo, MI: Medieval Institute Publications, 1991), p. 151.
51. Alan Levitan, "The Parody of Pentecost in Chaucer's *Summoner's Tale*," *UTQ* 40 (1971): 236–46 and V. A. Kolve, "Chaucer's Wheel of False Religion: Theology and Obscenity in 'The Summoner's Tale,'" in *The Centre and Its Compass: Studies in Medieval Literature in Honor of Professor John Leyerle*, ed. Robert A. Taylor, et al. (Kalamazoo, MI: Medieval Institute Publications, 1993).

52. John V. Flemming, "The Summoner's Prologue: An Iconographic Adjustment," *Chaucer Review* 2 (1967): 95–107.
53. Bakhtin, *The Dialogic Imagination: Four Essays*, ed. Michael Holquist, trans. Caryl Emerson and Michael Holquist (Austin: University of Texas Press, 1981), pp. 50–51 and 65. Chaucer's work offers especially interesting examples of "interanimation" as it continually introduces terms and phrases from Latin and continental writing, but, more importantly, as it recontextualizes language and imagery from disparate English discourse systems like the cooks who "turnen substaunce into accident" in the *Pardoner's Tale*, VI.539. See my *Chaucer and the Social Contest* (New York: Routledge, 1990) and Thomas Farrell's *Bakhtin and Medieval Voices* (Gainesville, FL: University of Florida Press, 1995).
54. Hutcheon, *A Theory of Parody*, pp. 16 and 32. Hutcheon alludes to the ambiguity of the prefix *para* in *parody*, which can mean either "counter" or "beside," with clear implications for the range of effects to be produced by the form (p. 32).
55. James Andreas calls on Bakhtin's descriptions of carnival to explain this feature of the *Summoner's Tale*: "sacred time and space are reversed but collapsed and deflated; they are familiarized but are rendered rehabiltable and manageable by common folk. The sacred, in short, is domesticated." ("'Newe Science' from 'Olde Bokes': A Bakhtinian Approach to the *Summoner's Tale*," *Chaucer Review* 25 [1990]: 138–51). Kendrick makes a similar point, also Bakhtinian: gargoyles and the like "stabilize the cultural structures [of cathedrals] not only by a kind of catharsis or exteriorization of dangerously destabilizing internal forces, but...through the mimesis of reversal, they also encourage a renewal of the forces necessary to maintain the structure.... This is the logic of Carnival" (*Chaucerian Play*, p. 158).
56. Hutcheon writes, "Even in mocking, parody reinforces; in formal terms, it inscribes the mocked conventions onto itself, thereby guaranteeing their cultural existence" (*Theory of Parody*, p. 75).
57. Lee Patterson, "'What Man Artow?': Authorial Self-Definition in *The Tale of Sir Thopas* and *The Tale of Melibee*," *Studies in the Ages of Chaucer* 11 (1989): 124.
58. I say "what we now call parody" because Joseph Dane has argued that parody only begins to appear in seventeenth- and eighteenth-century codifications. He writes: "My work on parody has made me very skeptical of claims for the universality of a parodic genre, subgenre, or even technique" (p. 5) and "Only after the genre was described and its definitive examples named...could it be discovered elsewhere—in ancient literature, in medieval and Renaissance literature" (p. 205). *We* may regard *Sir Thopas* as a parody, but "Chaucer could not have written it as a 'parody,' 'burlesque,' or 'travesty' if these words and the generic categories which these words tend to create did not exist." See *Parody: Critical Concepts Versus Literary Practices, Aristophanes to Sterne* (Norman: University of Oklahoma Press, 1988). Melissa Furrow observes that English instances of

fabliau were not numerous enough to establish the genre before Chaucer, but the effects of certain tales match those of their French counterparts ("Middle English Fabliaux and Modern Myth," *ELH* 56 (1989): 1-18). Both fabliau and parody remain useful categories for analysis.

59. Bradbury, "Chaucerian Minstrelsy: *Sir Thopas, Troilus and Criseyde* and the English Metrical Romance," in *Tradition and Translation in Medieval Romance*, ed. Rosalind Field (Cambridge: D. S. Brewer, 1999), p. 119. Bradbury's conclusion is that the "language of English romance is only one stream in the confluence of Chaucerian styles, but it clearly had its uses" (p. 124). The belatedness issue in general is related to Frye's general dictum that parody occurs when "certain vogues…are getting worn out" (Frye, *Anatomy of Criticism*, p. 103).
60. Frye, *Anatomy of Criticism*, p. 277.
61. Lerer, "'Now holde youre mouth': The Romance of Orality in the *Thopas-Melibee* Section of the *Canterbury Tales*," in *Oral Poetics in Middle English Poetry*, ed. Mark Amodio (New York: Garland, 1994), pp. 185–212; "narrator errant" is on p. 186. It is even possible that sophisticated arithmetic proportions are involved in the poetics of *Thopas*: "in what is on the face of it his most chaotic work Chaucer, more completely than in any of his other compositions, mimics the divinely ordered act of creation 'by measure number, and weight.'" See E. A. Jones, "'Loo, Lordes Myne, Heere is a Fit!': The Structure of Chaucer's *Sir Thopas*," *RES* 51 (2002): 249. Whether the arrangement of the lines in the three fits (the diapason, which signifies cosmic order) would have produced aesthetic force for many in early audiences is of course doubtful, but the ploy may have reached an inner circle. Derek Brewer found the "arithmetical component" dominant in Chaucer's mentality; see "Arithmetic and the Mentality of Chaucer," in *The Literature of Fourteenth-Century England*, ed. Piero Boitani and Anna Torti (Tubingen, Germany, 1983), pp. 155–64.
62. Patterson "What Man Artow?" 147. See also Lerer, "Romance of Orality," pp. 194–95. It is in anticipating problems like this one that Dane's warnings against considering parody a "universal" genre come in handiest *Parody*, p. 5).
63. Mary Carruthers locates the mode of thought invoked in *Melibee* as central to medieval subjectivity, in describing Heloise as calling up "her whole florilegium of texts" to meet the crisis of her taking the veil; *The Book of Memory*, p. 182. See also chapter 4 above.
64. Patterson, "What Man Artow," 154.
65. More lines in the *Nun's Priest's Tale* are given to ornament than in other tales—plotting only accounts for about one tenth of them, as Helen Cooper points out (*Oxford Guide*, p. 342).
66. Kendrick argues that the Freudian bribe would work even for women looking at this basically antifeminist offering. Its self-conscious fictionality enables the Priest to get away with his male-privileging tale, not just to Harry Bailly, but to the rest of the world, in and outside the frame

tale (*Chaucerian Play*, p. 38). Larry Scanlon agrees about modern readings: "During the 1950's the *Nun's Priest's Tale* abruptly became the quintessential Chaucerian text." See "The Authority of Fable: Allegory and Irony in the *Nun's Priest's Tale*," in *Critical Essays on Geoffrey Chaucer*, ed. Thomas Stillinger (New York: G. K. Hall, 1998), p. 173.

67. Robertson, *Preface*, p. 252.
68. Cooper, *Oxford Guide*, pp. 348–49.
69. Kant, *CJ*, p. 179. This is Kant's position on aesthetic judgment, but he allows that the beautiful object may also be treated as a source of conceptual reasoning, moral, or otherwise: "the beautiful permits also of being understood and reduced to concepts (although in aesthetic judgments it is not so)" p. 117. As I have stressed before, Kant presents the good as understood conceptually: "having a concept of the thing represented is not necessary for calling it beautiful, but to call a thing good, there must be a concept of what it is" (*CJ*, p. 46).
70. Patterson, "'For the Wyves Love of Bathe': Feminine Rhetoric and Poetic Resolution in the *Roman de la Rose* and the *Canterbury Tales*," *Speculum* 58 (1983): 658. Note Patterson's pun on "solicit"; he is eliding a feminine with an aesthetic function here. James Andreas uses the term *sermon joyeux* for the *Summoner's Tale* ("Newe Science," 145).
71. "In this active mimicking, the Wife reveals most powerfully that these glossators' concerns are indeed carnal; she has made her own self-interest explicit, and her act of appropriating their methods for openly carnal purposes indicate their motivations as similarly carnal" (Dinshaw, *Chaucer's Sexual Poetics*, p. 124).
72. See my "Alisoun Looms" in *Social Contest*, pp. 114–28.
73. Besserman calls some of what she says "her unorthodox but powerful exploitation of contradiction and inconsistency" in Paul's letters; see *Chaucer's Biblical Poetics* (Norman, OK: University of Oklahoma Press, 1998), p. 106. He concludes that the Wife "shares some of Chaucer's most profound concerns about validity in biblical interpretation in general and the problematic appropriation of the enforcing power of biblical authority for institutional purposes in particular" (p. 113). Patterson writes as if she is simply wrong ("Wyves Love," 677).
74. Dinshaw, *Sexual Poetics*, p. 120.
75. Kierkegaard, *Concluding Unscientific Postscript*, p. 81.
76. Owst, *Literature and the Pulpit in Medieval England* (Cambridge: Cambridge University Press, 1933), Chap. 7.
77. A Wycliffite sermon charges that "bastard dyvynes sien algates that thes wordis of Crist ben false, and so no wordis of Crist bynden, but to the witt that gloseris tellen." See John Wyclif, *Select English Works*, ed. Thomas Arnold (Oxford: Clarendon Press, 1869–71), I.367.
78. Leicester and Patterson both think she is lying about this accord, but I don't see how they know. Alisoun is perfectly willing to admit to lying, so this marriage (as the telling invites us to consider it) might actually have been a happy one.

79. I am in agreement here with Dinshaw who writes that the wife mimics, not to destroy patriarchal discourse, but to reform it (*Sexual Poetics*, p. 116). I choose the word "refresh" to mimic Alisoun herself.
80. Langer, *Feeling and Form: A Theory of Art* (New York: Charles Scribner's Sons, 1953), p. 340.

7 Imagining Community

1. Wittgenstein, *Philosophical Investigations*, p. 19.
2. *Troilus and Criseyde*, I.1065–71.
3. Anderson, *Imagined Communities: Reflections on the Origin and Spread of Nationalism* (London: Verso, 1983), p. 15. Hereafter cited in the text as *IC*.
4. Helgerson, *Forms of Nationhood: The Elizabethan Writing of England* (Chicago, IL: University of Chicago Press, 1992), p. 13. Helgerson's phrasing seems a bit too certain of this, a bit too neglectful of natural and constitutional elements in our sense of ourselves, but it cannot be gainsaid that *collective* identity is in large part culturally constructed and inheres in people's imaginations, often through the cultural objects they attend to, which is one reason why aesthetic force must be part of this picture.
5. Ricoeur, *From Text to Action*, trans. Kathleen Blamey and John B. Thompson. (Evanston, IL: Northwestern University Press, 1991), p. 174. The second phrase is from Andreea Ritivoi's *Paul Ricoeur: Rhetoric in the Modern Era* (Albany, NY: SUNY Press, 2005).
6. Plato, *The Republic*, Book 10.
7. Eagleton, *Ideology of the Aesthetic*, p. 28.
8. Ricoeur, *From Text to Action*, pp. 170–71.
9. Muscatine notes Chaucer's "tireless capacity for definition and comparison.He has a passion for relationships, and the over-all structure of the work, the linear sequence of discrete stories in various styles, meets his passion perfectly" (*Chaucer and the French Tradition*, p. 223).
10. Nicholas Watson attributes Hoccleve's claim for Chaucer's priority among English poets (1412) to the refusal of his texts to be reduced to any particular social program. Even though Langland was more widely read, Chaucer was seen as speaking to and about all the echelons of English society; *The Idea of the Vernacular*, ed. Jocelyn Wogan-Browne, Nicholas Watson, Andrew Taylor, and Ruth Evans (Exeter, UK: Exeter University Press, 1999), pp. 348–49.
11. Here, once more, is the passage from *Boece*: "Also ymaginacioun, albeit so that it takith of wit [sense impressions] the bygynnynges to seen and formen the figures, algates althoughe that wit ne were nat present, yit it envyrowneth and comprehendith alle thingis sensible, nat by resoun sensible of demyng, but by resoun ymaginatyf" (V. Prosa 4, 200–210).
12. Imagination, in Anderson's account, has practical effects. In Ricoeur's account, effects are seen as ontological: "'seeing as,' which sums up the

power of metaphor, could be the revealer of a 'being as' on the deepest ontological level (*Time and Narrative*, I.ix).

13. Marion Turner (*Chaucerian Conflict: Languages of Antagonism in Late Fourteenth-Century London* [Oxford: Oxford University Press, 2007]) regards Chaucer's overall vision as "defiantly anti-social." She counts Criseyde's love-betrayal as commensurate with the treasons of Antenor and Calchas, and those three betrayers are scapegoats for "the chaos within Trojan society" throughout its ranks (p. 51). I think this misreads the tone of Chaucer's nuanced treatment of his Trojan characters, but when this "heart of darkness" is said to produce the *Tales* as well, the approach seems unmindful of the element of imaginative play that is characterizes art.
14. If, as Stephen Greenblatt writes, language is the "greatest collective creation" a culture fashions ("Culture," in *Terms for Literary Study*, p. 230), Chaucer's decision to use English for his poetry greatly enhanced that collective cultural achievement. Derek Pearsall frames the issue as a bold choice Chaucer made: "an extraordinary decision for a writer attached to the English court of the 1360s. At least it must have seemed extraordinary at the time.... English, though it may have lacked the finesse in polite discourse of French and the abstract and conceptualizing vocabulary of Latin, was, after all the mother-tongue, with more immediate access to the deeper well-springs of emotional experience" (*The Life of Geoffrey Chaucer: A Critical Biography* [Cambridge, MA: Harvard University Press, 1992], p. 73).
15. Cole concludes that the polarization of thinking about the use of English is a mistake, that the "gentry in Chaucer's circle were reading Wycliffite texts with interest—Chaucer included." The Prologue to the *Astrolabe* suggests that Chaucer and his fellow translators are the "noble clerkes" who make new ideas available locally ("Chaucer's English Lesson," *Speculum* 77 [2002]: 1167).The position of the moderate reformer Thomas Ullerston supports Cole's contention that a contemporary conversation was being conducted. Ullerston took the side of judicious Englishing against Arundel's harsh prohibitions of the early fifteenth century. See Vincent Gillespie, "Vernacular Theology," in *Middle English*, ed. Paul Strohm (Oxford: Oxford University Press, 2007), pp. 401–20. Wycliffites and those who sympathized with them *in this matter* were answered that the English language was too crude to embody abstract ideas and laypeople too carnal to understand them; see Watson, *The Idea of the Vernacular*, pp. 343–45.
16. Evans, "The Notion of Vernacular Theory," in *The Idea of the Vernacular*, p. 326.
17. Cannon, *The Making of Chaucer's English: A Study of Words* (Cambridge: Cambridge University Press, 1988), p. 170. It is not necessary to claim a pattern of Chaucerian lexical first instances to see his work as linguistically influential in its broad aesthetic appeal, early and later.
18. Lerer, *Inventing English: A Portable History of the Language* (New York: Columbia University Press, 2007), p. 84.

19. Baswell, "Latinitas," in *The New Cambridge History of English Literature*, ed. David Wallace (Cambridge: Cambridge University Press, 1999), p. 123.
20. Helgerson, *Forms of Nationhood*, p. 3.
21. Anderson notes the Wycliffite "vernacular *manuscript* Bible" translation, but consigns it, along with the English used in courts and in opening Parliament to state, rather than national, interests and notes that this state encompassed some non-English-speaking terrain (*IC*, p. 45).
22. Translation was debated early in the Christian West; in *On Christian Doctrine*, Augustine argues that the readings of the Septuagint, the translation of the Hebrew Old Testament into Greek, should be preferred to the Hebrew where the two conflict, since the Holy Spirit guided the translators (2.15.22).
23. Christopher Baswell observes that from the thirteenth century on, "growing emphasis was placed on clerical ability not only to use the Latin liturgy but also to explain it in the vernacular.... By the late 1250s, Matthew Paris reports, Archbishop Sewald of York resisted papal candidates forbishoprics if they did not have good English" (p. 147). Baswell's findings also suggest that Latin in England is itself "an array of increasingly disparate, specialized language practices" ("Latinitas," p. 123).
24. Justice, *Writing and Rebellion: England in 1381* (Berkeley and Los Angeles: University of California Press, 1994), p. 30.
25. For example, Chaucer joins other English writers in preserving the distinction between "*trouthe* (subjective) and objectively verifiable *soothe*." See Green's *A Crisis of Truth: Literature and Law in Ricardian England* (Philadelphia: University of Pennsylvania Press, 1999), p. 28.
26. Barron, "The Uses of Literacy in Medieval London," Medieval Academy Meetings, April 4, 2002.
27. Strohm, *Social Chaucer* (Cambridge, MA: Harvard University Press, 1989), p. 63.
28. Carruthers makes a somewhat different critique of the Summoner's Latin, contrasting his inert phrases with the Man of Laws' ability to fuse his Latin learning with other kinds of knowledge, and thus use in practice what he knows (*Book of Memory*, p. 20).
29. Duffy, *The Stripping of the Altars: Traditional Religion in England 1400–1580* (New Haven, CT: Yale University Press, 1992), pp. 221–22. Duffy does not read this distance between the words and the worshipper's grasp of them as reducing in any way the efficacy of the prayers and sacraments for the spiritual well-being of the laity.
30. Carruthers, *Book of Memory*, pp. 60 and 71.
31. Duffy, *Stripping of the Altars*, p. 218.
32. Steven Rappaport, *Worlds within Worlds: The Structure of Life in Sixteenth-Century London* (New York: Cambridge University Press, 1988), p. 35. See my discussion of this sense of *free* in *Time-Bound Words* (New York: St. Martin's Press, 2000), pp. 59–61.
33. Ricoeur, *Time and Narrative*, I.79.

34. Auerbach, *Mimesis*, trans. Willard Trask (Garden City, NY: Doubleday, 1957), p. 64.
35. Haidu continues "even where intentionally established to function in subordination to an ideological superstructure [a Neoplatonic Form or Idea], [it] is inherently subversive of such vehiculation, and betrays that externally imposed purpose by its very nature. It must immediately be acknowledged that, in spite of this constitutive contradiction, exemplary narrative continued to function as a predominant fictional mode, even in vernacular literature, throughout the Middle Ages." ("Repetition," 886).
36. Bede, *Ecclesiastical History of the English People*, trans. Leo Sherley-Price, rev. edn. (New York: Penguin, 1990), pp. 129–30.
37. Le Goff, *Time, Work, and Culture in the Middle Ages*, trans. Arthur Goldhammer (Chicago and London: University of Chicago Press, 1980), p. 31. Later Le Goff writes of an "economy dominated by agrarian rhythms, free of haste, careless of exactitude, unconcerned by productivity—and of a society created in the image of that economy, *sober and modest*, without enormous appetites, undemanding, and incapable of qualitative efforts" (p. 44).
38. Ricoeur, *Time and Narrative*, I.65.
39. Ricoeur, *Time and Narrative*, I.67.
40. Ricoeur, *Time and Narrative*, I.29.
41. Strohm, *Social Chaucer*, p. 112.
42. The fact that surviving manuscripts offer conflicting orders does not detract from this conclusion. A meaning-bearing sequence can be based on either of the likeliest orders and the fact that discussion of the issue has been so vigorous suggests that modern readers consider the frame to be dependent on a modern sense of "empty time."
43. The *Merchant's Tale* is similar in both plotting and narrative style. For example, the Merchant leaves "Damyan about his need, / And in my tale forth I wol procede" (IV.2020). Even the narrator in *Troilus and Criseyde* signals his shifts from one perspective to another, using Anderson's very phrase "al this mene while" (III.50; see also I.1086, II.687 and 932, and IV.144).
44. *The Physician's Tale* is especially interesting here, since it is so difficult to see what general point is being made. If tragic irony is intended in that Virginius acted too quickly and the people might have saved his daughter if he had let them, the expository section on Virginia's moral excellence is wasted. If Virginius is to be seen as a noble Roman, able to sacrifice for principle, the specifically Christian moral edge of the plot is blunted. The puzzling moral of this tale may of course be part of the characterization of the Physician.
45. Le Goff, *The Medieval Imagination*, trans. Arthur Goldhammer (Chicago, IL and London: University of Chicago Press, 1985), p. 78.
46. Le Goff, *Medieval Imagination*, pp. 79–80.
47. Britton Harwood refers to "the modest but significant presence of productive capital," to the prevalence of wage labor in towns and even on

farms in the late fourteenth century (340–41), and to the Yeoman as, "apparently the only wage laborer anywhere in Chaucer—the only person hired to make a commodity" (343). See "Chaucer and the Silence of History: Situating *The Canon's Yeoman's Tale*," *PMLA* 102 (1987): 338–47.

48. *Work* appears only twice in the *General Prologue*, in neither instance meaning "perform labor." The Parson, though poor, is said to be "riche...of hooly thoght and werk" (I.479) and the Host does tell the pilgrims, in another sense of *work*, to "werken as I shal yow seye," that is, "do as I tell you" (779).
49. There is clearly a division of labor in the lab. Marx's comment is: "Division of labor within the workshop implies the undisputed authority of the capitalist over men.... the lifelong annexation of the worker to a partial operation" (Karl Marx, *Capital: A Critique of Political Economy*, trans. Ben Fowkes, intro. Ernest Mandel [New York: Random House, 1977], pp. 476–77).
50. "DissemiNation," in *Nation and Narration*, ed. Homi K. Bhabha (London and New York: Routledge, 1990), p. 279.
51. This passage is found in *Commentarium in Dionysii De Divinis Nominibus*, quoted by Eco in *The Aesthetics of Thomas Aquinas*, p. 28.

BIBLIOGRAPHY

Abelard, Peter. *The Story of Abelard's Adversities.* Trans. J. T. Muckle. Toronto, Canada: Pontifical Institute of Medieval Studies, 1992.

Adorno, Theodor. *Aesthetic Theory.* Ed. and trans. Gretel Adorno and Rolf Tiedemann, translator's intro. Robert Hullot-Kentor. Minneapolis: University of Minnesota Press, 1997.

Aers, David. "Chaucer's Criseyde: Woman in Society, Woman in Love," in *Chaucer, Langland and the Creative Imagination.* London: Routledge and Kegan Paul, 1980.

———. *Chaucer, Langland and the Creative Imagination.* London: Routledge and Kegan Paul, 1980.

———. "Criseyde: Woman in Medieval Society." *Chaucer Review* 13 (1979): 177–200; Rept. in Benson, pp. 128–48.

Allen, Judson Boyce. *The Ethical Poetic of the Later Middle Ages: A Decorum of Convenient Distinction.* Toronto, Canada: University of Toronto Press, 1982.

Altieri, Charles. *Canons and Consequences: Reflections on the Ethical Force of Imaginative Ideals.* Evanston, IL: Northwestern University Press, 1990.

Ancrene Riwle. The English Text of the Ancrene Riwle. Ed. A. C. Baugh. EETS 232. London: Oxford University Press, 1956.

Ancrene Wisse: A Corrected Edition of the Text in Cambridge, Corpus Christi College, MS 402, with Variants from Other Manuscripts. Ed. Bella Millett. EETS 325. Vol. 1. Oxford: Oxford University Press, 2005.

Anderson, Benedict. *Imagined Communities: Reflections on the Origin and Spread of Nationalism.* London: Verso, 1983.

Andreas, James. "'Newe Science' from 'Olde Bokes': A Bakhtinian Approach to the *Summoner's Tale.*" *Chaucer Review* 25 (1990): 138–51.

Aquinas, Thomas. *Summa Theologiae.* Blackfriars. Edition Vol. 12. New York and London: McGraw-Hill, 1968.

Armstrong, Isobel. *The Radical Aesthetic.* Oxford: Blackwell, 2000.

Astell, Ann W. *The Song of Songs in the Middle Ages.* Ithaca, NY: Cornell University Press, 1990.

Auerbach, Erich. *Mimesis.* Trans. Willard Trask. Garden City, NY: Doubleday, 1957.

Augustine, Saint. *City of God.* Trans. Henry Bettenson. London: Penguin Classics, 1984.

Aquinas, St. Thomas. *Summa Theologiae*. Blackfriars. New York and London: McGraw-Hill, 1968.

Augustine, Saint. *Confessions*. Trans. John K. Ryan. Garden City, NY: Doubleday, 1960.

———. *De Doctrina Christiana*, 2.6.8; *Corpus Christianorum; On Christian Doctrine*. Trans. D. W. Robertson Jr. Indianapolis, IN: Bobbs-Merrill, 1958.

Bakhtin, M. M. *The Dialogic Imagination: Four Essays*. Ed. Michael Holquist. Trans. Caryl Emerson and Michael Holquist. Austin: University of Texas Press, 1981.

Barker, Francis. *Tremulous Private Body*. London: Methuen, 1984.

Barney, Stephen. *Chaucer's Troilus: Essays in Criticism*. Hamden, CT: Archon Books, 1980.

———. "Troilus Bound." *Speculum* 47 (July 1972): 445–58.

Barron, Caroline M. "The Uses of Literacy in Medieval London." Medieval Academy Meetings, April 4, 2002.

Baswell, Christopher. "Latinitas," in *The New Cambridge History of English Literature*. Ed. David Wallace. Cambridge: Cambridge University Press, 1999.

Bauschatz, Cathleen. "Montaigne's Conception of Reading," in *The Reader in the Text*. Ed. Susan Suleiman and Inge Crosman. Princeton, NJ: Princeton University Press, 1980.

Bede, Saint. *Ecclesiastical History of the English People*. Trans. Leo Sherley-Price. Rev. edn. New York: Penguin, 1990.

Belsey, Catherine. *The Subject of Tragedy*. London: Metheun, 1985.

Benjamin, Walter. *The Origins of German Tragic Drama*. Trans. John Osborne. London: NLB, 1977.

Benson, C. David. *Chaucer's Troilus and Criseyde*. London: Unwin Hyman, 1990.

———. *Critical Essays on Chaucer's Troilus and Criseyde and His Major Early Poems*. Toronto, Canada: University of Toronto Press, 1991.

Bergson, Henri. *Laughter: An Essay on the Meaning of the Comic*. Trans. Cloudesley Brerston and Fred Rothwell. New York: Macmillan, 1912.

Berry, Craig. "Borrowed Armor/Free Grace: The Quest for Authority in *Faerie Queene* and Chaucer's *Tale of Sir Thopas*." *Studies in Philology* 91 (1994): 136–66.

Besserman, Lawrence. *Chaucer's Biblical Poetics*. Norman: University of Oklahoma Press, 1998.

Bestul, Thomas. "The Man of Law's Tale and the Rhetorical Foundations of Chaucer's Pathos." *Chaucer Review* 9 (1975): 216–26.

Bhabha, Homi K. "DissemiNation," in *Nation and Narration*. Ed. Homi K. Bhabha. London and New York: Routledge, 1990.

Biernhoff, Suzannah. *Sight and Embodiment in the Middle Ages*. Basingstoke, UK, and New York: Palgrave Macmillan, 2002.

Biggs, Fredrick M. and Laura L. Howes. "Theophany." *MAE* 65 (1996): 270–73.

Bloch, Howard. "Chaucer's Maiden's Head: *The Physician's Tale* and the Poetics of Virginity." *Representations* 28 (Fall 1989): 113–34.

———. *Medieval Misogyny and the Invention of Romantic Love*. Chicago, IL: University of Chicago Press, 1991.

Bloom, Harold. *Shakespeare: The Invention of the Human*. New York: Penguin, 1998.

Bloomfield, Morton. "Chaucerian Realism," in *The Cambridge Chaucer Companion*. Ed. Piero Boitani and Jill Mann. Cambridge: Cambridge University Press, 1986.

———. *An Introduction to the History of a Religious Concept*. East Lansing: Michigan State University Press. 1952.

De Bolla, Peter. *Art Matters*. Cambridge, MA: Harvard University Press, 2001.

Bonaventure, Saint. *Itinerarium Mentis in Deum*. Ed. Philotheus Boehner, *Works of Saint Bonaventure*. Vol. 11. New York: Franciscan Institute, 1956.

———. *The Mind's Road to God*. Trans. George Boas. Indianapolis, IN: Bobbs-Merrill, 1953.

Borges, Jorge Luis. "Funes the Memorious," in *Ficciones*. New York: Grove Press, 1962. Pp. 107–15.

Bourdieu, Pierre. *Distinction: A Social Critique of the Judgement of Taste*. Trans. Richard Nice. Cambridge, MA: Harvard University Press, 1984.

Bradbury, Nancy Mason. "Chaucerian Minstrelsy: *Sir Thopas, Troilus and Criseyde* and the English Metrical Romance," in *Tradition and Translation in Medieval Romance*. Ed. Rosalind Field. Cambridge: D. S. Brewer, 1999. Pp. 115–24.

Brenner, William H. *Wittgenstein's Philosophical Investigations*. Albany: State University of New York Press, 1999.

Brown, Peter. *Reading Dreams: The Interpretation of Dreams from Chaucer to Shakespeare*. Oxford: Oxford University Press, 1999.

———. "'Shot Window' (*Miller's Tale* I.3358 and 3695): An Open and Shut Case." *Medium AEvum* 69 (2000): 96–103.

Bundy, Murray Wright. *The Theory of Imagination in Classical and Medieval Thought*. Urbana: University of Illinois Press, 1927.

Burckhardt, Jacob. *Civilization of the Renaissance in Italy*. London: Phaidon, 1965.

Burke, Kenneth. *Counter Statement*. Berkeley and Los Angeles: University of California Press, 1931.

Burrow, J. A. *Gestures and Looks in Medieval Narrative*. Cambridge: Cambridge University Press, 2002.

Burton, T. L. and Rosemary Greentree. *Chaucer's Miller's, Reeve's, and Cook's Tales: The Chaucer Bibliographies*. Toronto, Canada: University of Toronto Press, 1995.

Bynum, Carolyn Walker. *Holy Feast and Holy Fast: The Religious Significance of Food to Medieval Women*. Berkeley and Los Angeles: University of California Press, 1987.

Camargo, Martin. "Rhetorical Ethos and the *Nun's Priest's Tale*." *Comparative Literature Studies* 33, 2 (1996): 172–86.

Carruthers, Mary. *The Book of Memory: A Study of Memory in Medieval Culture*. Cambridge: Cambridge University Press, 1990.

———. *The Craft of Thought: Meditation, Rhetoric, and the Making of Images 400–1200*. Cambridge: Cambridge University Press, 1998.

———. "The *Gentilesse* of Chaucer's Franklin." *Criticism* 23 (1981): 283–300.

Carruthers, Mary. "Sweetness." *Speculum* 81 (October 2006): 999–1013.

Cascardi, Anthony J. "The Difficulty of Art." *boundary* 2, 25 (Spring 1998): 35–65.

Chandrasekhar, S. *Truth and Beauty: Aesthetics and Motivations in Science*. Chicago, IL: University of Chicago Press, 1987.

Chapin, Arthur. "Morality Ovidized: Sententiousness and the Aphoristic Moment in the *Nun's Priest's Tale*." *Yale Journal of Criticism* 8 (1995): 7–33.

Chaucer, Geoffrey. *The Riverside Chaucer*. Ed. Larry D. Benson. 3rd edn. Boston, MA: Houghton Mifflin, 1987.

Chrétien de Troyes. "Erec and Enid" and "The Story of the Grail," in *Arthurian Romances*. Trans. William Kibler. Harmondsworth, UK: Penguin Books, 1991.

Cole, Andrew. "Chaucer's English Lesson." *Speculum* 77 (2002): 1128–67.

Cooper, Helen. *Oxford Guide to Chaucer: The Canterbury Tales*. 2nd edn. Oxford: Oxford University Press, 1996.

———. "Responding to the Monk." *SAC* 22 (2000): 425–33.

———. *The Structure of the Canterbury Tales*. Athens: University of Georgia Press, 1983.

Cottino-Jones, Marga. "Fabula vs. Figura." *Italica* 50 (1973): 38–52.

Courtenay, William. "Nominalism and Late Medieval Religion," in *The Pursuit of Holiness in Late Medieval and Renaissance Religion*. Ed. Charles Trinkaus and Heiko Oberman. Leiden, The Netherlands: Brill, 1974. Pp. 26–59.

Crane, Mary Thomas. *Shakespeare's Brain: Reading with Cognitive Theory*. Princeton, NJ: Princeton University Press, 2001.

Crane, Susan. "The Franklin as Dorigen." *Chaucer Review* 24 (1990): 236–52.

———. *The Performance of Self: Ritual, Clothing, and Identity during the Hundred Years War*. Philadelphia: University of Pennsylvania Press, 2002.

Croce, Benedetto. *Aesthetic as Science of Expression and General Linguistics*. Trans. Douglas Ainslie. London: Macmillan, 1922.

Daileader, Celia. "The Thopas-Melibee Sequence and the Defeat of Antifeminism." *Chaucer Review* 29 (1994): 26–39.

Damasio, Antonio. *The Feeling of What Happens: Body and Emotion in the Making of Consciousness*. New York: Harcourt Brace, 1999.

Dane, Joseph A. *Parody: Critical Concepts versus Literary Practices, Aristophanes to Sterne*. Norman: University of Oklahoma Press, 1988.

Delany, Sheila. "Run Silent, Run Deep," in *Medieval Literary Politics: The Shapes of Ideology*. Manchester, UK: Manchester University Press, 1990. Pp.1–18.

———. "Techniques of Alienation." *Chaucer's Troilus and Criseyde "Subgit to alle Poesye" Essays in Criticism*. Ed. R. A. Shoaf. Binghamton, NY: Center for Medieval and Early Renaissance Studies, 1992.

Dennett, Daniel C. *Consciousness Explained*. Boston, MA: Little, Brown, 1991.

———. *Elbow Room: The Varieties of Free Will Worth Wanting*. Cambridge, MA: MIT Press, 1985.

Denomy, Alex J. C. S. B. "The Two Moralities of Chaucer's *Troilus and Criseyde*," and "*Chaucer Criticism:* Troilus and Criseyde *and the Minor Poems*."

Ed. Richard J. Shoeck and Jerome Taylor. Notre Dame, IN: Notre Dame University Press, 1961. Pp. 147–59.

Dillard, Annie. "Sight into Insight," in *Popular Writing in America*. Ed. Donald McQuade and Robert Atwan. New York: Oxford University Press, 1977. Pp. 247–51.

Dinshaw, Carolyn. *Chaucer's Sexual Poetics*. Madison: University of Wisconsin Press, 1989.

———. *Getting Medieval: Sexualities and Communities, Pre- and Postmodern*. Durham, NC: Duke University Press, 1999.

Dollimore, Jonathan. *Radical Tragedy: Religion, Ideology and Power in the Drama of Shakespeare and His Contemporaries*. Chicago, IL: University of Chicago Press, 1986.

Donaldson, E. Talbot. *Swan at the Well*. New Haven, CT: Yale University Press, 1985.

Donoghue, Denis. *Speaking of Beauty*. New Haven, CT: Yale University Press, 2003.

Doran, Madeleine. *Endeavors of Art: A Study of Form in Elizabethan Drama*. Madison: University of Wisconsin Press, 1954.

Duby, Georges. *Medieval Marriage*. Baltimore, MD: Johns Hopkins University Press, 1978.

———. *The Three Orders: Feudal Society Imagined*. Trans. Arthur Goldhammer. Chicago and London: University of Chicago Press, 1978.

Duffy, Eamon. *The Stripping of the Altars: Traditional Religion in England 1400–1580*. 2nd edn. New Haven, CT: Yale University Press, 2005.

Dunn, Allen. "Who Needs a Sociology of the Aesthetic? Freedom and Value in Pierre Bourdieu's *Rules of Art*." *boundary* 2, 25 (Spring 1998): 87–110.

Eagelton, Terry. *The Ideology of the Aesthetic*. Oxford: Blackwell, 1990.

Eco, Umberto. *The Aesthetics of Thomas Aquinas*. Cambridge, MA: Harvard University Press, 1988.

———. *Art and Beauty in the Middle Ages*. Trans. Hugh Bredin. New Haven, CT: Yale University Press, 1986.

Eden, Kathy. *Hermeneutics and the Rhetorical Tradition: Chapters in the Ancient Legacy and Its Humanistic Reception*. New Haven, CT: Yale University Press, 1997.

Edwards, Robert R. *Ratio and Invention: A Study of Medieval Lyric and Narrative*. Nashville, TN: University of Tennessee Press, 1989.

Encyclopedia of Aesthetics. Ed. Michael Kelly. New York and Oxford: Oxford University Press, 1998.

Encyclopaedia of Religion and Ethics. Ed. James Hastings. New York: Scribners, 1928.

Evans, Ruth, Jocelyn Wogan-Browne, Nicholas Watson, and Andrew Taylor. "The Notion of Vernacular Theory," in *The Idea of the Vernacular*. Ed. Jocelyn Wogan-Browne, Nicholas Watson, Andrew Taylor, and Ruth Evans. Exeter, UK: Exeter University Press, 1999. Pp. 314–30.

——— "Virginities," in *The Cambridge Companion to Medieval Women's Writing*. Ed. Carolyn Dinshaw and David Wallace. Cambridge: Cambridge University Press, 2003.

Everest, Carol A. "Sex and Old Age in Chaucer's *Reeve's Prologue*." *Chaucer Review* 31 (1996): 99–114.

Felperin, Howard. "'Tongue-Tied Our Queen?': The Deconstruction of Presence in *The Winter's Tale*," in *Shakespeare and the Question of Theory*. Ed. Patricia Parker and Geoffrey Hartman. New York: Methuen, 1985. Pp. 3–18.

Ferrante, Joan. *Woman as Image in Medieval Literature from the Twelfth Century to Dante*. Rept. Durham, NC: Labyrinth Press, 1985.

Fineman, Joel. "The Structures of Allegorical Desire," in *Allegory and Representation*. Ed. Stephen Greenblatt. English Institute Essays, 1979–1980. Baltimore, MD: Johns Hopkins University Press, 1981.

Finlayson, John. "Petrarch, Boccaccio, and Chaucer's *Clerk's Tale*." *Studies in Philology* 97 (2000): 255–75.

Fisher, Philip. *Wonder, the Rainbow, and the Aesthetics of Rare Experiences*. Cambridge, MA: Harvard University Press, 1998.

Flemming, John V. "The Summoner's Prologue: An Iconographic Adjustment." *Chaucer Review* 2 (1967): 95–107.

Fletcher, Angus. *Allegory: The Theory of a Symbolic Mode*. Ithaca, NY: Cornell University Press, 1964.

———. "Iconographies of Thought." *Representations* 28 (Fall 1989): 99–112.

Foucault, Michel. *The History of Sexuality I*. New York: Random House, 1980.

———. *The Order of Things*. New York: Vintage Books, 1973.

Foxe, John. *Acts and Monuments*. (London, 1583). Rept. New York: AMS Press, 1965.

Frank, Robert Worth. "The *Reeve's Tale* and the Comedy of Limitation," in *Directions in Literary Criticism: Contemporary Approaches to Literature*. Ed. Stanley Weintraub and Philip Young. University Park: Pennsylvania State University Press, 1973. Pp. 53–69.

Freud, Sigmund. *The Interpretation of Dreams II*. Standard edn. Vol. 5 (1900–1901). Trans. James Strachey. London: Hogarth Press, 1953.

———. *Jokes and Their Relation to the Unconscious*. Standard edn. Vol. 8 (1905). Trans. James Strachey. London: Hogarth Press, 1960.

Frye, Northrop. *Anatomy of Criticism: Four Essays*. Princeton, NJ: Princeton University Press, 1957.

Furrow, Melissa. "Middle English Fabliaux and Modern Myth." *ELH* 56 (1989): 1–18.

Gadamer, Hans Georg. *Philosophical Hermeneutics*. Trans. and ed. David E. Linge. Berkeley: University of California Press, 1976.

———. *The Relevance of the Beautiful and Other Essays*. Trans. Nicholas Walker. Ed. and intro. Robert Bernasconi. Cambridge: Cambridge University Press, 1986.

———. *Truth and Method*. Second rev. edn. Trans. Joel Weinsheimer and Donald Marshall. New York and London: Continuum Books, 2003.

Gallagher, Catherine and Stephen Jay Greenblatt. *Practicing New Historicism*. Chicago, IL: University of Chicago Press, 2000.

Gans, Eric. "Aesthetics and Cultural Criticism." *boundary* 2, 25 (Spring 1998): 67–85.

Georgianna, Linda. "Lords, Churls, and Friars: The Return to Order in the *Summoner's Tale*," in *Rebels and Rivals: The Contestive Spirit in* The Canterbury Tales. Ed. Susanna Greer Fein, David Raybin, and Peter Braeger. Kalamazoo, MI: Medieval Institute Publications, 1991.

Gibson, John. "Reading for Life," in *The Literary Wittgenstein*. Ed. John Gibson and Wolfgang Huemer. New York: Routledge, 2004. Pp. 109–24.

Gibson, John and Wolfgang Huemer, eds. *The Literary Wittgenstein*. New York: Routledge, 2004.

Gillespie, Vincent. "Vernacular Theology," in *Middle English*. Ed. Paul Strohm. Oxford: Oxford University Press, 2007. Pp. 401–20.

———. "The Study of Classical Authors from the Twelfth Century to 1450," in *Cambridge History of Literary Criticism,* Vol. 2: *The Middle Ages*. Ed. Alastair Minnis and Ian Johnson. Cambridge: Cambridge University Press, 2005.

Gilson, Etienne. *The Arts of the Beautiful*. New York: Scribners, 1965.

Ginsberg, Warren. *Chaucer's Italian Tradition*. Ann Arbor: University of Michigan Press, 2002.

le Goff, Jacques. *The Medieval Imagination*. Trans. Arthur Goldhammer. Chicago and London: University of Chicago Press, 1985.

Gombrich, E. H. *Art and Illusion*. Princeton, NJ: Princeton University Press, 1960.

Green, Richard Firth. "Chaucer's Victimized Women." *Studies in the Age of Chaucer* 10 (1988): 3–21.

———. *A Crisis of Truth: Literature and Law in Ricardian England*. Philadelphia: University of Pennsylvania Press, 1999.

Greenblatt, Stephen. *Renaissance Self-Fashioning*. Chicago, IL: University of Chicago Press, 1980.

———. *Shakespearean Negotiations*. Berkeley and Los Angeles: University of California Press, 1988.

Guerin, Dorothy. "Chaucer's Pathos: Three Variations." *Chaucer Review* 20 (1985): 90–112.

Hahn, Thomas and Richard Kaeuper. "Text and Context in Chaucer's *Friar's Tale*." *SAC* 5 (1983): 67–102.

Haidu, Peter. "Humor and the Aesthetics of Medieval Romance." *Romanic Review* 64 (January 1973): 54–68.

———. "Repetition: Modern Reflections on Medieval Aesthetics." *MLN* 92 (December 1977): 875–87.

Hansen, Elaine Tuttle. *Chaucer and the Fictions of Gender*. Berkeley: University of California Press, 1991.

Harrison, Bernard. "Imagined Worlds and the Real One," in *The Literary Wittgenstein*. Ed. John Gibson and Wolfgang Huemer. New York and London: Routledge, 2004.

Harwood, Britton. "Chaucer and the Silence of History: Situating *The Canon's Yeoman's Tale*." *PMLA* 102 (1987): 338–50.

———. "Psychoanalysis as Politics." *ELH* (2001): 1–27.

Helgerson, Richard. *Forms of Nationhood: The Elizabethan Writing of England*. Chicago, IL: University of Chicago Press, 1992.

Henry of Lancaster. *Livre de Seintz Medicines*. Ed. J. Arnould. (Anglo-Norman Text Society, Oxford: Blackwell, 1940). Rept. New York: Barnes & Noble, 1966.

Hill, John. *Chaucerian Belief: The Poetics of Reverence and Delight*. New Haven, CT: Yale University Press, 1991.

Hoerner, Fred. "Church Office, Routine, and Self-exile in Chaucer's Pardoner." *SAC* 16 (1994): 69–98.

Hofstadter, Albert and Richard Kuhns, eds. *Philosophies of Art and Beauty*. New York: Random House, 1964.

Hofstadter, Douglas. *Gödel, Escher, Bach*. New York: Vintage Books, 1980.

Holland, Norman. *5 Readers Reading*. New Haven, CT: Yale University Press, 1975.

Hutcheon, Linda. *A Theory of Parody: The Teachings of Twentieth-Century Art Forms*. New York: Methuen, 1985.

Iser, Wolfgang. "The Reading Process: A Phenomenological Approach." *New Literary History* 5 (1974): 279–99.

Jameson, Fredric. *The Cultural Turn: Selected Writings on the Postmodern*. London: Verso, 1998.

Jauss, Hans Robert. "The Alterity and Modernity of Medieval Literature." *NLH* 10 (1979): 181–229.

———. *Question and Answer: Forms of Dialogic Understanding*. Ed. and trans. Michael Hays. Minneapolis: University of Minnesota Press, 1989.

———. *Toward an Aesthetic of Reception*. Trans. Timothy Bahti. Minneapolis: University of Minnesota Press, 1982.

Jerome, Saint. *Selected Letters*. Ed. F. A. Wright. London: Loeb Classical Library, 1954.

Johnson, Lynn Staley. "Chaucer's Tale of the Second Nun and the Strategies of Dissent." *SP* 89 (1992): 314–33.

Jones, E. A. "'Loo, Lordes Myne, Heere Is a Fit!': The Structure of Chaucer's *Sir Thopas*." *Review of English Studies* 51 (2002): 248–52.

Justice, Steven. *Writing and Rebellion: England in 1381*. Berkeley and Los Angeles: University of California Press, 1994.

Kaelin, Eugene. *An Existentialist Aesthetic: The Theories of Sartre and Merleau-Ponty*. Madison: University of Wisconsin Press, 1962.

Kamuf, Peggy. *Fictions of Female Desires: Disclosures of Heloise*. Lincoln: University of Nebraska Press, 1982. Pp. 1–43.

Kant, Immanuel. *The Critique of Judgement*. Trans. James Creed Meredith. Oxford: Clarendon Press, 1952.

Kendrick, Laura. *Chaucerian Play: Comedy and Control in the* Canterbury Tales. Berkeley and Los Angeles: University of California Press, 1988.

Kennedy, Beverly. "Cambridge MS. Dd.4.24: A Misogynous Scribal Revision of the *Wife of Bath's Prologue*?" *Chaucer Review* 30 (1996): 343–58.

———. "The Rewriting of the *Wife of Bath's Prologue* in Cambridge Dd.4.24," in *Rewriting Chaucer: Culture, Authority, and the Idea of the Authentic Text, 1400–1602*. Ed. Thomas A. Prendergast and Barbara Kline. Columbus: Ohio State University Press, 1999. Pp. 203–33.

Kenny, Anthony. *Wittgenstein.* Cambridge, MA: Harvard University Press, 1973.

Kenshur, Oscar. "The Rhetoric of Demystification," in *Aesthetics and Ideology.* Ed. George Levine. New Brunswick, NJ: Rutgers University Press, 1994. Pp. 57–78.

Kierkegaard, Søren. *Concluding Unscientific Postscript.* Trans. David F. Swenson and Walter Lowrie. Princeton, NJ: Princeton University Press, 1941.

Kittredge, G. L. *Chaucer and His Poetry.* Cambridge, MA: Harvard University Press, 1915.

———. "Chaucer's Pardoner," in *Chaucer: Modern Essays in Criticism.* Ed. Edward Wagenknecht. (1893) Rept. New York: Galaxy, 1959.

Knapp, Peggy A. "Alisoun of Bath and the Reappropriation of Tradition." *Chaucer Review* 24 (1989): 45–52.

———. *Chaucer and the Social Contest.* New York: Routledge, 1990.

———. "The Nature of Nature: Criseyde's 'Slydyng Corage.'" *Chaucer Review* 13 (1978): 133–40.

———. *Time Bound Words: Semantic and Social Economies from Chaucer's England to Shakespeare's.* New York: St. Martin's Press, 2000.

Knight, Stephen. *Geoffrey Chaucer.* New York: Blackwell, 1986.

Kolve, V. A. *Chaucer and the Imagery of Narrative: The First Five Canterbury Tales.* Stanford, CA: Stanford University Press, 1984.

———. "Chaucer's Wheel of False Religion: Theology and Obscenity in 'The Summoner's Tale,'" in *The Centre and Its Compass: Studies in Medieval Literature in Honor of Professor John Leyerle.* Ed. Robert A. Taylor, et al. Kalamazoo.: Medieval Institute Publications: 1993.

Kruger, Steven. *Dreaming in the Middle Ages.* Cambridge: Cambridge University Press, 1992.

Lambert, Mark. "*Troilus,* Books I–III: A Criseydan Reading," in *Essays on Troilus and Criseyde.* Ed. Mary Salu. Cambridge: D. S. Brewer and Totowa; New Jersey: Rowan and Littlefield, 1979. Pp. 105–25 .

Langer, Susanne. *Feeling and Form.* New York: Scribners, 1953.

Le Goff, Jacques. *The Medieval Imagination.* Trans. Arthur Goldhammer. Chicago, and London: University of Chicago Press, 1985.

———. *Time, Work, and Culture in the Middle Ages.* Trans. Arthur Goldhammer. Chicago, and London: University of Chicago Press, 1980.

Leicester, H. Marshall. *The Disenchanted Self: Representing the Subject in the Canterbury Tales.* Berkeley and Los Angeles: University of California Press, 1990.

———. "Synne Horrible: The Pardoner's Exegesis of His Tale and Chaucer's," in *Acts of Interpretation.* Ed. Mary Carruthers and Elizabeth Kirk. New York: Pilgrim Books, 1982.

Lentricchia, Frank and Thomas McLaughlin. *Critical Terms for Literary Study.* 2nd edn. Chicago, IL: University of Chicago Press, 1995.

Lerer, Seth. *Inventing English: A Portable History of the Language.* New York: Columbia University Press, 2007.

Lerer, Seth. "'Now holde youre mouth': The Romance of Orality in the *Thopas-Melibee* Section of the *Canterbury Tales*," in *Oral Poetics in Middle English Poetry*. Ed. Mark Amodio. New York: Garland, 1994. Pp. 181–205.

Levine, George, ed. *Aesthetics and Ideology*. New Brunswick, NJ: Rutgers University Press, 1994.

Lloyd, David. "Kant's Examples." *Representations* 28 (Fall 1989): 34–54.

Lochrie, Karma. *Covert Operations: The Medieval Uses of Secrecy*. Philadelphia: University of Pennsylvania Press, 1999.

Lorand, Ruth. "Bergson's Concept of Art." *British Journal of Aesthetics* 39 (October 1999): 400–414.

Lynch, Kathryn. "Despoiling Griselda." *SAC* 10 (1988): 41–70.

———. *The High Medieval Dream Vision*. Stanford, CA: Stanford University Press, 1988.

Lyotard, Jean-Francois. *Lessons on the Analytic of the Sublime*. Trans. Elizabeth Rottenberg. Stanford, CA: Stanford University Press, 1994.

Machan, Tim William, ed. with the assistance of Alastair Minnis. *Sources of the Boece*. Athens: University of Georgia Press, 2005.

Malcolm, Norman. *Nothing Is Hidden: Wittgenstein's Criticism of His Early Thought*. Oxford: Basil Blackwell, 1986.

de Man, Paul. "Pascal's Allegory of Persuasion," in *Allegory and Representation*. Ed. Stephen Greenblatt. Selected Papers from the English Institute Essays, 1979–1980.

Mann, Jill. *Chaucer and Medieval Estates Satire*. Cambridge: Cambridge University Press, 1973.

Marcuse, Herbert. *The Aesthetic Dimension*. Boston, MA: Beacon Press, 1978.

Marx, Karl. *Capital: A Critique of Political Economy*. Trans. Ben Fowkes. Intro. Ernest Mandel. New York: Random House, 1977.

McAlpine, Monica. "Criseyde's Prudence." *SAC* 25 (2003): 199–224.

———. *The Genre of* Troilus and Criseyde. Ithaca, NY: Cornell University Press, 1978.

Mehl, Dieter. "The Audience of *Troilus and Criseyde*," in *Chaucer's Troilus: Essays in Criticism*. Ed. Stephen Barney. Hamden, CT: Archon Books, 1980. Pp. 211–29.

Meredith, George. "An Essay on Comedy," in *Comedy*. Ed. Wylie Sypher. Garden City, NY: Doubleday, 1956.

Middleton, Anne. "The Clerk and His Tale: Some Literary Contexts." *SAC* 2 (1980): 121–50.

Miller, Mark. "Naturalism and Its Discontents." *ELH* 67 (2000): 20.

———. *Philosophical Chaucer: Love, Sex, and Agency in the Canterbury Tales*. Cambridge Studies in Medieval Literature. Ser. 55. Cambridge: Cambridge University Press, 2004.

Minnis, A. J. *Medieval Theory of Authorship*. 2nd edn. Philadelphia: University of Pennsylvania Press, 1988.

Minnis, A. J. and Ian Johnson, eds. *Cambridge History of Literary Criticism*. Vol. 2: *The Middle Ages*. Cambridge: Cambridge University Press, 2005.

Mitchell, J. W. T. *Iconology: Image, Text, Ideology*. Chicago, IL: University of Chicago Press, 1986.

———. "Representation," in *Critical Terms for Literary Study*. Ed. Frank Lentricchia and Thomas McLaughlin. 2nd edn. Chicago, IL: University of Chicago Press, 1995.

Monk, Ray. *Ludwig Wittgenstein: The Duty of Genius*. London: Penguin Books, 1990.

Moravec, Hans. *Mind Children: The Future of Robot and Human Intelligence*. Cambridge, MA: Harvard University Press, 1988.

———. *Robot: Mere Machine to Transcendent Mind*. New York: Oxford University Press, 1999.

Morey, James H. "The Cultour in the *Miller's Tale: Alison as Iseult*." *Chaucer Review* 29 (1995): 373–81.

Morse, Charlotte. "The Exemplary Griselda." *SAC* 7 (1985): 51–86.

Muscatine, Charles. *Chaucer and the French Tradition*. Berkeley and Los Angeles: University of California Press, 1957.

———. "The Emergence of Psychological Allegory in Old French Romance." *PMLA* 68 (1953): 1160–83.

Newman, Barbara. "Authority, Authenticity, and the Repression of Heloise." *JMRS* 22 (1992): 121–57.

Nicholson, Marjorie Hope. *Mountain Gloom, Mountain Glory*. New York: Norton, 1959.

Niehamas, Alexander. "Plato on the Imperfection of the Sensible World." *American Philosophical Quarterly* 12 (1975): 105–17.

Novelli, Cornelius. "Sin, Sight, and Sanctuary in the *Miller's Tale: Why Chaucer's Blacksmith Works at Night*." *Chaucer Review* 33 (1998): 168–75.

O'Brien, Timothy. "'Ars-Metrik': Science, Satire, and Chaucer's Summoner." *Mosaic* 23 (1990): 1–22.

O'Connell, Robert J. *Art and the Christian Intelligence in St. Augustine*. Cambridge, MA: Harvard University Press, 1978.

O'Hara, Daniel T. and Alan Singer. "Thinking through Art: Reimagining the Aesthetic Within Global Modernity." *boundary* 2, 25 (Spring 1998): 1–5.

Olson, Glending. "The End of *The Summoner's Tale* and the Uses of Pentecost." *SAC* 21 (1999): 209–45.

———. *Literature as Recreation in the Later Middle Ages*. Ithaca, NY, and London: Cornell University Press, 1982.

Owst, G. R. *Literature and the Pulpit in Medieval England*. Cambridge: Cambridge University Press, 1933.

Panofsky, Erwin. *Idea: A Concept in Art Theory*. Trans. Joseph J. S. Peake. New York: Harper and Row, 1968.

———. *Gothic Architecture and Scholasticism*. London: Meridian Books, 1957.

Parry, Joseph D. "Female Agency in the *Miller's Tale* and *Merchant's Tale*." *PQ* 80 (2001): 133–67.

Partner, Nancy. "No Sex, No Gender." *Speculum* 68 (April 1993): 419–43.

———. "Reading *The Book of Margery Kempe*." *Exemplaria* 3 (Spring 1991): 21–66.

Pasnau, Robert. *Thomas Aquinas on Human Nature: A Philosophical Study of* Summa Theologiae 1a. 75–89. Cambridge: Cambridge University Press, 2002.

Patterson, Lee. *Chaucer and the Subject of History.* Madison: University of Wisconsin Press, 1991.

———. "'For the Wyves Love of Bathe': Feminine Rhetoric and Poetic Resolution in the *Roman de la Rose* and the *Canterbury Tales.*" *Speculum* 58 (July 1983): 656–95.

———. "On the Margin: Postmodernism, Ironic History, and Medieval Studies." *Speculum* 65 (January 1990): 87–108.

———. "Perpetual Motion: Alchemy and the Technology of Self." *SAC* 15 (1993): 25–57.

———. "'What Man Artow?': Authorial Self-Definition in *The Tale of Sir Thopas* and *The Tale of Melibee.*" *Studies in the Ages of Chaucer* 11 (1989): 117–75.

Payne, Robert. *The Key to Remembrance.* New Haven, CT: Yale University Press, 1963.

Pearsall, Derek. "Chaucer's Pardoner: The Death of a Salesman." *Chaucer Review* 17 (1983): 358–65.

———. *The Life of Geoffrey Chaucer: A Critical Biography.* Cambridge, MA: Harvard University Press, 1992.

Petrarch, Francesco. Letter to Boccaccio, quoted in Mark Musa and Peter Bondanella's Norton Critical Edition of *The Decameron.* New York: W. W. Norton, 1977. Pp. 184–87.

Poovey, Mary. "Aesthetics and Political Economy in the Eighteenth Century: The Place of Gender in the Social Construction of Knowledge," in *Aesthetics and Ideology.* Ed. George Levine. New Brunswick, NJ: Rutgers University Press, 1994.

Pound, Ezra. *Selected Prose 1909–1965.* Ed. William Cookson. New York: New Directions, 1973.

———. *Gaudier Brzeska: A Memoir.* New York: New Directions, 1970.

Prudentius. *Psychomachia,* in *Prudentius with an English Translation.* Trans. H. J. Thomson. Cambridge, MA: Harvard University Press, 1949.

Pulsiano, Phillip. "The Twelve-Spoked Wheele of *The Summoner's Tale.*" *Chaucer Review* 29 (1995): 382–89.

Quilligan, Maureen. "Allegory, Allegoresis, and the Deallegorization of Language," in *Allegory, Myth, Symbol.* Ed. Morton Bloomfield. Cambridge, MA: Harvard University Press, 1981.

———. *The Language of Allegory.* Ithaca, NY: Cornell University Press, 1979.

Rampersad, Arnold. "Values Old and New," in *Aesthetics and Ideology.* Ed. George Levine. New Brunswick, NJ: Rutgers University Press, 1994. Pp. 31–39.

Rancière, Jacques. *The Politics of Aesthetics.* Trans. Gabriel Rockhill. London and New York: Continuum Books, 2004.

Reames, Sherry. "The Cecilia Legend as Chaucer Inherited It and Retold It." *Speculum* 55 (1980): 38–57.

Reiss, Timothy J. *Knowledge, Discovery, and Imagination in Early Modern Europe.* London: Cambridge University Press, 1997.

Reynolds, Suzanne. *Medieval Reading*. Cambridge: Cambridge University Press, 1996.

Ricoeur, Paul. *From Text to Action*. Trans. Kathleen Blamey and John B. Thompson. Evanston, IL: Northwestern University Press, 1991.

———. *Time and Narrative*. Trans. Kathleen McLaughlin and David Pellauer. 3 vols. Chicago and London: University of Chicago Press, 1983.

Ritivoi, Andreea. *Ricoeur: Rhetoric in the Modern Era*. Albany, NY: SUNY University Press, 2005.

Robertson Jr., D. W. "Some Observations on Method in Literary Study." *NLH* 1 (1970): 21–33.

———. *A Preface to Chaucer*. Princeton, NJ: Princeton University Press, 1962.

Rosmarin, Adena. *The Power of Genre*. Minneapolis: University of Minnesota Press, 1985.

Rubin, Gayle. "The Traffic in Women: Notes on the 'Political Economy' of Sex," in *Toward an Anthropology of Women*. Ed. R. R. Reiter. New York: Monthly Review Press, 1975.

Salu, Mary. *Essays on Troilus and Criseyde*. Cambridge: D. S. Brewer and Totowa, NJ: Rowman and Littlefield, 1979.

Scanlon, Larry. "The Authority of Fable: Allegory and Irony," in *Nun's Priest's Tale. Critical Essays on Geoffrey Chaucer*. Ed. Thomas Stillinger. New York: G. K. Hall, 1998.

Scarry, Elaine. *On Beauty and Being Just*. Princeton, NJ: Princeton University Press, 1999.

Schibanoff, Susan. "The New Reader and Female Textuality in Two Early Commentaries on Chaucer." *SAC* 10 (1988): 71–108.

———. "Taking the Gold Out of Egypt: The Art of Reading as a Woman," in *Gender and Reading: Essays on Readers, Texts, and Contexts*. Ed. Elizabeth Flynn and Patrocinio P. Schweickart. Baltimore, MD: Johns Hopkins University Press, 1986.

Shoaf, R. A. *Chaucer's Troilus and Criseyde "Subgit to alle Poesye" Essays in Criticism*. Ed. with the assistance of Catherine S. Cox. Binghamton, NY: Center for Medieval and Early Renaissance Studies, 1992.

Sim, Stuart. *Beyond Aesthetics: Confrontations with Poststructuralism and Postmodernism*. Toronto, Canada: University of Toronto Press, 1992.

Singer, Alan. "Beautiful Errors: Aesthetics and the Art of Contextualization." *boundary* 2, 25 (Spring 1998): 7–34.

Singer, Alan. *The Subject as Action*. Ann Arbor: University of Michigan Press, 1993.

Spearing, A. C. "Introduction" to *Reading Dreams*. Ed. Peter Brown. Oxford: Oxford University Press, 1999.

Spearing, A. C. "*The Canterbury Tales IV*: Exemplum and Fable." "Chaucerian Realism," in *The Cambridge Chaucer Companion*. Ed. Piero Boitani and Jill Mann. Cambridge: Cambridge University Press, 1986.

———. *Medieval Dream Poetry*. Cambridge: Cambridge University Press, 1976.

Steiner, Peter. *Russian Formalism: A Metapoetics*. Ithaca, NY: Cornell University Press, 1984.

Steiner, Wendy. *The Scandal of Pleasure: Art in an Age of Fundamentalism*. Chicago, IL: University of Chicago Press, 1995.

———. *Venus in Exile: The Rejection of Beauty in 20th-Century Art*. London: Free Press, 2001.

Stewart, Susan. *On Longing: Narratives of the Miniature, the Gigantic, the Souvenir, the Collection*. Durham, NC: Duke University Press, 2003.

Strohm, Paul. *Social Chaucer*. Cambridge, MA: Harvard University Press, 1989.

———. "Some Generic Distinctions in the *Canterbury Tales*." *Modern Philology* 68 (1971): 321–28.

———. "Storie, Spelle, Geste, Romaunce, Tragedie: Generic Distinctions in the Middle English Troy Narratives." *Speculum* 46 (April 1971): 348–59.

Stugrin, Michael. "Richardian Poetics and Late Medieval Cultural Pluriformity: The Significance of Pathos in the *Canterbury Tales*." *Chaucer Review* 15 (1980): 155–67.

Sypher, Wylie. "The Meanings of Comedy," in *Comedy*. Ed. Wylie Sypher. Garden City, NY: Doubleday, 1956.

Taylor, Andrew. *Textual Situations*. Philadelphia: University of Pennsylvania Press, 2002.

Tilghman, B. R. *Wittgenstein, Ethics and Aesthetics: The View from Eternity*. Albany, NY: SUNY Press, 1991.

Tupper, Frederick. "Chaucer and the Seven Deadly Sins." *PMLA* 29 (1914): 93–128.

Turner, Marion. *Chaucerian Conflict: Languages of Antagonism in Late Fourteenth-Century London*. Oxford: Oxford University Press, 2007.

Turner, Victor and Edith Turner. *Image and Pilgrimage in Christian Culture: Anthropological Perspectives*. New York: Columbia University Press, 1978.

Turville-Petre, Thorlac. *England the Nation: Language, Literature, and National Identity 1290–1340*. Oxford: Clarendon Press, 1996.

Tuve, Rosemond. *Allegoical Imagery: Some Medieval Books and Their Posterity*. Princeton, NJ: Princeton University Press, 1966.

Vaszily, Scott. "Fabliau Plotting Against Romance in Chaucer's *Knight's Tale*." *Style* 31 (Fall 1997): 523–42.

Vinsauf, Geoffrey of. *Poetria Nova*. Trans. Margaret Nims. Toronto, Canada: Pontifical Institute of Medieval Studies, 1967.

Wallace, David. *Chaucerian Polity: Absolutist Lineages and Associational Forms in England and Italy*. Stanford, CA: Stanford University Press, 1997.

Warnock, Mary. *Imagination*. Berkeley and Los Angeles: University of California Press, 1976.

Waswo, Richard. *Language and Meaning in the Renaissance*. Princeton, NJ: Princeton University Press, 1987.

Watson, Nicholas. "Desire for the Past." *SAC* 21 (1999): 59–97.

———. "The Politics of Middle English Writing," in *The Idea of the Vernacular*. Ed. Jocelyn Wogan-Browne, Nicholas Watson, Andrew Taylor, and Ruth Evans. Exeter, UK: Exeter University Press, 1999. Pp. 330–52.

Watt, Ian. *The Rise of the Novel*. Berkeley and Los Angeles: University of California Press, 1957.

Weinberg, Steven. *Dreams of a Final Theory*. New York: Pantheon, 1992.

White, Hayden. *Figural Realism: Studies in the Mimesis Effect*. Baltimore, MD: Johns Hopkins University Press, 1999.

Whitman, Jon. *Allegory: The Dynamics of an Ancient and Medieval Technique*. Cambridge, MA: Harvard University Press, 1987.

Williams, Raymond. *Marxism and Literature*. Oxford: Oxford University Press, 1977.

Witmore, Michael. *Culture of Accidents: Unexpected Knowledges in Early Modern England*. Stanford, CA: Stanford University Press, 2001.

Wittgenstein, Ludwig. *Philosophical Investigations*. Trans. G. E. M. Anscombe. 3rd edn. Oxford: Basil Blackwell, 2001.

Wogan-Browne, Jocelyn, Nicholas Watson, Andrew Taylor, and Ruth Evans, eds. *The Idea of the Vernacular*. Exeter, UK: Exeter University Press, 1999.

Wyclif, John. *Select English Works*. Ed. Thomas Arnold. Oxford: Clarendon Press, 1869–1871.

INDEX

CPSIA information can be obtained at www.ICGtesting.com
Printed in the USA
BVOW071739170112

280751BV00002B/13/P